10643850

STANIER PACIFICS
AT WORK

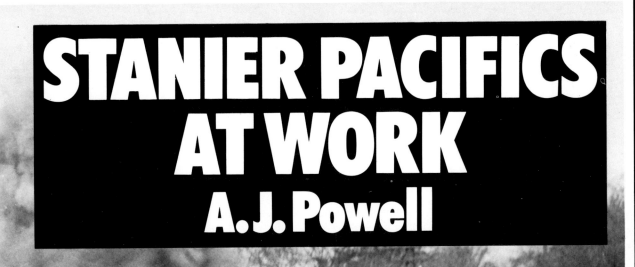

STANIER PACIFICS AT WORK
A.J. Powell

IAN ALLAN LTD

Contents

Previous page:
No 46207 *Princess Arthur of Connaught* emerges smokily from Kilsby Tunnel on an up Liverpool train on 7 April 1953. *J. F. Henton*

Below right:
***City of St Albans* is unusually on the up 'Pines Express' from Manchester at Handforth Sidings.** *T. Lewis*

Front endpaper:
The southbound 'Coronation Scot' approaches Clifton & Lowther behind No 6224 *Princess Alexandra*. *Eric Treacy/P. B. Whitehouse collection*

Rear endpaper:
No 6203 *Princess Margaret Rose* is nearly at the top of the long rise from Watford as she emerges from Northchurch Tunnel on a down Liverpool express. *E. R. Wethersett*

Rear cover, bottom:
At the Liverpool end, No 46208 *Princess Helena Victoria* is being coaled at Edge Hill from the unique coaling plant fed direct from wagons above. *Eric Treacy/ P. B. Whitehouse collection*

Rear cover, top:
No 6223 *Princess Alice* wheels the up 'Coronation Scot' past Euxton Junction. *Eric Treacy/P. B. Whitehouse collection*

First published 1986

ISBN 0 7110 1534 1

All rights reserved. No part of this book may be reproduced or transmitted in any form or by any means, electronic or mechanical, including photo-copying, recording or by any information storage and retrieval system, without permission from the Publisher in writing.

© A. J. Powell 1986

Published by Ian Allan Ltd, Shepperton, Surrey; and printed by Ian Allan Printing Ltd at their works at Coombelands in Runnymede, England

Preface

The title *Stanier Pacifics at Work* may well invoke different expectations in different people. It is therefore incumbent on the author to mark out his ground.

'Stanier' is a name which can only command the highest respect, for Sir William was directly responsible for the most profound turnround in the fortunes (an inappropriate word, on reflection, for luck played little or no part in it) of locomotive engineering on the LMS Railway. But he has been the subject of at least two biographies, and there is very little that I can add to them.

'Pacifics' is evocative of the largest passenger locomotives performing the most public and noteworthy work. There have been numerous publications which have dealt with them in factual terms or have glorified them in pictorial splendour. Much of the historical information needs no repetition here, and only a smattering will be found in this book; the photographic content of a number of albums has been assembled by people with an eye for composition and visual effect which I can hardly hope to rival, and so the pictures here are some of those which appeal to me as epitomising the 'presence' of the Pacifics.

But the 'at Work' element of the title has been much less fully dealt with by others, and very much piecemeal; there have been areas of the overall field of design, performance and maintenance which have only been sketchily covered, and not always by those with practical experience of the subject. So the aim of this book is to draw a comprehensive picture of the life of the Stanier Pacifics from their birth on the drawing board to their withdrawal. It is not a work of unquestioning adulation, even though I see the later Pacifics as probably the finest overall steam locomotives for heavy express passenger work produced in Britain. They had their faults and weaknesses, and a frank evaluation of these has been attempted.

In writing this book I have received help from many sources. The writings of Cecil J. Allen and O. S. Nock have been exhaustively consulted for documented runs and comment. In presenting the tabulated runs, I have made calculations of the average Equivalent Drawbar Horsepower (EDBHP) exerted over selected sections; this is the total usable horsepower output of the locomotive, both in hauling the train and in lifting itself on rising gradients. The figures, which take account of gradients and acceleration/deceleration, are given to the nearest 10hp; they depend on published times and speeds, which are themselves sometimes sufficiently inconsistent or inaccurate to need correction, and include allowance for the diminishing weight of the tender as coal and water are used. Train resistance is based on figures published by BR in 1953 for a 10mph 45° headwind, which does not necessarily apply to actual conditions at the time. So no spurious accuracy should be attributed to calculated EDBHP values, which are no more than a fair guide to locomotive output and can be a clue to how the locomotive was being worked.

To those youthful readers who have been brought up on diesel and (even more so) electric traction on the West Coast main line, many of the speeds quoted in steam runs may look pretty small beer. In the 1950s, to get over Tring with a heavy train at 70mph was the exception, and meant that the fireman was working both intelligently and hard; nowadays the round 100 is the norm and selected trains are passing there at 110. But a 'Duchess', kept running by one pair of sturdy arms, could never aspire to the 5,000hp output of a Class 87 locomotive drawing on the resources of a power station.

I have again received unstinting help from Phil Atkins and his staff at the library of the National Railway Museum, York; Chapter 10 is based on a paper which he prepared, and used with his permission though I have modified it considerably in the light of comments from E. S. Cox, to whom I am indebted. I am also grateful for anecdotes from Ken Cameron, Laurie Taylor and Bob Watt.

My freedom of action in selecting photographs for this book was affected by the sad and premature death of that great recorder, Derek Cross. As a result I have had only limited access to his enormous library of Stanier Pacific photographs, though his brother had helped me in this field. I am extremely grateful to Pat Whitehouse, who has given me the opportunity to use the pictures of the late Bishop Eric Treacy. Many other contributors are also acknowledged, notably W. J. V. Anderson, who has looked out some previously unpublished photographs for me, and J. H. Cooper-Smith, whose pictures of preserved steam are of the highest order.

Two Stanier Pacifics live on in condition to haul trains on selected BR routes. No 6229 *Duchess of Hamilton* in particular has been putting up performances in the 1980s which, notwithstanding the enginemen's limited experience of big steam engines, are in no way inferior to their best work of 30 years ago. Long may it continue.

A. J. Powell,
Dalmeny
South Queensferry,
West Lothian EH30 9JZ.

1

Introduction

The year 1932 was a very significant one for the locomotive policy of the LM&S Railway. At the beginning of January, William A. Stanier came from Swindon to be the new Chief Mechanical Engineer at Euston. And at the beginning of November, J. E. Anderson retired as Superintendent of Motive Power in the Chief General Superintendent's Department at Derby, a post he had filled for the first 10 years of the LMSR's existence.

Stanier came from a railway which, in the 1930s, possessed a locomotive fleet with a high degree of standardisation and of an overall quality clearly superior to that of the other three main line companies. Developed from the Churchward era, GWR locomotives used a small number of standard boilers, cylinders, wheel sizes and other main components, of thoroughly modern design, and assembled them rather like Meccano, to build lengthy runs of a limited range of express passenger, mixed traffic and freight locomotives that were masters of the work required of them at the time.

The fleet for which Stanier took over responsibility was a very different affair. The 9,052 locomotives[1] were predominantly of pre-grouping designs; indeed, no more than 2,027 locomotives had been built in the nine years since the grouping, and only 607 of these could be said to represent post-grouping LMS design. On the express passenger side the only engines of modern conception were the 70 'Royal Scots' and the two 'Baby Scots' ('Patriots' as they were to become, and themselves officially classed as 'Claughton' rebuilds). Construction under the LMS had mostly been of ex-MR 4-4-0 and 0-6-0 types which had been given a modest facelift but were inherently 20-year-old concepts.

Which brings us to the influence of Anderson, who as Superintendent of Motive Power was a key figure in formulating the requirements of the operators to run the service and to discuss with the Chief Mechanical Engineer how these requirements could best be met. Anderson was a locomotive-trained engineer who had joined the Midland Railway in 1903, had been Chief Locomotive Draughtsman, Works Manager at Derby, acting Chief Mechanical Engineer during World War 1 and, from 1919 until he joined the operating fold in 1923, Deputy CME. His experience of Midland locomotive philosophy and design, gained in these posts, carried over powerfully into his LMS appointment. As E. S. Cox wrote in 1945[2] of George Hughes, the first CME of the LMS, and his plans for a 4-6-2 express passenger engine:

> 'Hughes knew the value of the big engine, master of its job. . . . It was his misfortune, however, to have to work with a newly formed Operating Department imbued with the small engine outlook so that his intentions in that respect did not come to fruition'.

The result of this Midland influence was that in those nine years prior to Stanier's arrival, apart from the 72 modern passenger 4-6-0s already mentioned, no less than 298 modest-sized 4-4-0s of dated design had been turned out along with pre-grouping 4-6-0s of inherently short life expectancy. Stanier's inheritance was not a very happy one.

LMS first-line passenger locomotives in 1932
For working the heavier and/or harder services without inordinate piloting, only the 'Royal Scots' and two 'Patriots', with 15 more of the latter already in the 1932 building programme, were available. Behind them were 127 'Claughtons', 20 of which had been reboilered with the larger G9½S boiler also used on the 'Patriots'; their fundamental mechanical weaknesses had already led to a decision not to give them any further General Repairs, and no less than 24 were scrapped in 1932 in line with this policy. The 70 'Dreadnoughts' of L&YR design, which had been built up to 1925 and had been used with limited success between Crewe and Carlisle, until displaced by 'Royal Scots', were not very economical on fuel, and maintenance costs were relatively high; by 1934 withdrawal was in full swing, some after a life of only 10 years, and but for World War 2 the class would have been extinct by 1940.

The 'Royal Scots' in their early years had been less than thoroughly dependable, partly due to the onset of serious steam leakage past the broad Schmidt piston valve rings, and acceleration of passenger services was deferred until this problem was solved. Much of the express running on the LMS was pedestrian and unenterprising; it was very much a '55mph railway', mainly on 'Limited Load' timings, on which the 'Royal Scots' could lumber along on heavy trains without needing to exert more than about 1,000DBHP. If there was no 'Scot' available, a rebuilt 'Claughton' or some double-headed combination had to deputise. But by the time of Stanier's arrival, the decision had been taken to bring about the demise of the '8¼hr' agreement on journey times for the day Anglo-Scottish expresses, which had stood for over 30 years; in May the 'Royal Scot' was accelerated by 20min to and from Glasgow, and the summer service in July reduced the time further, to 7hr 40min. The 'Mid-day Scot' similarly was accelerated by 25min Down and 20min Up, bringing it to an 8hr timing with several intermediate stops. Permitted load unassisted over Shap and Beattock was 425 tons with 'Limited Load' timings. LMS thinking favoured long through locomotive working where possible, and on Anglo-Scottish trains this invariably meant between Euston and Carlisle (299 miles), or Crewe and Glasgow (243 miles). 'Royal Scot' 4-6-0s were rostered to work the Crewe-Glasgow leg throughout on no less than five trains each way on weekdays, and in addition they also hauled the 'Royal Highlander' through between Crewe and Perth (292 miles), with long non-stop runs from Warrington to Carlisle (117 miles) and thence to Stirling (118 miles).

It took a little while for enginemen to adapt to these accelerations, as one might expect. The best of them took the harder running in their stride; in August 1932, Cecil J. Allen gave details[3] of some typical running on the accelerated down 'Mid-day Scot', when with 436 tons tare a 'Royal Scot' reached Rugby (82.6 miles) in barely 86½min, maintaining 51mph and developing close on 1,100EDBHP on the climbs to Bushey and Tring. Farther north, another engine of the same class, with the train now reduced to 353 tons tare, ran from Lancaster to Carlisle, 69.1 miles in 80½min (83min allowed) despite a permanent way check to 30mph approaching Tebay which ruined the climb to Shap Summit and cost about 3min in running. Output on Grayrigg and Shap inclines was of the order of 1,240EDBHP. Others, however, took longer to get the measure of what was needed, even though still more would be demanded — and met — in subsequent years. Referring to another occasion when No 6149 has a 15-coach train grossing 490 tons[3] Allen commented that it was 'a little too onerous for timekeeping'. At the same time the 'Royal Scots' were working other accelerated trains with conspicuous success; the Up 'Mancunian', allowed 172min for the 176.9 miles from

The need for a new engine

Conditions were changing. The economic depression of the 1930s was demanding ruthless economies which tended to increase train weights on the West Coast route. At the same time the competitive position, notably *vis-à-vis* the LNER, was calling for higher speeds and reduced journey times. These factors would combine to tax the 'Royal Scots' to the limit and beyond on the Anglo-Scottish workings. Stanier was thus given an early remit by the LMS Board to produce a new locomotive which would be capable of working right through between London and Glasgow (thus avoiding the Carlisle engine change) with loads of 500 tons tare, and with potential for considerable further acceleration. To meet this remit, with its substantial coal consumption, the need to keep combustion rates on the grate down to moderate levels, and to provide adequate ashpan capacity for such a long run (coal burnt on such a journey would contain up to ½-ton of ash), there was no satisfactory alternative to a wide firebox and a 4-6-2 wheel arrangement to carry it.

The Pacific concept had had a limited, and mixed, history in this country. Stanier was familiar with the first such engine, the GWR's *The Great Bear* of 1908 (Fig 1), for he had been Divisional Locomotive Superintendent at Paddington for the first four years of the *Bear's* life, and was then at Swindon Works for the remainder of its existence as a 4-6-2 (it was 'rebuilt' as a 4-6-0 in 1924). The only other Pacifics actually

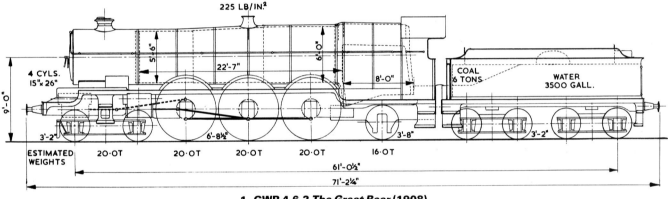

1 GWR 4-6-2 *The Great Bear* (1908).

Wilmslow to Euston, and the 17.25 Liverpool-Euston on its fast timing of 142min from Crewe to Willesden (152.6 miles) were cases which prompted Allen to write[4] that 'the work that is being got out of the "Royal Scots" at the present time is such as to make rapid schedules like these almost easy'. But on the Anglo-Scottish trains, engine crews took a little longer to get the last bit out of these engines; when they did, the result could be positively brilliant.

built were the Gresley 'A1s' on the LNER (Fig 2), together with their higher-pressure developments as Class A3, and the five ex-NER Pacifics of Class A2 (Fig 3), withdrawal of which started in 1936. Only the Gresley engines, particularly when modified with long-lap valves, could be deemed a success.

Others had produced schemes for 4-6-2 engines which had not come to fruition. On the Caledonian, J. F. McIntosh had, in 1913, caused two outline designs to be produced for

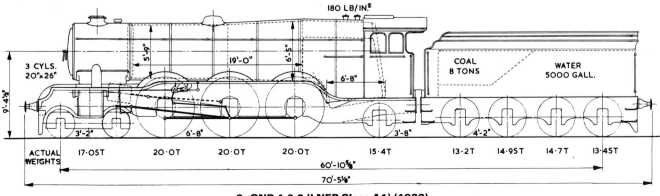

2 GNR 4-6-2 (LNER Class A1) (1922).

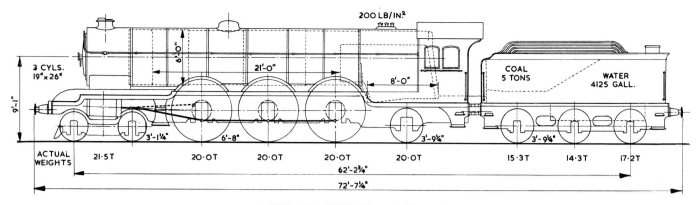

3 NER 4-6-2 (LNER Class A2) (1922).

four-cylinder Pacifics,[5] though of very modest size and power; Fig 4 shows the semi-wide firebox version, but it had been preceded by a *narrow*-firebox scheme! Both boilers would have been seriously deficient, and could only have continued the CR reputation for large-engine mediocrity.

On the LMS itself, two of Stanier's predecessors had also considered Pacific designs. In 1924 George Hughes, following up earlier L&YR work at Horwich, had produced several schemes for a powerful four-cylinder 4-6-2 for the West Coast route, culminating in that shown in Fig 5. The design was generally enlightened, and the boiler proportions sound, but it was killed by operating prejudice. Henry Fowler in 1926 fell at the same hurdle with a design for a four-cylinder compound Pacific (Fig 6) which actually got as

far as the cutting of frame plates and the casting of a few cylinders before being stopped in October 1926. Again the boiler was fairly well proportioned, but the use of low-pressure cylinders 23⅝in diameter between the frames made it impossible to provide adequate coupled axle journals[6] and mechanical performance would have suffered. No doubt information on these two designs was given to Stanier by the Derby drawing office as he pondered the shape of his new locomotive, and full details of the Gresley engines was readily available. At the same time he was familiar with all the features of the GWR 'King' class 4-6-0s, and the 'Royal Scots' were increasingly occupying his time. Thus was the scene set for the production of his second locomotive class.

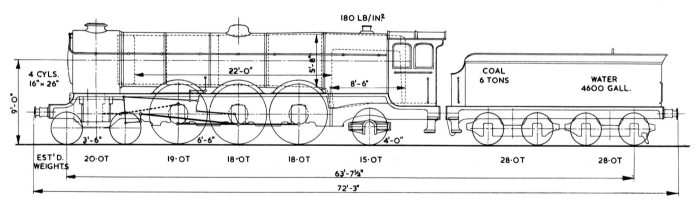

4 Projected CR McIntosh 4-6-2 (1913).

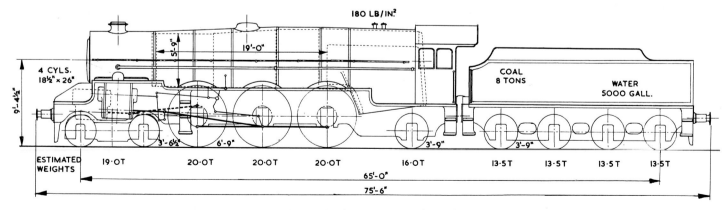

5 Projected LMS Hughes 4-6-2 (1924).

8

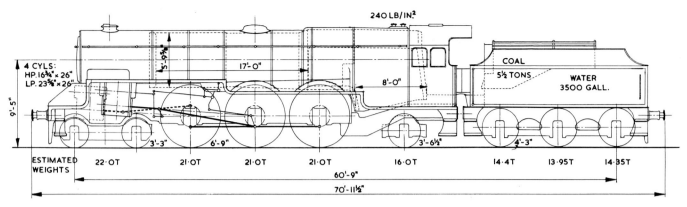

240 LB/IN.²

4 CYLS:
HP.16¾" × 26"
LP. 23⅝" × 26"

9'-5"

COAL
5½ TONS

WATER
3500 GALL.

5'-9⅝"

17'-0"

8'-0"

3'-3"   6'-9"

3'-6½"

4'-3"

ESTIMATED
WEIGHTS

22·OT   21·OT   21·OT   21·OT   16·OT   14·4T   13·95T   14·35T

60'-9"

70'-11½"

6 Projected LMS Fowler compound 4-6-2 (1926).

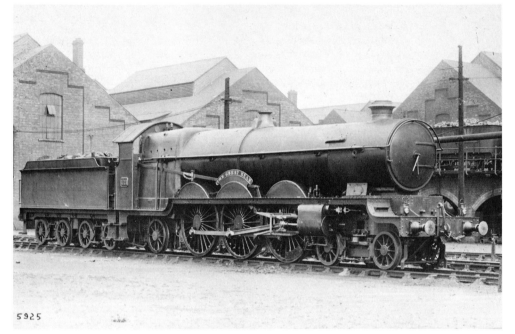

5925

Left:
**GWR No 111 *The Great
Bear.*** *Ian Allan Library*

Below:
**LNER Class A3 No 4480
Enterprise. Built at
Doncaster in 1923, she was
fitted with 220lb/in² boiler
(with 43-element
superheater) in 1927, the
form in which she appears
here.** *Ian Allan Library*

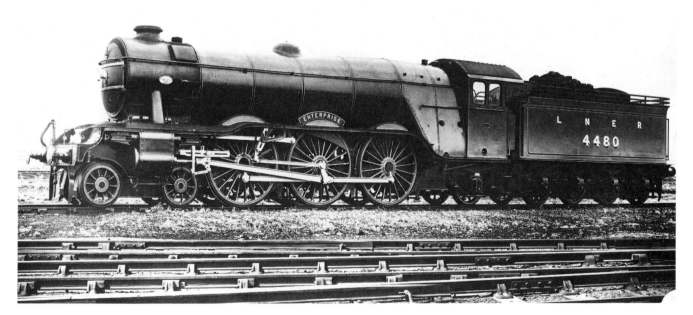

Left:
LNER Class A2 No 2400 *City of Newcastle*. Later engines of the class had outside bearings for the trailing axle. *Ian Allan Library*

Below:
'Royal Scot' No 6139 *Ajax* on a down express passing Hatch End about 1933. She has been fitted with smoke deflectors — though not yet inclined inwards at the top — but retains bogie brakes and the original 3,500gal tender, now fitted with coal rails. In 1936 she was renamed *The Welch Regiment*. *Real Photos*

2
The Birth of the 'Princesses'

Stanier's small design team at Euston quickly produced two initial schemes for 4-6-2 passenger locomotives to fulfil the remit; they were for engines with the usual 6ft 9in diameter coupled wheels and a large boiler having a wide Belpaire firebox with 45sq ft of grate, in alternative three-cylinder (Fig 7) and four-cylinder versions. The mechanical elements of the three-cylinder engine owed a lot to the 'Royal Scot' design, while the four-cylinder scheme leaned towards the GWR 'Kings'. Stanier opted for four cylinders, and the Derby development drawing office started to look in more detail at the boiler proportions in the light of Stanier's views on low superheat. This work led to a revision of the initial scheme, using 6ft 6in diameter wheels (allowing the boiler to be pitched 1in lower) and with the length between tube-plates reduced from 22ft 0in to 20ft 9in by providing a short 'combustion chamber' (Fig 8). Three of these Pacifics were authorised in the 1933 Building Programme, the Crewe order being No 371, but in the event the third engine was deferred, and appeared two years later in rather different form (Chapter 4). The first of the new engines emerged from

Crewe Works in late June 1933 as No 6200 (Fig 9) and came up to Euston station, for inspection by LMS officers on 28 June, still in her works photographic grey colour-scheme. In fact this trip caused quite a panic, because on arrival at Rugby on the previous afternoon one of the outside crossheads was found to have run hot at the top slipper.[7] Rugby depot was apparently not trusted to remetal and machine the crosshead, and because of the solid fit, without draw, of the piston rod cone end in the crosshead it was decided to replace piston head, rod and crosshead complete with the equivalent parts from No 6201 under construction at Crewe. These were rushed to Rugby, fitted during the evening, and the engine worked up to Euston overnight for exhibition next day. It was another month before she went back into the paint shop to receive her proper maroon livery. Five months elapsed before No 6201 came out to keep her sister company.

With such a radical departure from previous practice, no further 'Princesses' were ordered for two years, while the pair were assessed in traffic and enginemen got the measure

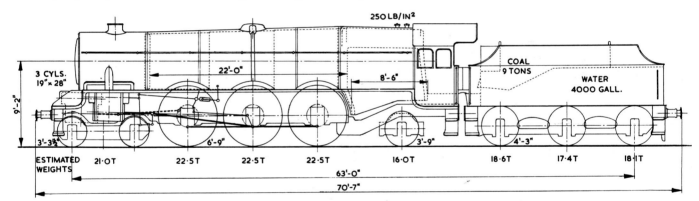

7 Preliminary scheme for Stanier three-cylinder 4-6-2.

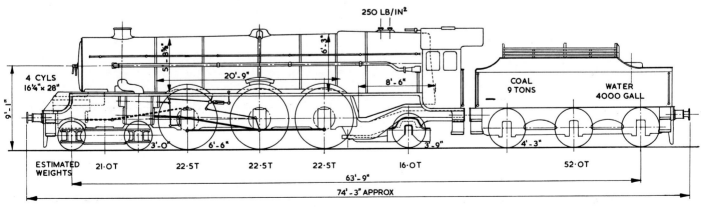

8 Early scheme for Stanier four-cylinder 4-6-2.

11

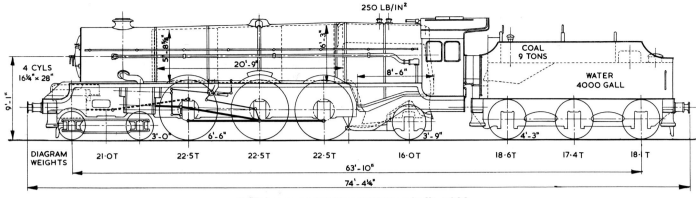

9 'Princess' 4-6-2 Nos 6200/1 as built, 1933.

of them. Then, in the 1935 Building Programme, a further 10 Pacifics were authorised, the Crewe order being No 395. These engines, built between July and October 1935, incorporated significant changes from their predecessors dictated by operating experience (Fig 10).

Design Features

1 Frames

The frames were robust; those of Nos 6200/1 were of 1¼in plate, but to save weight (see item 14) the frames of Nos 6203-12 were of 1⅛in high-tensile plate. There were plenty of vertical stretchers, but only two horizontal ones to prevent racking — the bogie centre pin casting and another between intermediate and trailing coupled axles. Separate axlebox guides were used rather than hornblocks, with the horn-stays studded up under the guides rather than bolted

direct to the frames. Cross-stays were fitted between the axlebox guides at intermediate and trailing coupled axles. Due to rivet loosening, new leading and intermediate axlebox guides were provided from 1956, with broader flanges taking 12 rivets instead of eight.

Under the firebox, a four-plate structure was spliced to the mainframes, which finished immediately behind the trailing coupled wheels; this concept was inherited directly from the Fowler Pacific design of 1926. Here, too, the plate thickness was reduced on Nos 6203-12 to save weight.

This overall frame design (Fig 11) proved reasonably satisfactory in service. There was very little fracturing at the horngaps (which was such a feature of the 'Royal Scots' and Class 5s early in their life). However, the mounting of the outside cylinders over the trailing bogie axle, where there was no horizontal bracing, was a weak spot; flexure caused fractures behind the cylinder rear flanges, as well as looseness

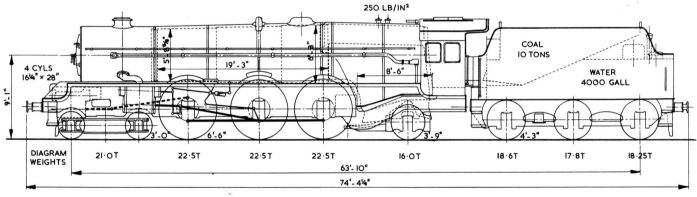

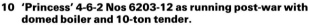

10 'Princess' 4-6-2 Nos 6203-12 as running post-war with domed boiler and 10-ton tender.

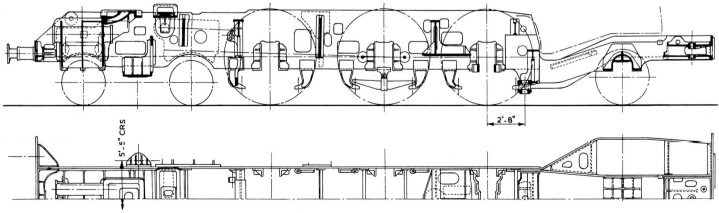

11 Frame arrangement, Nos 6200/1 as built.

of the cylinders on the frame, which could be relied upon to cause leakage of the smokebox steam pipe joints, a sure recipe for poor steaming.

To overcome this trouble, two steps were taken in the early 1950s. First, loosening of the outside cylinders was tackled by welding heavy buttress strips to the frames fore and aft of the cylinder flanges, with fitted inserts welded in. Then, as an aid to production, this modification was incorporated in a complete renewal of the front end of the frames as far as the leading coupled axle horngap; a complete sub-assembly, with cylinders and stretchers, was maintained as a 'spare' to be welded on to the cut-back frames at General Repairs as required. Minor modifications to the frames in front of the firebox were made to Nos 6200/1 in 1952 to allow them to carry the later boilers with 19ft 3in tubes.

2 Coupled Axleboxes

Stanier's excellent cast steel coupled axleboxes were fitted, having a pressed-in horseshoe brass with a thin whitemetal bearing surface and mechanical lubrication delivered on the horizontal journal centrelines. The coupled journals were 10in diameter×10in long. These boxes gave exemplary service and heated bearings were very rare.

3 Springs

Stanier's standard laminated springs using rolled silico-manganese steel plates of ribbed section, secured in the buckle by dimples and a wedge cotter,[8] were used on all axles, with screwed tension links. After a period in service, adjustment of these links was almost impossible due to fretting corrosion of the knuckle threads. However, there was no regular weight check (very few places other than the works had weighing apparatus) so that this difficulty only really affected those on the Works stripping pits.

4 Cylinders

The 16¼in×28in cylinders were of sound design; the exhaust passages were reasonably direct, but inevitably somewhat long because of the cylinder positions relative to the blastpipe. The outside cylinders were flat-faced to the frame plates, the exhaust passages being continued in a small smokebox saddle casting, while the inside cylinder casting incorporated a forward saddle with exhaust passages above the valve chests. A heavy blastpipe casting linking the two saddles brought the two flows together. (This made it comparatively simple to fit a double blastpipe on No 6201 in 1934, with the unusual feature that the inside cylinders

exhausted up the front blastpipe and the outside cylinders up the rear one.) It was an inelegant arrangement, and problems with alignment, cylinder movement and frame flexure caused fractures of the exhaust passages. Starting in 1953, therefore, a change was made to cast steel inside cylinders, with cast iron liners, and these were fitted as part of the front end frame renewal.

The piston valves were 8in diameter (no more than adequate for a fast passenger engine), driven by independent Walschaerts valve gears giving travels of over 7in in full gear; steam lap was 1¾in and lead ¼in, with no exhaust clearance. The steam distribution left little to be desired, but while the 'Princesses' could be driven quite happily on short cut-offs where loads allowed, they seemed to need at least 18% cut-off to really produce results. Lubrication to cylinders and valves was from mechanical lubricators, that to the valves being via Stanier's standard atomiser controlled by the cylinder cock linkage; this was very effective and cylinders and valves remained very clean in service.

Stanier's original form of piston, screwed on to the piston rod direct, proved unsatisfactory due to fatigue fractures at the thread roots in the rod, and from 1943 this was replaced by a piston head pulled up to a flat collar on the piston rod by twin nuts with opposed threads.

The cylinder drain cocks were of the usual LMS poppet valve type; they were operated from the cab by mechanical linkage, which was of necessity rather complex and subject to wear of numerous pin joints and to whip of the long rods. It was troublesome to keep in order by normal standards of shed maintenance, and in 1956 it was decided to replace the whole arrangement by BR standard steam-operated cylinder cocks.

5 Valve Gear and Motion

The Walschaerts valve gear mostly followed normal LMS practice, using the four-stud return crank fixing on the crankpin, but the eccentric rod drive to the expansion links was through stub pins low on the outside of the links, an unusual arrangement for outside motion. From No 6203 onwards the more usual offset tails on the foot of the outside links were adopted. Fig 12 shows the inside motion on Nos 6203-12, and Appendix 3 gives details of the valve events.

Nos 6200/1 were built with bronze motion bushes, but from No 6203 onwards needle roller bearings with grease lubrication (a maintenance staff responsibility) were applied to motion pins and ball bearings to the return crank/eccentric

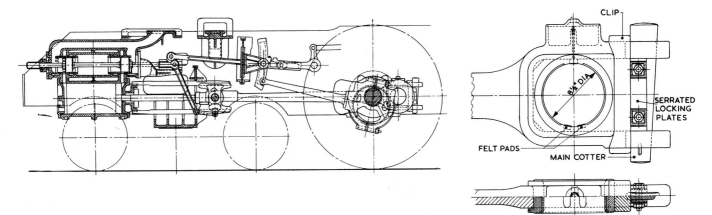

12 Inside motion arrangement and big end, Nos 6203-12.

rod pins, much to the delight of enginemen whose preparation did not need to take in the difficult access to the top joints of the inside combination levers. Wartime shortages, however, dictated a reversion to bronze bushes on motion pins on these 10 engines, though retaining grease lubrication.

The inside big ends were of a design long used at Swindon but new to the LMS, the connecting rods having an open fork in which the brasses were retained by a heavy clip and tapered cotter (Fig 12). As built, with long felt oil pads, the upper one set in a through slot in the joint face of the brasses, a gradual breakdown of the big end could occur due to looseness from fretting of the very small top 'feet' of the brasses;[9] if this occurred in service without the driver becoming aware, the brasses could (and not infrequently did) disintegrate, causing dire secondary damage. From 1951, therefore, 'stink bombs' were fitted in the inside crankpins to give warning of heating, but these were by no means infallible and, of course, did nothing to eliminate the cause. The long-term cure proved to be the use of smaller circular felt oil pads staggered across the width of the brasses.

The reversing gear was unusual; to get the reversing rod past the wide firebox, it was positioned well out towards the platform edge, with a short intermediate shaft to line up the front reversing rod to the reversing shaft arm. On Nos 6200/1 this intermediate shaft was behind the trailing splasher, giving a front reversing rod about 13ft long, unsupported and rather 'whippy'. On Nos 6203-12 this shaft was moved to the front of the trailing splasher, shortening the front rod to about 9ft 6in long, and the longer rear rod was given a steadying bracket. To link this reversing rod position to the reversing handle in the cab it was necessary to provide a geared drive.

The use of four sets of valve gear was a nuisance in drivers' preparation, and added to costs. In May 1938, therefore, one engine, No 6205, was modified by removing the inside valve gears and driving the inside valves by rocking levers from the outside gears. New and massive outside slidebar brackets, carrying the expansion link trunnions, were fitted to take the increased thrust from driving two piston valves. The rocking levers had to be in front of the outside cylinders, and thus the setting of the inside valves was affected by thermal expansion of the outside valve spindles. This clearly introduced problems at works overhauls, for No 6205 never ran with the same mechanical sweetness as the others. The reversing rods were also altered at this time.

6 Balancing

Fifty per cent of the reciprocating masses was balanced, the balance being equally divided between the three coupled axles. The balance weights in the wheels comprised steel plates riveted over the spokes into which molten lead/ antimony mixture was selectively poured while on the high-speed balancing machine with equivalent weights on the crankpins, to give smooth running. Contrary to what has been stated elsewhere,[10] the crank axle webs were extended opposite the crankpins for rotating balance.

7 Leading Bogie

This, too, was an import to the LMS though more or less standard on Swindon four-cylinder engines. It was of bar frame construction with axlebox guide pedestals riveted to the top bar, the bottom bar forming the hornstay; this gave a very light form of non-loadbearing construction for its long wheelbase of 7ft 6in. Engine weight was transferred to the bogie through side bolsters set wide apart at 5ft 5in centres, with friction pads sliding on flat brass liners on the wings of the bogie centre casting. Helical side control springs fore and aft of the centre casting gave an initial centring force of 4 tons.

8 Trailing Truck

The design of this truck originated with Fowler's Pacific scheme of 1926. It was of plate construction, with cast steel radius arm, and here too the weight was transferred through side bolsters, though in this case they were set on the axle centreline, between the wheels, on a heavy frame stretcher. The side control spring arrangement followed the same general lines as on the bogie, giving 1.44 tons initial centring force. The standard of riding given by this bogie and truck combination was exemplary, and comparable with that of coaching stock.

9 Boiler and Firebox

The three original boilers (Nos 6048-50) used by Nos 6200/1 had fireboxes with short combustion chambers giving a length between tubeplates of 20ft 9in. All subsequent boilers were built with extended combustion chambers, cutting the length between tubeplates to 19ft 3in. The fireboxes of the original boilers were never altered to reduced tube length, and from 1950 these boilers gravitated to any of the 12 'Princesses' as availability dictated.

The wide Belpaire fireboxes were a masterpiece of the draughtsman's skill allied to the professionalism of the Crewe boiler shop staff, which was of a high-order. Eric Langridge has set down in some detail[11] the development of the design, notably in the blending of curves on the sloping throatplate and the continuous curvature of outer and inner firebox wrapper plates, and the close co-operation with the boiler shop in exploiting production techniques. Staying followed Stanier's early practice, pioneered on the parallel boilers of the 'Royal Scots', of riveted copper stays except in the side breaking zones and the firebox crown, where steel stays, nutted on the fireside, were used. The wide firebox was trapezoidal in shape, the grate being 7ft 7¾in long, tapering from 6ft 1in wide at the front to 5ft 6¼in at the back. Grate area was 45sq ft.

In view of its great length and weight, intermediate support was necessary on the first and third rings of the barrel, in addition to flat sliding feet on the foundation ring at the throatplate. A diaphragm steadying plate bolted to the rear of the foundation ring and to the dragbox prevented lateral movement while allowing normal expansion. In practice this simple device was a source of much maintenance trouble. Its fixing bolts were difficult to keep tight and not infrequently sheared, resulting in loud thumping noises below the footplate. This was a cause of much premature shopping.

Low superheat was originally provided, there being 16 superheater flues of standard 5⅛in diameter and 170 small tubes of 2¼in diameter. Two small tubes were soon replaced by washout plugs in the smokebox tubeplate to facilitate washing out of the tube bank, leaving 168. The critical ratio of cross-sectional area to gas-swept surface (A/S) for the small tubes was 1/498, a very long way from the optimum of 1/400, while the total free gas area was only 5.11sq ft, almost identical with that of the 'Royal Scots', and only 11.4% of the grate area. This was not a recipe for a free-steaming boiler commensurate with the engine's cylinder power. Interestingly, some weeks after a description of the new engine had been published in the *Railway Gazette*, the editor reproduced a letter[12] from an engineer on the Buenos Ayres Western Railway, which concluded:

'I consider, therefore, that the new engines will not better the performance of the "Royal Scot" class, and that they would have been infinitely better if fitted with a 36in combustion chamber and at least 32 elements'.

Prophetic words indeed!

There were three increases in the size of the original superheater. This was finalised at 32 elements, though boilers Nos 9101-4 went through an intermediate stage of 24 elements, and the special boiler No 9236, one of the spares used particularly on the 'Turbomotive' until 1950, had an even larger 40-element superheater. Several types of elements were used over the years; before World War 2 the most common type was of Stanier's bifurcated design with 1¼in diameter tubes. In 1935 there was a trial of 'Sinuflo' elements (the results were disappointing, and are covered in Chapter 3) confined to one engine and of short duration. In the postwar years the Superheater Co's standard return loop elements, 1¼in diameter, were increasingly used, though lengths, and hence the heating surface, varied. Likewise, the 2¼in diameter small tubes were replaced within a few years by tubes of 2⅜in diameter, in varying numbers; in the 19ft 3in boilers these had an A/S ratio of 1/435, which was much nearer the ideal. The boiler ratios which resulted are recorded in Appendix 4.

10 Regulator

The boilers were domeless (the apparent small dome housing the top feed clackboxes) and the regulator valves were housed in the superheater header, with access gained very awkwardly through a front cover. The regulator valves required lubrication from a small displacement lubricator in the cab. The operating rod from the driver's handle was about 32ft long, and lacked sensitivity; this could cause slipping in starting, and difficulty in closing if any major carryover of water occurred. This general arrangement was abandoned by Stanier in his other classes for new building by the end of 1935, and indeed spare boiler No 9236, used as first replacement on 'Turbomotive', was built new in 1935 with dome containing a horizontal regulator; boiler No 6030, the third of the 1933 order, also had a dome regulator from new. The remaining boilers retained their smokebox regulators until fitted with domes in the 1952-5 period, but the superheater headers were not replaced. The latter gave some trouble from cracking, necessitating works repair, but a satisfactory welding technique for the cast iron was developed.

11 Ashpan

To get ample primary air to the fire, three normal dampers (front, back, and at the front of the hump over the truck axle), *plus* full length side dampers immediately under the foundation ring, were provided (Fig 13). All were operated from the cab; the controls for the normal dampers were of

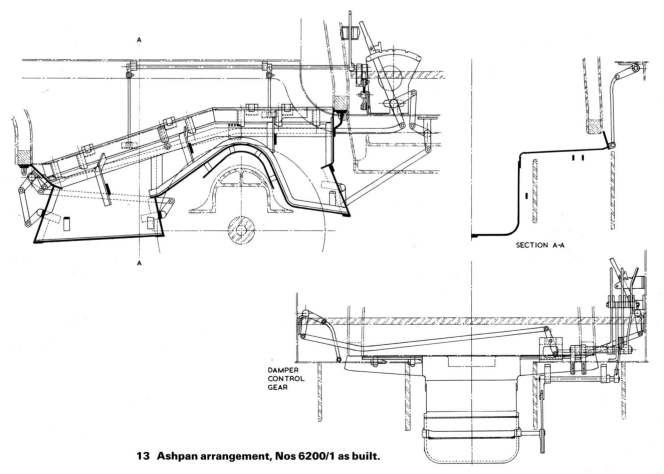

SECTION A-A

DAMPER CONTROL GEAR

13 Ashpan arrangement, Nos 6200/1 as built.

the quadrant type at floor level, but the retaining catches were poor and needed 'help' by a variety of unofficial devices. The side dampers were extremely useful for raking ash accumulations off the side sheets of the ashpan, which had to be nearly horizontal to clear the trailing frames. Their large area, however, could result in excess air if used in conjunction with one or more of the other dampers, with adverse effects on steaming and superheat. From 1942, therefore, the cab operating gear for the side dampers was removed and local retaining catches fitted. The centre damper was also welded up as superfluous.

12 Sanding Gear
Stanier's original dry gravity sanding, supplemented by water desanding jets behind the coupled wheels, was fitted to all 'Princesses' when new, but quickly came into disfavour, and the standard LMS steam sanding gear replaced it from 1936 onwards.

13 Cab
The cab was very roomy, being some 8ft 11in wide. As one driver commented[13] on the similar 'Duchess' cabs, 'there seemed almost enough room to ride one's bike around it', although it was only about 5in wider than those on, for example, the 4-6-0s. There were hinged glass draught screens on the cab sides for use when running. For such a large boiler, the cab front windows were surprisingly large, and gave a reasonably good forward view — always a problem on the largest locomotives.

As built the firehole doors were of the too-free roller-suspended type, which has the infuriating habit of partly closing while firing (though on the smooth-riding 'Princesses' this was not such a problem as on a run-down 4-6-0). Nevertheless, they were mostly replaced over the years by the simple sliding type with thicker doors providing more secondary air over the fire.

Most steam valves originally had straight handles; these were replaced quite early on by either wheels with tails, or by spanner squares, as most appropriate. The 'Dreadnought'-type combined vacuum/steam brake valve, with pull-down handle and integral ejector steam valves, also gave way to the very indifferent Midland combined brake valve with separate large/small ejector steam valves above it.

14 Engine Weight
All engine diagrams for the 'Princesses' showed the weights as originally estimated, with 22.5 tons on each coupled axle and a total engine weight of 104.5 tons in working order. This was a travesty of the truth, presumably for the Chief Civil Engineer's delusion. Ken Cameron, who was a foreman in charge of new construction at this time, has related to the author how, when No 6200 was placed new on the Crewe Works weigh-tables, the coupled axles sent the machine pointers hard against the stops at 24 tons, their maximum capacity, and it was only by spring adjustment to transfer weight to the bogie and trailing truck that the actual weight, revealed by Eric Langridge as 119.9 tons,[14] became known. The extra load put on the trailing truck led to several cases of hot axleboxes there; eventually it was Stanier personally, with his keen interest in, and knowledge of, journal finish and lubrication, who instructed that strips of the finest grade emery cloth be stitched to the face of the worsted axlebox oil pads and the engine run up to Carlisle and back like this. On

the engine's return the boxes were cool and the journals were, as Cameron recalls, 'polished just like chromium plate'. Steps were taken to lighten the engine, by new or enlarged lightening holes in frame plates and stretchers, by thinning of castings, and other modifications. These were also applied to No 6201, being partly responsible for the five months' delay before she appeared, and got the total weight down to 108 tons. With judicious adjustment this enabled the coupled axles to be kept down to about 23 tons.

15 Tender
With the remit to work throughout between Euston and Glasgow in mind, and the generous provision of water troughs south of Carlisle (nine sets — only in Scotland was there the long stretch of 65½ miles from Mossband to Pettinain) a new tender was designed holding 9 tons of coal and 4,000gal of water. But it was unimaginative, being little more than an enlarged ex-Midland 3,500gal tender, complete with vertical handbrake and water pickup columns and the fireirons stowed — if that is not too precise a term — on top of the coal. As in the Fowler design the bunker profile did not ensure the delivery of coal to the shovelling plate, the rear end being altogether too flat. This proved to be a real weakness on a long run; O. S. Nock described a footplate trip on No 6200 in the spring of 1934, working through from Glasgow,[15] when from Crewe onwards:

> '. . . in between spells of firing (the fireman) was having to enter the tender and shovel coal forward. After Stafford, the driver took his share in the task, not only doing a considerable amount of firing, but while his mate was observing signals and taking an occasional brief rest, he too went to the back of the tender and got large quantities of coal forward . . . for a spell of two hours it was touch and go whether the fire could be kept replenished'.

Clearly this could not go on, and from 1935, as a stop-gap, these tenders were replaced by the familiar Stanier 4,000gal tenders. The bunker shape of this tender was infinitely better, although with certain types of large coal this, too, could wedge and hang back, requiring an attack with the coal hammer to move it forward. The 9-ton capacity also proved barely adequate. Meanwhile, a new tender design specifically for the Pacifics was produced and built in 1936, in which the bunker slope was extended back over the water pickup dome, to hold 10 tons, and the sides raised. Even then, under adverse conditions it could be touch-and-go on the long through Anglo-Scottish workings, and one tender (attached to No 6206) was fitted with a steam-operated coal pusher as a prototype for the subsequent 'Duchesses'.

From about 1948, standard external feed-water sieve boxes were fitted between leading and middle axles and were useful; the sieve plates could be cleaned without emptying the tank. Their only disadvantage was a proneness to freeze and fracture in bitterly cold weather.

16 Preparation and Disposal
There was no national agreement with the trade unions on preparation time which specifically referred to engines of this size; the standard allowance of 60min for engines with a heating surface greater than 1,500sq ft was clearly inadequate

for a locomotive with 45sq ft of grate on which to build a fire, and four sets of valve gear amongst other features. A special allowance of 75min was therefore negotiated.

Crossheads, slidebars and the bottom of the combination levers for the inside cylinders could be oiled from outside through a large hole in the frames, but the remainder of the gear was only accessible from the pit. By setting the inside big ends on the bottom quarters these were easily got at, but an incursion between bogie centre and rear axle and over the inside motion plate was necessary to reach the area of the valve spindle crossheads (see item 5 above), an unpleasant pursuit in a zone where every surface was coated in oily dirt.

At least a couple of tons of coal was needed to make up the fire. For this reason, on such longer and harder turns as the Euston-Perth sleeper, worked by a Pacific from Crewe, it was common practice to make up the fire and then go back under the coaling plant for a top up — another reason for a longer preparation time.

Disposal was always an Armstrong job, unaided by self-cleaning smokeboxes, rocking grates and the like. Smokebox char was very moderate, even when the engine had been worked hard, but the smokebox was over 8ft long and with an obstructed base for the shovel. The dirty fire and clinker was usually pushed down through a few lifted firebars into the ashpan, which had to be raked through both front and back dampers because of the centre hump. However the back section was at least accessible from the track side rather than the pit. The side dampers enabled the side slope sheets to be conveniently raked.

17 Firing

Few firemen attempted to run with a thin fire, which needed a very carefully maintained pattern of all-over firing with evenly-broken coal if the firebed was not to become uneven and lumpy, and correct damper settings were all-important to limit the excess air through the fire (which would adversely affect steaming). A rather thicker fire was the preferred practice, somewhat saucer-shaped with the greater thickness on the horizontal rear section of the grate. At the firehole the bed would be about 2ft thick, tapering off down the sides to more like 15-18in on the slope and at the throatplate. With a grate of this size, a good technique called for 12-15 shovels at a firing, mainly to the back corners, sides and under the door. There was a feeling amongst some firemen that large slabs of coal, provided they could be got through the firehole, would make a long-lasting basis for the fire while saving much coal hammer work — and some depots, Camden amongst them, seemed to get a high proportion of their Grade 1 coal in enormous lumps — but inevitably this led to unevenness and often to excess air through the resulting voids.

Getting coal into those back corners was a real art, for they were a couple of feet round from the side of the firehole and under the sides of the smokeplate. Some selection of this coal was desirable — lumps about the size of two fists were ideal — if it was to be placed there by wrist action with the shovel, without too much prodding. All this time the fireman's hands were exposed to the fierce heat of the fire at close quarters. To make this tolerable, firemen usually wore wrist-length leather gloves (such as welders use, but cut short), and a firing under the door immediately before filling the back corners would shield them from some of the radiant heat. Another firing technique which the author has seen used successfully was to fire alternate sides of the box.

Left:
The frames of the first 'Princess' in the erecting shop at Crewe in 1933. The two diamond-shaped holes behind the buffer beam were for by-pass valves for the inside cylinders, which in the event were never fitted.
Crown Copyright, National Railway Museum

Below left:
No 6209 of the second batch nearly completed in the erecting shop, 18 August 1935. Leading and intermediate coupled wheels are set on rollers ready for valve setting.
W. L. Good

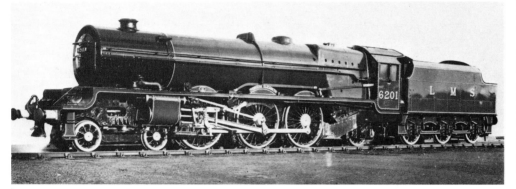

Above left:
No 6200, still in photographic grey paint, arrives at Euston for official inspection on 28 June 1933. There appears to be a steam blow, probably from the right inside piston rod packing. *Ian Allan Library*

Left:
No 6201 fitted with experimental double chimney in 1934. She still has the original tender, dry sanding gear and vacuum pump. *Crown Copyright, National Railway Museum*

Below left:
***Princess Elizabeth* with domed long-tube boiler and later 9-ton tender, fresh from General Repair in December 1935. This is the condition in which she made the high-speed test runs in November 1936.**
Real Photos (47503)

Below:
No 46205 *Princess Victoria*. This clearly shows the modifications to eliminate the inside valve gears — the massive motion girder, rocking lever in front of the outside cylinder, the short links coupling it to the outside valve spindle, and the altered reversing rods.
Real Photos (R2443)

3
The Golden Years of the 'Princesses'

The 'Princess' class locomotives, as we have seen, came into being to meet a specific operating need to work through between Euston and Glasgow on 500-ton trains, unassisted over the formidable climbs over Shap and Beattock. Representing, as they did, a fundamental change from their predecessors, they did not immediately emerge as the answer to all prayers. Important weaknesses became apparent as the first pair of engines began to make mileage on these long through workings, notably a need for very sympathetic handling to avoid steaming problems and the unsuitability of the tender. But a cross-section of the enginemen at Camden, Crewe North, Upperby and Polmadie was gaining experience in the handling techniques, particularly for the fireman in dealing with the wide firebox and the critical firing of the back corners. By 1935, when the additional 10 engines came into traffic with the early lessons incorporated, engines and men were ready to be put to the test. Thereafter, the operators increasingly called for them to perform work of an extremely high order — indeed, their confidence in the 'Princesses' led them to impose duties which taxed them to the very limit of their capability, and even beyond that on occasion. For it is true to say that the history of the timetable developments with the West Coast Anglo-Scottish expresses in the last four prewar years was intimately bound up with the prowess of these engines.

There was a preliminary test run with No 6200 on 23 July 1933, after her public viewing at Euston and while temporarily based at Crewe North. She worked a 502-ton train of empty stock from Crewe to Carlisle and back, on timings of 170min northbound and 174min back (slower than 'Limited Load'). The steaming on Grimethorpe coal proved excellent on the more level sections of line, but could not be maintained against the injector on the heavier grades. Some highly surprising consumption figures were derived:

Coal, lb/mile	41.5
lb/DBHP hr	2.68
lb/sq ft grate/hr	44.1
Water, gal/mile	35.0
lb/DBHP hr	22.6
Evaporation, lb/lb coal	8.42

These figures were quite unaccountably low, a similar phenomenon to the tests on 'Jubilees' a year later. It was assessed that, had steam heating been in use, the coal consumptions would have been 44.7lb/mile and 2.89lb/ DBHP hr. The results were not circulated as an official report.

The first outing in the full glare of publicity, however, was hardly a triumph. No 6200 was introduced to the press on an inaugural special run on 15 August 1933, having run some 5,000 miles during the six weeks since new. It was nominally a dynamometer car test, working to 'Special Limit' timings on a 165min schedule from Euston to Crewe with 532 tons.[16] The start out of Euston up to Camden No 1 box, without banking assistance and on 55% cutoff, caused C. J. Allen to enthuse[17] that:

'. . . the new giant simply soared up the 1 in 77 and the 1 in 105 . . . without an atom of slip. . . . Never previously have I witnessed such an unassisted exit from the terminus, even with trains considerably lighter than this'.

Outline details of the running are shown in Table 1. As was to be expected with the dynamometer car in use, the

Table 1
Dynamometer Car Test Run: Euston-Crewe, 15 August 1933

Locomotive: Class 7P 4-6-2 No 6200 *The Princess Royal*
Load, coaches: 15
    tons tare/gross: 532/540
Enginemen: Dvr A. Parsons, Fmn H. Betley (Crewe N)

Distance miles		'Special Limit' Sched (min)	Actual Time min sec	Speeds
0.0	EUSTON	0	0.00	—
1.0	mp 1		3.08	—
5.4	WILLESDEN JN	9	8.47	58½
8.1	Wembley		11.26	61½
13.3	Hatch End		16.56	54
17.4	WATFORD JN	22	21.16	61½
24.5	Hemel Hempstead		28.31	54
28.0	Berkhamsted		32.33	50
31.7	Tring	38	37.12	47½
36.1	Cheddington		41.30	75
46.7	BLETCHLEY	51	50.13	—
59.9	Roade	63	62.22	55½
75.3	Welton		75.40	56½
82.6	RUGBY	86	84.11	40*
97.1	NUNEATON	101	99.56	69
			pws†	40
110.0	TAMWORTH	114	113.01	—
116.3	LICHFIELD	120	119.30	—
118.8	Elmhurst		122.42	—

Calculated average Equivalent DBHPs:
Wembley-Hatch End	1,420
Watford-Hemel Hempstead	1,070
Hemel Hempstead-Berkhamsted	1,030

* Permanent speed restriction
† Polesworth pitfall slack, allowed for in schedule

emphasis was on conforming closely to the timings with no spectacular running. Indeed, after the very limited crew familiarisation it would have been unrealistic to attempt it. The engine was worked very easily, generally on 17% cutoff on the level stretches, with the regulator half open, but once or twice the cutoff was shortened to 12½% (sic). Minimum boiler pressure was 230lb/sq in. Nemesis struck, however, beyond Lichfield, when the enginemen detected a hot trailing coupled axlebox, and the test had to be terminated at the next signalbox, Elmhurst Crossing, from where the train limped to Crewe largely on the slow line. As a result, no useful consumption figures were produced. The return was handled creditably by a 'Royal Scot'.

A month later, on 22 September, and now transferred to Camden, *The Princess Royal* took up her intended work, the through London-Glasgow working of the 'Royal Scot' train. With the entry into service of sister No 6201 in November, based at Polmadie, the two engines took over the train; for a time they were expected to cover an intensive diagram involving 1,612 miles in three days, as follows:

Day 1	10.00 Euston-Glasgow	The 'Royal Scot'
	22.45 Glasgow-Euston	
Day 2	13.30 Euston-Glasgow	The 'Mid-day Scot'
Day 3	10.00 Glasgow-Euston	The 'Royal Scot'

This proved to be somewhat ambitious, and was eased to a four-day diagram covering a single trip each day. Some settling down was needed, not least by drivers and firemen, on such long continuous runs. Particularly in the down direction, where heavy work was required on Shap and Beattock banks after 5-6hr of steaming, with the fire beginning to get dirty, the best technique needed to be learned. On the first day,[18] the 141.0 miles from Crewe to Carlisle were run in 159½min with a load of 431 tons tare and a minimum speed of 24½mph at Shap Summit, while the 10.0 miles from Beattock to Summit were taken comfortably in 19¾min with a minimum of 25½mph.

The second 'Princess', No 6201, was also run in from Crewe North, and on Sunday 17 December 1933 made a trial run with dynamometer car to Carlisle and back. Again a 502-ton train of empty stock was taken, on 'Limited load' timings of 167min (down) and 169min (up), and using Grimethorpe coal as usual. There were delays due to fog in the early stages, and on the return there were serious operating delays after Preston. The engine was worked with full regulator, 15% cutoff sufficing on the easier sections but increased to 35% on Grayrigg and a maximum of 40% on Shap; southbound 35% was used to Southwaite and 30% thence to the Summit. The steaming was excellent throughout. The consumption figures were very different from those for No 6200 five months earlier, and much more credible:

Coal, lb/mile	50.9
lb/DBHP hr	3.22
lb/sq ft grate/hr	46.8
Water, gal/mile	42.8
lb/DBHP hr	27.0
Evaporation, lb/lb coal	8.41

The steam temperatures, however, were abysmal, averaging 475-480°F in the steam chest, with a maximum of 500°F.

An illuminating account of the engine working at this period was given by O. S. Nock,[19] reporting on a footplate trip on No 6200 with the up 'Royal Scot' on 3 April 1934 from Symington — a station now vanished almost without trace, where the Edinburgh section was attached — through to Euston. Extracts from this run are given in Table 2. It is

Table 2
The 'Royal Scot', Glasgow-Euston. 3 April 1934

Locomotive: Class 7P 4-6-2 No 6200 *The Princess Royal*
Load, coaches: 15
 tons tare/gross: 465/500
Enginemen: Symington-Carlisle. Dvr Harrison, Fmn Hill (Polmadie)
 Carlisle-Euston. Dvr L. Earl, Fmn Lubnow (Camden)

Distance miles		Sched (min)	Actual Times min sec	Speeds
0.0	SYMINGTON	0	0.00	—
3.7	Lamington		5.40	61½
9.1	Abington		11.22	53min
11.6	Crawford		14.10	55/47½
14.3	Elvanfoot		17.18	55
17.2	Beattock Summit	22	21.05	34½min
27.2	BEATTOCK	32	30.43	70½/56
41.1	LOCKERBIE	45	43.43	66/56
		62	pws	40
58.3	Gretna Jn	62	60.18	70½
66.9	CARLISLE	71	70.30	—
4.9	Wreay		10.57	29½
7.4	Southwaite		15.11	41
10.8	Calthwaite		20.00	44½ (mp60)
13.1	Plumpton	21	23.06	40 (mp57¼)
17.9	PENRITH	27	28.22	64½
22.2	Clifton		32.50	47
26.2	mp43		39.04	33½
29.5	Shap		45.23	30
31.5	Shap Summit	49	48.53	32¼
37.0	TEBAY	55	55.35	72½
50.0	OXENHOLME	67	67.21	74 max
			pws	25
			pws	45
			sigs	15
90.1	PRESTON	108	109.15	*
141.1	CREWE	168	167.30	*
145.8	Betley Road		175.08	44½
151.6	Whitmore	182	182.35	53
165.6	STAFFORD	196	195.35	72/30*
182.9	LICHFIELD	214	213.31	64½/74
			pws	40†
202.0	NUNEATON	233	233.22	64½/57½
216.6	RUGBY	249	248.03	64½/35*
239.3	Roade	272	271.28	69/62½
252.5	BLETCHLEY	284	282.35	77½
259.0	Leighton Buzzard		288.38	61
263.1	Cheddington		292.42	58½
267.5	Tring	301	297.47	48
281.7	WATFORD JN	314	310.38	75 max
293.8	WILLESDEN JN	325	320.55	77½ max
			sigs	
299.2	EUSTON	334	329.45	—

 Net time 324

Calculated average Equivalent DBHPs:
Lamington-Abington	1,220
Elvanfoot-Beattock Summit	1,300
Wreay-Calthwaite	1,170
Clifton-mp43	1,300
Betley Road-Whitmore	1,370
Nuneaton-Bulkington	1,200
Cheddington-Tring	960

* Permanent speed restriction
† Polesworth pitfall slack, allowed for in schedule

worthy of note that, even six months after No 6200, and more than three months after No 6201 had taken up the 'Royal Scot' haulage, the Polmadie crew had never previously worked a 'Princess'.

> 'Less than a mile from the . . . start, Driver Harrison had brought the cutoff back to 15% and opened the regulator wide . . . cutoff was advanced to 18% at Wandelmill and to 20% at Abington . . . '.

which was enough to get the train to Beattock Summit slightly faster than scheduled; outputs ranged around 1,250EDBHP. From the Summit, 15% to 17% cutoff, with regulator not more than half open, enabled the 71-minute booking to be bettered by ½min, or 1½min net.

The running from Carlisle, now in the expert hands of Driver Laurie Earl, showed the most scrupulous adherence to the timetable. 'Limited Load' timings applied from Carlisle to Crewe (500 tons allowed to Shap Summit) and 'Special Limit' timings forward to Euston. All the way to Bletchley, the actual running time was never more than 2min 35sec different from schedule, and even that was the direct result of two permanent way slacks costing 2¾min between them! It also showed proper consideration for the fireman over a 5½hr stint, and the rather slow start probably reflected a need to build up the fire for the long climb to Shap Summit; Polmadie men had a reputation for handing over with a light fire.

> 'Apart from the start out of Carlisle, Earl used 25% cutoff all the way up to Shap Summit, but it was not until Clifton that the regulator was opened to full. Speed was being steadily maintained on the upper part of the 1 in 125 past Thrimby Grange; it was 33½mph at Milepost 43, 31½ at post 42, 30½ at 41 post and 30 at post 40 — not a high speed, but sufficient for timekeeping'.

After Lancaster, full regulator with 25% cutoff was employed along the almost level stretch to Preston, to produce 73½mph at Brock troughs. South of Crewe, 25% cutoff was used on Madeley bank, producing nearly 1,400EDBHP at a sustained 44½-45mph on the 1 in 177, but thereafter nothing more than 20% was used and no high power outputs produced; the final climb to Tring could only be described as leisurely, notwithstanding gaining 1¾min on the easy 17min sectional timing.

But C. J. Allen was constrained to comment:[19]

> 'It could be added . . . that during these first months . . . the performance of the new engines have not been unvaryingly of the same high standard. Shortly after . . . I came . . . on the same train, with the same engine and . . . load, but we reached Euston 30¾min late, after a late start of 2min. There were flashes of brilliance here and there . . . but . . . there were distinct symptoms of shortness of steam'.

This may well have been aggravated by the problems of coal not trimming down in the tender, to which reference has been made in the preceding chapter. It was evident that the lower-superheat 'Princess' boiler with 2¼in diameter small tubes was not free-steaming, for all its vital ratios were wrong. Stanier by this time had realised that Swindon practice did not readily transfer in its entirety to the LMS. As he modestly admitted a dozen years later in the discussion following an Institution of Locomotive Engineers paper:[21]

> ' . . . he thought, with his limited experience, that the Great Western was right and everyone else was wrong, and that a two-row superheater was all that was necessary. . . . He soon had grounds, however, for altering his opinion.'

So the first four 'Princesses' of the 1935 order came out with 24-element superheaters, and the remainder with 32-element boilers. The two original boilers, with 20ft 9in between tubeplates, were also modified to carry a 32-element superheater in 1935; the third boiler, No 6050, had been built with 32 elements. With the bigger superheater, most of the steaming problems vanished. All 12 engines were allocated to Camden.

From 27 May to 1 June 1935 No 6200 with her new boiler was tested between Euston and Glasgow on the 'Royal Scot', then allowed:

Euston-Crewe	170min	Glasgow-Symington	51min
Crewe-Carlisle	166min	Symington-Carlisle	71min
Carlisle-Glasgow	124min	Carlisle-Euston	330min

For the purpose she had been fitted with 'Sinuflo' elements for steam temperature comparisons with the standard 1¼in diameter 13swg elements. On the first three trips the 'original' 5¹¹/₁₆in diameter blastpipe cap was fitted, but for the last three days it was replaced by a 5½in diameter cap. On 31 May the train was specially loaded to 587 tons to Crewe and 493 tons to Symington, while on 11 June the engine brought 574 tons from Symington. Grimethorpe coal was used throughout.

Some details were given in Dynamometer Car Report No 56 of the engine working on the last two days. On 31 May the fire was not well prepared, and there were steaming problems until Roade. Despite this, no longer cutoff than 22% was used from Willesden to Tring, and 15-17% was the norm until Oxenholme; 22% sufficed on Grayrigg and a maximum of 40% was used on Shap and Beattock. Southbound nothing more than 26% was used between Penrith and Shap Summit. Steaming was generally good, with the 5½in diameter cap having the edge. But temperatures were very disappointing, as compared with the immediately following tests with the same engine on accelerated timings and with standard bifurcated elements. The 'Sinuflo' elements gave figures mainly in the 515-550°F range, with a maximum of 550°F, where the standard ones gave mainly 590-600°F. Consumption figures averaged:

	Down	Up
Coal, lb/mile	40.3	38.2
lb/DBHP hr	2.97	2.95
lb/sq ft grate/hr	47.8	45.7
Water, gal/mile	35.0	35.1
lb/DBHP hr	25.9	27.1
Evaporation, lb/lb coal	8.71	9.19

No conclusions were drawn, but the 5½in diameter blastpipe cap was standardised and the elements were not used again.

Less than a month later, between 25 and 30 June, No 6200 was out with the dynamometer car again,

'to investigate the possibility of working an accelerated service between Euston and Glasgow. . . hauling heavy trains',

in readiness for the 1936 'Mid-day Scot'. The timings postulated were:

Euston-Crewe	153min	Glasgow-Carlisle	112min
Crewe-Lancaster	76min	Carlisle-Lancaster	78min
Lancaster-Carlisle	72min	Lancaster-Crewe	78min
Carlisle-Glasgow	112min	Crewe-Willesden	142min

The Willesden timing arose only because, for convenience in pathing the tests, the Crewe-Euston leg was made on the 17.25 from Liverpool, which stopped there; an empty stock working from Crewe to Liverpool was used for balancing purposes. North of Crewe the tests were made by a special empty stock train of 461 tons on Sunday 30 June at 08.10 from Crewe and 15.00 from Glasgow, while south of Crewe the loads varied from 453 to 515 tons.

Dynamometer Car Report No 57 refers to the engine as '. . . fully capable of working to the accelerated times', and then mentions in unaccustomed language:

'. . . the exceptionally fine run between Crewe and Euston on Thursday 27 June . . . the train arrived at Euston 13½min before time, and the average speed was 70.7mph, the maximum . . . being 87mph'.

Further details of this run are given in Table 4.

'A remarkable running performance was also made over Shap . . . this being completed in 7min 20sec (Tebay-Shap Summit) which is approximately 4min below normal scheduled time. Beattock Summit was passed in 16½min (from Beattock) instead of . . . 20min. Again a very fine run was made on the return journey from Carlisle to Shap Summit, this taking 37min instead of . . . 48min'.

The Report notes that 1,500-1,600DBHP (not equivalent) was sustained for long periods, cutoffs between 15% and 25% on the more level stretches and 35-45% on the banks being used with the regulator wide open. Averages of 1,560DBHP from Tebay to Shap Summit, 1,530 from Penrith to Summit and 1,562 from Crewe to Whitmore were specifically mentioned, which was hard work indeed for a 'Princess'. Steaming was 'very satisfactory' against this demand with the 5½in diameter blastpipe cap. The outputs on the northern climbs have been superimposed on Figs 28 and 29 for comparison with later 'Duchess' performance. Consumptions were:

	25-27 June Euston-Liverpool and return	30 June Crewe-Glasgow and return
Coal, lb/mile	44.6	52.6
lb/DBHP hr	2.84	2.88
lb/sq ft grate/hr	57.5	68.1
Water, gal/mile	36.2	39.2
lb/DBHP hr	23.0	21.5
Evaporation, lb/lb coal	8.12	7.45

While the consumptions per mile were higher than a month before, as a result of the harder work involved, the specific figures per DBHP hr were some of the lowest ever recorded in Britain.

Even now the testing section was not finished with the 'Princesses'. Between 17 November and 3 December 1935 tests were run on the 'Royal Scot' between Euston and Glasgow to make a direct comparison of coal and water consumptions between engines with 24- and 32-element superheaters. Three days' testing was rejected owing to unsatisfactory loads or fog delays. Between Euston and Carlisle, Camden and Upperby crews alternated; Polmadie men worked north of Carlisle. The engines selected were Nos 6203 (24 elements) and 6209.

Dynamometer Car Report No 59 said that steaming was, in general, 'completely satisfactory', but on certain occasions with both engines was erratic, with pressures down to 160-170lb/sq in. This must have been due to crew errors, though on only one day was mismanagement of the fire blamed.

Steam temperatures averaged 520-535°F, with a maximum of 550°F, with the smaller superheater; with 32 elements the average was 550-575°F with a maximum of 595°F, the bigger superheater thus giving some 40°F higher steam temperatures. This was reflected in the coal and water consumption figures, which were:

	6203	6209	Difference in favour of 6209
Coal, lb/mile	46.4	44.3	−4.7%
lb/DBHP hr	3.23	3.07	−4.9%
lb/sq ft grate/hr	53.5	51.8	−3.2%
Water, gal/mile	38.1	35.7	−6.3%
lb/DBHP hr	26.4	24.9	−5.7%
Evaporation, lb/lb coal	8.20	8.11	−1.1%

But superheat retained its fascination for Stanier and his staff, and No 6209 figured in further tests, of a slightly bizarre nature, between Crewe and Carlisle from 29 November 1938 to 20 January 1939. Fresh from a General Repair and carrying 32-element boiler No 9106, she ran four trips between Crewe and Carlisle each way as a control, and was then stopped at Crewe North shed while insulation was applied to elements, superheater header and smokebox main steampipes. It was already apparent that the flue gas temperatures on leaving the large tubes were lower than the superheated steam temperatures, and thus heat was being *lost* from the steam at this stage. The last 4ft 6in of the element exit pipes was wound with asbestos tape, while the header and steam pipes were enclosed in plastic magnesia. True, it was found that the steam chest temperatures in lagged condition were up to 26°F higher than when unlagged (the higher increases being on the easier sections) but it was not a practicable application; in March 1939 Stanier wrote to his chief, Sir Harold Hartley, pointing out the drawbacks and discontinuing the experiment pending completion of the new Rugby Testing Station. But no 'Princess' got on to the rollers there, and the war imposed a 10-year delay anyway.

Service Accelerations

The test runs in June 1935 bore fruit in the 1936 summer timetable, which imposed a formidable task on the 'Princesses' with the acceleration of the 'Mid-day Scot'. The down train, leaving Euston at 14.00, was allowed 7hr 35min overall to Glasgow, a cut of 30min at one fell swoop. Four stops were included, at Crewe (in 163min, where a Birmingham section was attached, making a minimum load of 14 coaches but usually 16 or even more at weekends), Lancaster, Penrith and Carlisle (where Edinburgh and Aberdeen sections were detached, leaving about nine coaches to go forward to Glasgow). The timings south of the border were 'Special Limit' except for the Lancaster-Penrith portion, where a murderous 59min allowance was made for the 51.25 miles over Grayrigg and Shap banks — something of a counsel of perfection. Even here the Pacifics were expected to keep time with 17 coaches unassisted. The up train was more easily timed, in 7hr 50min, but could load every bit as heavily. At this time the down 'Royal Scot' was still a 7¾hr train, stopping only at Carlisle Kingmoor (to reman) and Symington (divide), while the up train was allowed 7hr 40min.

Some extraordinarily fine work was done on the 'Mid-day', and was undoubtedly the zenith of 'Princess' running. Such confidence did these engines engender that the operators continued the acceleration policy; the normal pattern was that some duplication of services took place in summer, allowing stops to be cut out and thus some acceleration, while reverting to combined trains with additional stops during the winter months. In the winter 1936 book the 'Royal Scot' came in for treatment; the down train came down by 5min to 7hr 40min to Glasgow, with Rugby, Crewe, Carlisle and Symington stops, while in the opposite direction the time was reduced by 15min, to 7hr 25min. It was a heavy train, seldom loading to less than 15 coaches.

In May 1937 these timings were nibbled at again. The down 'Royal Scot' came down to 7½hr, still non-stop to Kingmoor and then dividing at Symington, while the down 'Mid-day Scot' divided at Crewe, the first portion calling at Lancaster and Carlisle to reach Glasgow in 7½hr, while the lighter second portion called at Lancaster, Penrith, Carlisle and Symington with coaches for Edinburgh and Aberdeen. Still more change was wrought with the high summer timetable in July 1937, when the 6½hr 'Coronation Scot' was introduced. The 'Royal Scot' now made a Carlisle station stop in each direction, while the 'Mid-day Scot' at 14.00 assumed a new stop pattern; northbound it called at Crewe, Wigan (9min attaching Manchester-Glasgow and Edinburgh coaches), Lancaster (5min attaching coaches from Liverpool) and Carlisle, while in the up direction it picked up an Aberdeen section at Law Junction and an Edinburgh section at Symington before stopping at Carlisle, Lancaster and Crewe, still in 7½hr. But this operation was too complex for good timekeeping, and further changes were made.

In May 1938 the 'Royal Scot' became a 7hr train to and from Glasgow, with Pacifics limited to 420 tons; the down train called only at Carlisle, reached in 300min, and

Symington (to drop Edinburgh coaches), but in the up direction the Glasgow and Edinburgh trains ran separately. The first remanned at Carlisle No 12 box and then reached Euston in 302min, while the latter made the Carlisle station stop. With the winter timetable, however, additional stops were put into the 'Royal Scot' in the down direction, as usual, giving an overall time of 7hr 20min and intermediate times of:

Euston-Rugby	80min ('XL Limit')
Rugby-Crewe	75min ('XL Limit') detach Aberdeen section
Crewe-Carlisle	151min ('Special Limit')
Carlisle-Symington	79min detach Edinburgh coaches
Symington-Glasgow	43min

By contrast the up 'Royal Scot' was put back to 7hr 25min, running non-stop from Carlisle to Euston in 321min. All this time the 'Princesses' were the mainstay of the service, for it was not until May 1938 that the original five 'Coronation' Pacifics began to be supplemented by further building. In the last summer before World War 2 the 7hr timing of the 'Royal Scot' was restored, with the Euston-Carlisle time pared to 299min to just come into the 60mph category. Train loads were slightly curtailed and this, in conjunction with the more practical timetable, brought improved punctuality. Morale was high, the 'On Time' campaign was making its mark, and 15 'Coronation' Pacifics were now in service and beginning to relieve the 'Princesses' on the harder Anglo-Scottish turns. Locomotive performance was at a very high level.

Day-to-Day Running

As accelerations were made, so did the demand on the locomotives increase. Within reason this was beneficial, for a timetable seldom works better in practice by slowing trains and making the locomotive work easier. It will therefore be appropriate to look at a variety of performances to see how far they taxed the locomotive and crew in running according to the book or in recovering time. The bulk of 'Princess' work was done on the West Coast main line from Euston to Glasgow and Perth; they performed some limited filling-in turns elsewhere, notably from Perth to Aberdeen and Glasgow, but these were much less demanding. To illustrate the development of their performance it is enough to examine three specific sections:

- the easily-graded 158.1 miles between Euston and Crewe,
- the 69.1 mile Lancaster-Carlisle section, taking the severe banks over Grayrigg and Shap (915ft), and
- the Carlisle-Carstairs length of 73.5 miles, covering the rises to Kirkpatrick and Castlemilk before Beattock bank up to Beattock Summit (1,014ft).

1 Euston-Crewe

Four performances with the down 'Royal Scot' between 1936 and 1938 have been brought together in Table 3, all by the last batch of engines with 32-element superheaters. That in column 1[22] shows, from Rugby onwards, a 'Princess' on an already very heavy train being loaded up quite unreasonably by the addition of two empty vehicles being worked north by operating whim; the resultant load to Crewe was over

Table 3
Euston-Crewe. The 'Royal Scot'

		Winter 1936			Early 1937		Summer 1937			Summer 1938		
Year:		6211			6206		6212			6209		
Locomotive:												
Load, coaches:		17‡			16		16			13		
tons tare/gross:		539/565‡			492/515		493/520			394/420		
Enginemen:		Not recorded			Dvr L. Earl, Fmn Abey (Camden)		Dvr L. Earl (Camden)			Dvr Bishop (Camden)		
Distance miles		'Special Limit' Sched (min)	Actual Times min sec	Speeds	Actual Times min sec	Speeds	'Special Limit' Sched (min)	Actual Times min sec	Speeds	'XL Limit' Sched (min)	Actual Times min sec	Speeds
0.00	EUSTON	0	0.00	—	0.00	—	0	0.00	—	0	0.00	—
5.4	WILLESDEN JN	10	9.40	—	10.37	—	10	10.35	—	9	8.57	—
8.1	Wembley		—	62	13.22	59		—			—	—
11.4	Harrow		15.38		16.54	—		17.07			14.46	
13.3	Hatch End		—	57	—	55		—	52½		—	60½
17.4	WATFORD JN	23	21.50	—	23.10	62½	23	23.33		21	20.20	—
21.0	Kings Langley		—	65	26.35	61		—	62		—	69
24.5	Hemel Hempstead		28.44	—	30.05 / pws	60 / 15		30.27	—		26.42	—
31.7	Tring	38	36.28	53	41.59	—	38	37.48	58½	35	33.06	63
40.2	Leighton Buzzard		43.45	77	48.50	85/80½		44.36	80½		39.59	79
46.7	BLETCHLEY	51	49.00	—	53.33	83½/79	51	49.41	—	47	44.57	—
52.4	Wolverton		53.55	—	57.46	85		54.24	—		49.38	—
59.9	Roade	63	60.58	56½	63.33	72½	63	60.57	63½	58	56.04	63
62.8	BLISWORTH	66	63.55	—	65.66	76½	66	63.40	—	61	58.43	—
69.7	Weedon		70.05	68	71.12	79		69.42	—		64.21	—
75.3	Welton		75.30	56	75.36	70½		74.40	63		69.15	59
82.6	RUGBY	87	83.55	—	83.14	—	85	82.04	45*	79	76.30	45*
5.5	Brinklow		8.19	—				88.36	—		—	—
14.5	NUNEATON	16	16.39	79			101	96.47 / sig stop	—	93	90.46	74
19.7	Atherstone		20.50 / pws†	—				108.00 / pws†	— / 32		95.14	64*
27.4	TAMWORTH	30	28.28	—			115	117.22	66		101.35	74
33.7	LICHFIELD	36	34.45	59			121	123.09	64	110	106.46	62
41.7	Rugeley	43	42.18	72			128	130.01	76	117	113.53	72
51.0	STAFFORD	53	51.10	42*			138	138.35	70/55*	126	122.27	48*
56.3	Norton Bridge	60	57.54	50††			145	144.35	—	132	127.39	—
60.8	Standon Bridge		63.42	—				—	—		—	65
65.0	Whitmore	69	69.48	—			154	152.38	66	141	136.03	64
70.7	Betley Road		75.12	—				157.29	79		141.12	eased sigs
75.5	CREWE	80	81.15	—			164	162.45 / pass	20*	151	147.54 / pass	20*

	Winter 1936	Early 1937	Summer 1937	Summer 1938
Net Times	84+81¾	79	155¼	147
Calculated average Equivalent DBHPs:				
Wembley-Hatch End	1,510	1,300	1,310	1,300
Watford-Tring	1,330	1,410**	1,410	1,350
Castlethorpe-Roade	1,300	1,750	1,500	1,280
Standon Bridge-Whitmore	—	—	1,610	1,290

* Permanent Speed Restriction
† Polesworth pitfall slack, allowed for in schedule
‡ Load increased from Rugby to 19 coaches, 589/615 tons
** Kings Langley-Hemel Hempstead
†† From 50mph at Great Bridgeford, engine eased excessively for timekeeping

600 tons gross. As far as Rugby, with 17 coaches, some fairly hard work was done, with EDBHPs in the 1,300-1,500 range; the 'Special Limit' timing was bettered by 3min. From the restart the engine must have been worked very hard indeed to pass Nuneaton at 79mph and drop only 39sec on the difficult 16min timing. This good work continued to Stafford, where some liberty was taken with the 30mph limit then in force on Queensville curve. But from Great Bridgeford the speed fell off badly and Whitmore was breasted at no more than about 40mph, suggesting that the engine may have been 'winded' by its exertions; from being 2min to the good at

Stafford, Crewe was reached in 1¼min over the allowance.

The next run[23] was by that remarkable little driver Laurie Earl, and was on the down 'Royal Scot' a few months later, the engine working right through and the men going as far as Carlisle. Earl, as usual, showed a degree of early caution while getting the measure of his engine, and was barely keeping time when brought down to 15mph by a permanent way slack before Berkhamsted; he had used 30% cutoff on Camden bank, 25% from there to Willesden, and then 20% to the slack. From there, as O. S. Nock commented, 'the running . . . became spectacular indeed'. Thirty per cent cutoff was used to recover to Tring, from where 20% was the rule on the level and downhill sections, and 25% up to Roade and Kilsby; this gave EDBHPs up to 1,750, and almost certainly involved mortgaging the boiler.

Column 3 again featured Earl with a similar-sized train (well within the 'Special Limit' loading).[24] Again the start was taken easily, with just 25% cutoff while assisted up Camden bank and 20% from Primrose Hill. Speed probably did not reach 60mph by Milepost 7, at the start of the climb, fell away to 52½ at the crest, and did not exceed 62 at Watford. It was a well-judged opening, however, for with slightly harder work from Kings Langley, Tring was breasted at 58½mph and in 12sec less than the booking. At Wolverton no time was wasted in advancing cutoff progressively to 25% before speed fell very far on the rise to Roade, producing a

good minimum of 63½mph, and the work up to Kilsby Tunnel was very similar. After the Rugby slowing, Earl worked the engine easily, but he was now 4½min early and paid the penalty with a dead stand for signals at Hartshill box (mp 99½). Recovery was not pushed until after the pitfall slack beyond Polesworth, but then, with the train 2¼min late, *Duchess of Kent* was put to it strongly to be right time by Norton Bridge. In recovering from the, by this time, 55mph restriction at Stafford, 25% cutoff was used most of the way up to Whitmore, which was topped at the high speed of 66mph.

In column 4 in the summer of 1938, with the train now on 'XL Limit' timings and a load within 26 tons of the 420-ton limit,[24] the engine was working through to Glasgow and the men to Carlisle. Driver Bishop (who a year later went with

Table 4
Crewe-Euston. 17.25 ex-Liverpool Lime Street

Year:			1934		1935			1948	
Locomotive:			6200		6200			6200	
Load, coaches:			12		15			15	
tons tare/gross:			354/380		453/475			466/500	
Enginemen:			Dvr Parsons (Camden)		Not recorded			Dvr Walls, Fmn Foster (Edge Hill)	
Distance miles		Sched min	Actual Times min sec	Speeds	Actual Times min sec	Speeds	Sched min	Actual Times min sec	Speeds
0.0	CREWE	0	0.00	—	0.00	—	0	0.00	—
1.1	Basford Wood		—	—	2.35	40		—	—
4.8	Betley Road		6.45	59	6.47	60		8.00	52
8.0	Madeley		9.58	58½	10.06	58		11.45	51
10.5	Whitmore		12.26	62/66	12.33	64		14.33	—
24.5	STAFFORD	26	23.11	82/38*	23.34	80½/*	26	25.38	85½/52*
41.8	LICHFIELD	42	38.13	78/75	38.40	80/76	41	41.03	78½/74
48.1	TAMWORTH		42.45	85/79	43.19	85½		45.34	85½
			pws†	68	pws†	—		sig stop	
55.8	Atherstone		49.13	65	51.05	65		56.57	—
61.0	NUNEATON	60	53.35	76½	55.21	76	58	62.03	67½
66.7	Shilton		58.23	70½	60.00	73½		—	64½
			sigs	80½/15					
75.5	RUGBY	73	66.44	15	67.09	82/*	72	74.44	77/*
	Kilsby Tunnel North		—	57	—	55		—	56
88.4	Weedon		79.48	76½/72*	78.47	85½		86.58	80½
95.3	BLISWORTH	91	85.26	74	84.02	75	90	92.13	77½
98.2	Roade	94	87.57	68½	86.27	71½	93	94.37	72
105.7	Wolverton		93.40	85/72*	92.10	82		100.04	87½
111.4	BLETCHLEY	105	98.24	75/70½	96.43	75	104	104.20	77½/80
			sigs,	slight					
117.9	Leighton Buzzard		103.51	64	102.00	72		109.26	74½/76½
122.0	Cheddington		107.39	67/61½	105.23	71½		112.42	71½
126.4	Tring	119	112.09	55½	109.16	67	118	116.39	64½
137.2	Kings Langley		120.58	83½	117.25	86½		125.09	83½
								sig stop	
141.7	WATFORD JN		123.33	71½	119.55	75		136.18	—
150.0	Wembley		131.09	74	126.52	85½		145.10	80
			sigs	30					
152.7	WILLESDEN JN	142	134.37	—	129.33	—	140	147.16	—
								sigs	
158.1	EUSTON						148	155.40	—
	Net Times		132		129½			132‡	

Equivalent DBHPs:			
Basford Wood-Betley Road	1,550	2,000	—
Betley Road-Madeley	1,650	1,910	1,670
Nuneaton-Bulkington	1,260	—	1,540
Blisworth-Roade	1,030	1,610	1,460
Cheddington-Tring	950	1,550	1,450

* Permanent Speed restriction
† Polesworth pitfall, allowed for in schedule
‡ Net time to a Willesden stop

25

the 'Coronation Scot' to the USA) showed exemplary steady running at fairly constant output, about 1,300EDBHP being produced on the principal climbs. This required a steam rate of something like 25,000lb/hr, and coal at a rate of close on 3,000lb/hr, reckoned to be about the continuous firing limit for one man.

In the up direction, Table 4 sets out three runs on the 17.25 from Liverpool Lime Street, the fastest start-to-stop timing on the LMS before World War 2 and running on unique timings about 5min faster than 'XL Limit'. This carried a load limit of 420 tons. Until 1937 this train made a Willesden stop. The first run, made with No 6200 in original condition with two-row superheater, can be regarded as exceptionally good for that time with a normal 12-coach load. The start from Crewe up to Whitmore was very energetic, needing steam at over 28,000lb/hr. But such running brought the train 2¾min early by Stafford and 6½min early by Nuneaton; it could not go on. Signals reduced progress to 15mph all the way from Rugby No 7 box to the station — probably for no better reason than No 1 box putting a train over to the Northampton line. Now on clear signals Driver Parsons went hard at it again until Bletchley, but approaching Leighton he was sighting distant signals at caution and eased off on the climb to Tring. Even so, a net time of 132min betokens fine enginemanship.

The second run[27], made as part of the dynamometer car tests in June 1935, was really spectacular, and must constitute a record on this train. The load had been deliberately made up to 15 coaches including dynamometer car, some 33 tons over the limit for a 'Princess', and was clearly a pre-arranged effort for No 6200 (with 32-element superheater), for O. S. Nock wrote:[28]

'. . . arriving at Euston about 8.30pm I was surprised to see No 6200 come in to No 1 platform . . . 14min early . . . it was evident that something pretty exciting must have happened on the way up, particularly as I recognised Mr Riddles climbing off the footplate'.

Up to Whitmore the engine was driven very hard, as EDBHPs well over 1,900 confirm; this required steaming at a rate of about 32,000lb/hr but probably dropped the water level somewhat. All the short banks were taken in comparable manner, using the sheer capacity of the boiler for brief periods, while there were no less than eight separate bursts of speed into the 80s, with a maximum of 86½mph coming down from Tring. Even on the final rise from Cheddington the steaming rate was about 29,000lb/hr.

Little inferior to this, however, without the stimulus of Mr Stanier's Personal Assistant on the footplate, was the last run in the table,[29] also on The Princess Royal in 1938. The load was even heavier, at 500 tons gross — 46 tons over the limit for this train — but that did not worry a pair of highly competent Edge Hill men. It was not an uneventful trip, as a signal stop for 34sec at Polesworth due to sheep on the line, and a further signal stop at Watford Tunnel North box for 4min 16sec (doubtless due to a train in front stopping in Watford station) confirm. But intermediately the running was of the highest order; the main banks were attacked with EDBHPs up to 1,700, and there were seven 80s as well. A net time equivalent to 132min to a Willesden stop with 500 tons gross behind the tender in everyday traffic conditions would be very hard to surpass.

Table 5
Lancaster-Penrith. The 'Mid-day Scot' in 1936-8

Locomotive:			Class 7P 4-6-2		6203		6209		6212		6208	
Load, coaches:					14		14		16		16	
tons tare/gross			500/530		445/470		448/470		493/520		490/515	
Enginemen:			See note below		Not recorded		Not recorded		Not recorded		Not recorded	
Distance miles		Sched min	Calc Time min sec	Speeds	Actual Times min sec	Speeds	Actual Times min sec	Speeds	Actual Times min sec	Speeds	Actual Times min sec	Speeds
0.00	LANCASTER	0	0.00	—	0.00	—	0.00	—	0.00	—	0.00	—
6.3	CARNFORTH	8	7.52	63/67½	8.01	67	7.39	70½	8.40	64	7.52	71
9.5	mp9½		11.03	55	11.05	55	—	60	12.00	49½	—	55
13.6	Milnthorpe		14.51	71	14.53	67½	14.17	70½	16.05	66	14.33	67½
15.5	Hincaster Jn		16.38	60½	16.46	59	16.04	59	18.03	57½	—	—
19.1	OXENHOLME	21	20.04	58½/52	20.44	50	19.50	53½	22.23	45	20.25	52½
22.0	mp22		23.40	47/48½	24.29	—	—	45½*	26.18	43½	—	—
24.0	mp24		26.19	44½	27.19	42½	—	—	29.02	44½	—	45
26.1	Grayrigg		29.21	40	30.21	41	29.02	40½	32.06	40	29.21	42¼
32.2	TEBAY	36	35.16	70	36.31	66½	34.48	71½	38.09	70½	35.15	66½
35.0	mp35		38.25	40	39.41	—	38.18†	39½	41.24	—	—	—
37.7	Shap Summit	45	43.24	29	44.19	31½	43.10	—	46.30	27½	43.30	28½
47.0	Clifton & Lowther		—	—	53.06	78	52.17	76½	55.00	80½	—	80
51.2	PENRITH	59	—	—	57.34	—	56.24	—	59.26	—	56.10	—

Calculated equivalent DBHPs:

Carnforth-mp9½	1,730	1,660	1,870	1,500	1,570
Oxenholme-mp24	} 1,800	1,560	} 1,690	1,810	} 1,890
Mp24-Grayrigg		1,770		1,850	
Tebay-Shap Summit	1,590	1,790	1,550	1,710	1,840

Note: Theoretical performance based on Class 7P 4-6-2 'Duchess' working at 26,000lb/hr steam rate, from Lancaster start to mp7 and Grayrigg to Dillicar troughs, 30,000lb/hr elsewhere.
* At Hay Fell (22.6 miles)
† At Scout Green (35.2 miles)

2 Crewe-Carlisle

Never were the hill-climbing capabilities of the 'Princesses' better demonstrated than on the 'Mid-day Scot' on that gruelling section from Lancaster to Penrith on the 59min 1936 timing. In looking at them it should be borne in mind that before tackling this section they had already come 230 miles, and the same crew had to take the engine a further 120 difficult miles when they had finished it. Management of the boiler was critical. From passing Carnforth at little above sea level, the 31.4 miles to the 915ft of Shap Summit represents an *average* continuous grade of 1 in 183. To cover this at an average speed of 50.9mph required some 1,650EDBHP. To illustrate just how difficult this was in practice, the performance of a 'Duchess' 4-6-2 (for which comprehensive data is available) with a train of 530 tons gross has been calculated[30] as from the Lancaster start to Shap Summit. The start tends to be a little faster than in practice, but making allowance for this it was found that a close match to the booked times was given by a steam rate of 26,000lb/hr on the more level stretches and 30,000lb/hr on the major banks — the latter giving a coal rate of over 3,800lb/hr for the fireman to sustain for periods of about 21min and 8min. Not exactly a life of ease! These theoretical times and speeds are shown in the first column of Table 5.

Of the four actual runs in this Table, those in columns 2 and 4 were made during the first week of the accelerated service, and were the drivers' baptism on these timings. To set the scene, however, what C. J. Allen described at the time as the 'poorest attempt of the series'[31] during this first week involved No 6208 with a 14-coach train taking 48min 34sec to Shap Summit and reaching Penrith in 62¼min. Not very good, perhaps, in relation to the timetable, but this needed minimum speeds of 37½mph on Grayrigg and an admittedly not very good 23½ at Summit, the average EDBHPs being 1,200 up to Yealand, 1,570 on Grayrigg and 1,470 on Shap. And that was poor! No doubt the driver had underestimated somewhat the severity of the new timetable.

The run with No 6203 in the second column[32] was the only one of six to keep strict time during that first week, and it was a remarkable performance. Note how the speeds very closely tallied with the calculated figures, and how the intermediate times of the schedule were accurately kept. But the EDBHPs are something of an eyeopener, especially that on the climb to Shap. The third column sets out a run in July 1936[33] which surpassed even that of No 6203; drivers were now fully familiar with what was needed. Allen counted himself:

> '. . . fortunate to witness what I should barely have thought to be possible, and that is a gain in time, with the normal load . . . from every timing point to the next, without exception'.

The engine must have been opened out with a vengeance to rush the short hump to Yealand, and Grayrigg was taken well, but speed was allowed to fall away a little to Shap Summit, which was probably breasted at about 28mph .

No 6212 in column 4[34] had 16 coaches on the first day of the accelerations and started more slowly than the others, but then put up a magnificent showing with over 1,800EDBHP on Grayrigg bank and 1,710 on Shap; despite this output she was 1½min down at the Summit! However, a minute was pulled back by fast running down to Penrith. But undoubtedly the prize must go to the run of No 6208 in the final column,[35] when with 16 coaches the schedule was bettered by no less than 2¾min. No wonder that Allen described it at the time as 'a positively miraculous feat' — it was an apt appraisal of a run on which Yealand was topped at 55mph, Grayrigg at 42¼ and Shap Summit at 28½. This was enginemanship of the very highest order to produce EDBHPs corresponding to a steaming rate of 33-36,000lb/hr.

It is pertinent to point out, however, that everything depended on the skill of the enginemen. C. J. Allen noted[36] that:

> 'On my very next trip on the down "Mid-day Scot" we had No 6209 again and one coach more — 505 tons all found — but lost time steadily, taking 63min 39sec from Lancaster to Penrith'.

Put another way, the 59min schedule could not be adhered to, day in and day out, given the variability of loads, conditions and men.

In the opposite direction, the features that made or broke train running were the steep and continuous climbs from Carlisle to Milepost 57 above Calthwaite (11 miles varying from 1 in 131 to 1 in 228) and, after a still rising but broken nine miles through Penrith, the 10 miles from before Eden Valley Junction to Shap Summit, mostly on a continuous 1 in 125. As Driver P. G. Johnson has said,[37] 'It's a long drag up Shap in either direction with a green fire or a green fireman'. Over this difficult road, details of a single run are given[38] in Table 6, with No 6206 carrying her original 24-element boiler and working the 'Mid-day Scot' through from Glasgow to Euston in 1938.

In comparison with O. S. Nock's 1934 footplate trip on No 6200 (Table 2) the load was two coaches more, while the

Table 6
Carlisle-Lancaster. The 'Mid-day Scot'

Locomotive: 6206 *Princess Marie Louise*
Load, coaches: 17
      tons tare/gross: 532/570
Enginemen: Not recorded

Distance miles		Sched (min)	Actual Times min sec	Speeds
0.00	CARLISLE	0	0.00	—
4.9	Wreay		9.48	39
7.4	Southwaite		13.14	50
10.8	Calthwaite		17.23	48
13.1	Plumpton	20	20.11	57½/52
17.9	PENRITH	25	25.15	62½
22.1	Clifton & Lowther		29.37	52
26.1	mp43		35.00	41
28.1	mp41		37.56	41
29.4	Shap		39.43	42/48½
31.4	Shap Summit	44	42.29	42½
36.9	Tebay	50	47.20	82
50.0	OXENHOLME	62	58.50	64/75
			pws	40
62.8	CARNFORTH	74	71.00	77/65/76½
69.1	LANCASTER	81	77.34	—

Net Time	76¼

Calculated average Equivalent DBHPs:
Wreay-mp60	1,680
mp60-mp57¼	1,730
Clifton-mp43	1,820

schedule was 5min tighter. The engine was much faster away from Carlisle, reaching 39mph on the 1 in 131 past Wreay, 50 on the easier grades past Southwaite and falling only to 48 at Milepost 57. On the long 1 in 125 from Eden Valley Junction the engine settled down to an unvarying 41mph, producing more than 1,800EDBHP and needing steam at nearly 32,000lb/hr; she cleared Shap Summit at the excellent speed of 42½mph in just 42½min. Yet this fine effort only managed to undercut the schedule by 1½min.

3 Carlisle-Glasgow

North of the Border the two adverse stretches of 1 in 200 gradient from Mossband troughs (Milepost 7¼) to beyond Kirkpatrick, some 7¼ miles, and again from Milepost 17¾ (beyond Kirtlebridge) nearly to Castlemilk box, a little over four miles, were a testing forerunner of the main climb to Beattock Summit, particularly if the engine was not steaming freely. This is well illustrated in the last column of Table 7, giving three runs on the 'Mid-day Scot' from Carlisle to Carstairs or Symington.

The first run, with No 6209 in 1936,[39] was with the eight-coach Glasgow section, the Edinburgh coaches having been detached at Carlisle, and was the continuation of the journey shown in column 3 of Table 5. No time was wasted at the start, and with this moderate-weight train the first stretch of 1 in 200 was easily surmounted at 64mph with a power output on the bank of no more than 1,210EDBHP. Beattock

bank was taken easily, with EDBHPs not exceeding 1,220, which was sufficient to cut the 18min allowance for the 10.0 miles from Beattock to Summit by almost 2½min. To get through Lockerbie in under 'even time' despite a permanent way slack was smart work by any standard. After Summit it was a case of spinning out time.

By 1938, however, the 'Mid-day' was running through to Symington before division, and this posed a much harder task. No 6209 in column 2[40] had a 12-coach train, and after another fast start was badly hampered by a 20mph slowing near Kirtlebridge which prevented the 1 in 200 to Castlemilk being rushed. The approach to Beattock bank was very brisk, and on the bank itself the engine was putting out nearly 1,500EDBHP in the early stages, and was evidently 'dropped down' a little from Harthope to recover to 31mph at the top. Timekeeping was exemplary. With No 6200 in the last column,[41] however, the driver tried to get more from the engine than he and his mate knew how. To Nethercleugh the work was excellent, with minima of 57½ and 55mph on the 1 in 200 climbs and an EDBHP as high as 1,590 past Kirkpatrick. But this hard work had taken its toll of the boiler, and after Nethercleugh it had to be rallied for Beattock bank; enough was done to enable a very vigorous attack to be mounted, but by Greskine box the output began to tail off as pressure and water level fell. The last stage could only produce less than 1,200EDBHP and a speed of 21½mph at Summit. So a minute was dropped from Beattock station and was not recovered on the run down Clydesdale.

Table 7
Carlisle-Carstairs. The 'Mid-day Scot'

Year:			1936			1938			1938
Locomotive:			6209			6209			6200
Load, coaches:			8			12			13
tons, tare/gross:			253/265			394/420			432/460
Enginemen:			Not recorded			Not recorded			Not recorded

Distance miles		Sched min	Actual Times min sec	Speeds	Sched min	Actual Times min sec	Speed	Actual Times min sec	Speed
0.0	CARLISLE	0	0.00	—	0	0.00	—	0.00	—
8.6	Gretna	10	9.12	77½	11	9.33	76½	10.13	71½
13.0	Kirkpatrick		13.00	64		pws	20	14.42	57½
16.7	Kirtlebridge		16.17	76½		18.42	—	18.17	68
20.1	Ecclefechan		19.05	—		—	—	21.25	—
			pws						
22.7	Castlemilk		22.03	—		—	47½	—	55
25.8	LOCKERBIE	26	24.47	—	28	29.03	—	26.45	—
28.7	Nethercleugh		27.00	80½		—	77½	—	70½
34.5	Wamphray		31.39	72½/75		36.16	76	35.42	47†/70½
39.7	BEATTOCK	38	36.17	—	40	40.56	—	40.32	60
42.3	Auchencastle		39.22	—		43.53	45	43.28	41
45.4	Greskine		44.14	34		49.19	30	48.54	28
47.8	Harthope		48.27	34		54.06	29	54.27	23½
49.7	Summit	56	51.53	34	58	57.57	31	59.36	21½
57.8	Abington		60.58	—		—	79	—	77½
			pws						
63.2	Lamington		67.47	—		69.12	—	71.44	—
66.9	Symington		71.30	—	74	72.41	—	75.31	—
73.5	CARSTAIRS	80 pass	77.17 pass	*					

Net Times		72			69¾			75½	
Calculated average Equivalent DBHPs:									
Gretna-Kirkpatrick		1,210			—			1,590	
Kirtlebridge-Castlemilk		—			—			1,330	
Wamphray-Greskine		1,090			1,460			1,600	
Greskine-Summit		1,220			1,520			1,160	

* Permanent speed restriction
† Driver coasting: see text

28

Table 8
Symington-Carlisle. The 'Royal Scot'

Locomotive: Load, coaches: tons tare/gross: Enginemen:				6208 16 512/535 Not recorded		6207 17 541/570 Not recorded	
Distance miles		Sched min		Actual Times min sec	Speeds	Actual Times min sec	Speeds
0.0	SYMINGTON	0		0.00	—	0.00	—
3.7	Lamington			6.07	60	6.11	58
9.1	Abington			11.49	—	12.20	—
11.6	Crawford			14.36	—	15.25	—
14.3	Elvanfoot			17.42	—	18.51	45½/53
17.2	Beattock Summit	22		21.16	42	22.35	40
27.2	BEATTOCK	32		30.22	75	31.44	73
32.4	Wamphray			34.40	71	36.04	75
38.2	Nethercleugh			39.36	—	40.53	73
41.1	LOCKERBIE	45		42.15	—	43.27	—
44.2	Castlemilk			45.21	56	46.26	58
50.2	Kirtlebridge			50.50	74	51.40	73
53.9	Kirkpatrick			53.39	73	54.58	—
58.3	Gretna	62		57.46	71	58.30	75
				eased		eased	
66.9	CARLISLE	71		67.40	—	67.43	—

Calculated average Equivalent DBHPs:
Lamington-Beattock Summit   1,520   1,460

In the up direction, the climb to Beattock Summit is essentially a two-stage affair; the first section of 16 miles from Uddingston up to Craigenhill, with long stretches of 1 in 100 could be a sore trial for an engine with poorly-prepared fire or which was steaming badly, and in the 1940s there were two firebox explosions due to low water on this climb (see Chapter 11). However, while the practice of joining up sections at Symington continued, loads were moderate. From Symington heavy trains were faced with 12½ miles of climbing from the Clyde bridge at Lamington, gradually steepening to Elvanfoot and, after a short level relief, culminating in 1 in 99 to Beattock Summit; the fireman could expect little sitting down until the top was passed.

In Table 8 have been brought together two contrasting runs on the 'Royal Scot' in the early days of the second 10 'Princesses', in both cases with 32-element boilers, and with trains of 16 and 17 coaches. They merit comparison with Nock's early footplate trip on No 6200 (Table 2), on similar timings but with a slightly lighter load.

No 6208, on the lighter of the two trains,[42] got away smartly to Lamington, and was then driven hard to Summit, averaging just over 1,500EDBHP and taking steam at about 28,000lb/hr. The station-to-station averages suggest speeds of about 55 at Abington, 53 at Crawford and 51 before and 57 after Elvanfoot — first class work by any standard with this load. With the train over 1½min to the good by Beattock station, the easiest of running on to Carlisle was sufficient for an arrival over 3min early. On No 6207's trip,[43] with an extra coach, the start to Lamington was similar, but thereafter speed was allowed to fall away more rapidly, with the result that ½min was dropped to Summit. Faster running was thus called for from Beattock, and this got the train into Carlisle in an almost identical time.

The fastest timings of this road were made by No 6201 on her high-speed demonstration runs in November 1936. These were made with a firm schedule in mind, and were of a very different character from most 'Princess' work at that time. Accordingly, these trials will be covered where the author feels they belong, as groundwork for the design of the later Pacifics, in Chapter 5.

To sum up the first six years of these fine engines, therefore, it will have been seen that, after an early brief period while familiarisation took place and weaknesses were identified and eliminated — during which period the predictions of the BAWR engineer were uncannily fulfilled — they rose to remarkable heights of performance such as the LMS had not witnessed before. They inspired operator confidence which led to their being asked to perform near-miracles on a day-to-day basis, in a favourable climate of experienced crews, good quality coal and tail-high morale. The author is reminded of an apt opinion, offered by a friend about another class of Stanier engines: to get the best from a 'Princess', she needed to be treated with all the excitement, understanding and tact of a mistress — and that is in no way a reflection on the distinguished ladies whose names they carried — whereas the perhaps more detached attention often bestowed on a wife was not quite good enough.

In 1939 the concentration of all 'Princesses' on Camden shed was broken up as newer Pacifics entered service. Nos 6201 and 6206 were transferred to Longsight in July for working the heavy Euston-Manchester business expresses via Crewe (nothing heavier than Class 5XP engines was allowed over the 'Pots' line via Stoke at that time). But they hardly settled in on these trains before the outbreak of war in September scattered them more widely.

Above left:
No 6201, brand new and still unnamed, with indicator shelter at Crewe North in November 1933.
W. H. Whitworth

Left:
No 6201 *Princess Elizabeth* in Platform 2 at Euston after arrival with the up 'Royal Scot'. On the top lamp bracket she carries the Caledonian semaphore headcode.
Real Photos (T9423)

Below:
A Camden 'Princess', believed to be No 6210 *Lady Patricia*, accelerates a down afternoon express past Kilburn No 1 box in the late 1930s. *Eric Treacy/ P. B. Whitehouse collection*

Above left:
No 6208 *Princess Helena Victoria* approaches the junction at Edge Hill with an up Euston train about 1937. Every signal in sight is of LNWR origin. *Eric Treacy/ P. B. Whitehouse collection*

Above:
No 6203 *Princess Margaret Rose* passing Edge Hill shed on an up Euston train about 1937. *Eric Treacy/ P. B. Whitehouse collection*

Centre left:
No 6201 *Princess Elizabeth* approaches Clifton & Lowther on the up 'Mid-day Scot' in 1938. The train consists of 17 coaches (including two 12-wheel diners) and a 6-wheeled van, about 545 tons tare. The engine is being worked on at least 35% cutoff.
Eric Treacy/ P. B. Whitehouse collection

Left:
No 6209 *Princess Beatrice* approaching Eden Valley Junction with an up express. *Eric Treacy/ P. B. Whitehouse collection*

31

4

The 'Turbomotive'

Stanier decided to seek a variation in his 1933 Building Programme authority to build three 'Princesses', following a visit to Sweden in 1932 at the invitation of Metropolitan-Vickers Electrical Co (now part of GEC) to see a new 2-8-0 locomotive built for the Grangesberg-Oxelosund Railway with non-condensing geared steam turbine propulsion via a jackshaft. Dynamometer car tests with this locomotive had shown economies in coal consumption of over 7%, and in water of 15%, as compared with similar conventional locomotives. But the virtue of the Swedish engine was its simplicity, in making only one departure from an otherwise standard and proved machine, namely the turbine and transmission; this appealed to Stanier's engineering sense of how to conduct an experiment. In conjunction with Euston a preliminary design for a turbine-driven version of the 'Princess' was produced at Met-Vick (Fig 14); the turbines were to drive through double-reduction gearing on to 6ft 9in diameter wheels, and to accommodate the turbines and gear train the boiler was pitched 2in higher than the early

reciprocating engine proposal (Fig 8). The form of frame construction is not clear, having both bar and plate frame characteristics, while the rear end is even more obscure. An open quill drive and offset gearbox were shown. Further study led to the use of smaller turbines running at higher speeds, with triple-reduction gearing and the quill drive contained within the final gearwheel, the remainder of the locomotive being wherever possible standard with the 'Princesses' as built. In June 1935 this machine emerged from Crewe Works as No 6202 (Fig 15), and went into service shortly after from Camden. Bravely the LMS anticipated a 15% saving in coal consumption by comparison with a standard 'Princess'. The first cost, not a representative one for a one-off machine, was more than twice that of Nos 6203-12.

From the published information on the features of this unique locomotive, it will be appropriate here to concentrate on just six differences from the 'Princesses' which were directly relevant to the engine's work.

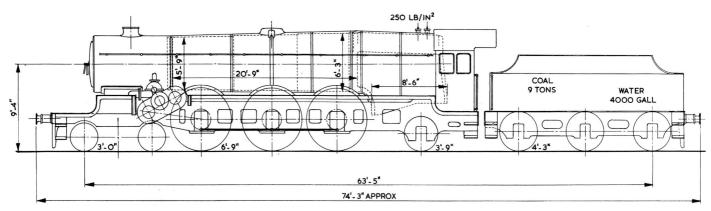

14 Preliminary scheme for turbine-driven 4-6-2, 1932.

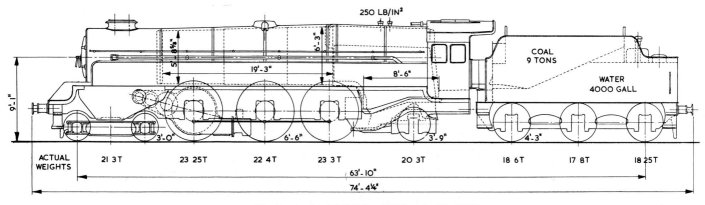

15 'Turbomotive' 4-6-2 No 6202 as built, 1935.

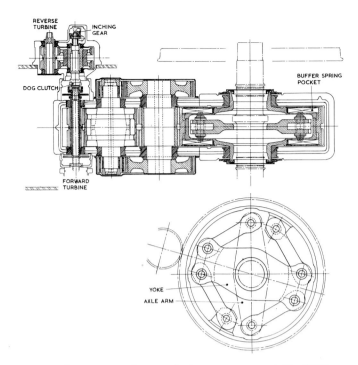

16 Gearcase and transmission arrangement, No 6202.

1 Turbines and Transmission

The turbines, rigidly mounted on the frames, drove the leading coupled axle through a gear train contained in a gearbox/oil bath also rigidly frame-mounted (Fig 16). To accommodate the rise and fall of the axle the final transmission gear was carried in bearings in the gearbox and surrounded the axle, the drive being transmitted through a yoke and resilient links to the ends of an axle-mounted arm. The 2,000hp forward turbine — it could in fact produce 2,600hp at 90mph — on the left side was permanently coupled to the gear train. The reverse turbine, on the right side, was much less powerful — in fact, the original was inadequate to propel an empty train from Euston up Camden bank — and connected to the gear train by another reduction gear; this was engaged through splines and a dog clutch. The clutch was only engaged for reverse running, originally by a steam-operated servo mechanism; after some years (and failures) this was replaced by a manual control from the cab. A ratchet 'inching gear' was provided to enable the clutch to be engaged if the dogs stopped opposite each other. The turbine bearings and gears were force-lubricated from two steam-operated oil pumps — which sounded rather like Westinghouse brake pumps when working — and a gear pump in the gearbox well. In 1942 a further steam-operated oil pump was fitted to improve lubrication of the reverse turbine bearings. In some quarters the engine was nicknamed 'Gracie Fields' from the 'sing-as-we-go' hum from the gear train.

Power control of each turbine was by multiple steam inlet valves — six for the forward turbine and three for the reverse one — mounted on the smokebox sides and cam-operated by shafts from the cab. The main regulator in the superheater header was kept fully open during forward running. There were thus discrete steps in power output, but this was not a problem for drivers in practice.

2 Roller Bearings

Engine and tender were fitted with oil-lubricated Timken roller bearing axleboxes throughout; those on the

intermediate and trailing coupled axles were of cannon type. The resultant coupled axle horn gaps were very wide, and this, together with the large frame cutouts over the bogie for turbine mounting and exhaust passages, dictated the use of 1¼in thick high tensile frame plates.

3 Draughting

The even exhaust from a turbine, at low pressure, was held to make conventional draughting proportions unsuitable, and so a double blastpipe and chimney were adopted, somewhere between the plain design later used on several LMS classes and the more complex 'Kylchap' design (Fig 17). Cylindrical chokes were mounted between the blastpipe caps and petticoats; the cap areas were variable by means of axial coned spindles, caused to rise and fall in the caps by a cam and linkage from the forward steam valve control. This increased the cap area with the number of valves in use. This linkage was not ideal, and was probably responsible for some early steaming problems; after some years it was discarded and the central cones permanently fixed in the most

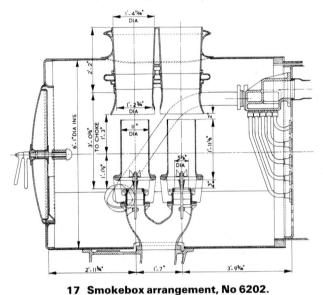

17 Smokebox arrangement, No 6202.

restrictive position. In 1946 the cylindrical chokes were removed.

The draught was very soft and quiet, and this gave rise to crew complaints of drifting exhaust interfering with signal sighting and of extremely dirty cab conditions due to smoke being sucked in from the tender. In 1936 Stanier had thoughts about streamlining the engine, which would probably have stopped this nuisance, but in the event traditional smoke deflectors were fitted in 1939.

4 Boiler and Firebox

No 6202 was built with boiler No 9100, originally intended for the first of the 1935 'Princesses', No 6203. This boiler had the extended combustion chamber, 19ft 3in between tubeplates, and a 32-element superheater with bifurcated elements. Contemporary press releases spoke of a designed steam temperature of 750°F, but this proved highly optimistic and in practice fell more than 100°F short of this figure. The engine only ran 45,668 miles with this boiler before she went into Crewe Works and emerged in July 1936 with the last spare boiler, No 9236, specially fitted with a 40-element superheater with 'Turbomotive' in mind; this had separate dome and topfeed, with regulator in the dome. The elements were trifurcated and 1in diameter, and this superheater came much nearer to producing the required steam temperature, averaging close on 700°F. The relevant proportions of the two boilers, including later changes, are given in Appendix 4.

5 Cab Controls

While the cab was generally similar to that of the 'Princesses', the steam and reversing controls were very different. The reversing screw was replaced by a control box, having three main controls:

- on top, a reversing handle
- facing the driver, a driving handle which rotated clockwise for forward movement and anticlockwise for reverse, and which controlled the turbine steam valves, and
- below the driving handle, a safety handle with 'running' and 'locking' positions.

On the side of the box was a forward/reverse indicator, while on top was a pointer showing the number of valves open. The inching gear control was also on the control box. A number of additional gauges was fitted — steam chest pressure, lube oil pressure, sump contents, back pressure and oil temperature. There was interlocking of controls to prevent incorrect engagement and operation of the turbines.

Because 'Turbomotive' ran so smoothly, giving drivers little concept of speed, she was always fitted with a speedometer, even when these had been removed from other steam locomotives.

6 Manning

The differences from the other 'Princesses', and general complexity, suggested that the handling of the engine should, if possible, be confined to a minimum number of drivers, but the normal link workings could not make such provision, and for various reasons change could not be effected. It was therefore considered prudent for selected fitters, specially trained, to accompany the locomotive at all times in traffic. This also dictated its allocation to Camden and its regular use on a single out-and-home working.

'Turbomotive' on Test

The engine had been built barely a month when preliminary dynamometer car trials were made, on 16-19 July 1935. The trains used were the 09.27 Crewe-Carlisle and 15.57 return; the down train was really a semi-fast with eight stops and loaded to 357-382 tons as far as Preston and 413-423 tons onwards, while the up train made only three stops and varied more widely in weight between 321 and 399 tons to Preston and 377-457 tons on to Crewe. Timings were 'Limited Load', putting the actual loads well within allowable tonnages; Grimethorpe Grade 1 coal was used.

The steaming of the engine was stated[44] to be 'completely satisfactory throughout . . . climbing to Shap Summit in both directions three and four valves were mainly in operation, the fifth and sixth valves being opened for short periods on the 09.27 train approaching the Summit'. This produced times ranging from a minimum of 25½min (with 416 tons) to a

maximum of 27min (with 423 tons) from the Oxenholme start to Shap Summit, 18.5 miles, compared with 29min allowed. In the up direction, times from the Penrith start to pass Shap Summit, 13.5 miles, lay between 20min 25sec (with 337 tons) and 22min 5sec (a poor effort with 321 tons, for on another occasion 21min 50sec was taken with 399 tons). The DBHP developed on the banks was between 1,100 and 1,300, with a maximum of 1,600 approaching the summit, corresponding to about 2,000EDBHP.

On the easier parts of the route between 900 and 1,000EDBHP sufficed. Superheat temperature was quoted as averaging 610°F with a maximum of 630°F — curious in the light of later testing. Coal and water consumptions over the four days averaged:

Coal	lb/mile	39.4
	lb/DBHP hr	2.94
Water	gal/mile	34.0
	lb/DBHP hr	25.4
Evaporation	lb/lb coal	8.64

The harder the engine worked, the lower were the specific consumption figures.

The engine now settled down at Camden to work a regular diagram involving a morning Euston-Liverpool express — the time varied between 08.30 and 10.40 over the years — and returning with the very fast 17.25 train with a load limit of 420 tons. But three further series of dynamometer car tests were made over the next two years, two of which were run in direct comparison with standard 'Princesses'. All three, oddly, were run on the Euston-Carlisle-Glasgow route, and not on the Liverpool line which was to be No 6202's regular territory.

The second series, between 20 April and 14 May 1936, was designed to compare coal and water consumptions of No 6202 with those of 'Princess' No 6212 when working the 'Royal Scot' between Euston and Carlisle and throughout to and from Glasgow; two trips were run each week. No 6202 had run just over 32,000 miles from new, still carrying her 32-element boiler, while No 6212 had run 54,763 miles from new and 19,511 miles since a very premature Service Repair. Both engines were handled by Driver Wardle of Crewe North throughout the tests. Again the coal used was Grimethorpe Grade 1. The loads were heavy. In the down direction they ranged from 530 to 569 tons to Crewe, and forward to Carlisle/Symington from 468 to 507 tons; after division at Symington the Glasgow portion was usually a little over 300 tons. On no occasion were the trains banked out of Euston. In the up direction, again, loads of 305-331 tons were hauled to Symington, where the trains were made up with the Edinburgh portion to a load of 472-503 tons to Euston.

Working with full regulator where practicable, the number of valves (on No 6202) and cutoffs (No 6212) were typically:

Down	6202	6212
Willesden-Tring	4-5	25%
Bletchley-Roade	4	21%
Blisworth-Welton	4	23%
Stafford-Whitmore	4-5	25-23%
Carnforth-Grayrigg	4-5	18-35%
Tebay-Shap Summit	4-5	20-45%
Beattock-Summit	6	25-50%

Up	6202	6212
Uddingston-Cleghorn	4	20-25%
Symington-Beattock Summit	5	25-45%
Carlisle-Plumpton	5-4	30-20%
Penrith-Shap Summit	3-5	20-30%
Lancaster-Preston	4	20-17%
Crewe-Whitmore	5	25-20%
Rugby-Kilsby Tunnel	4	20%
Bletchley-Tring	3-4	18%

Coal and water consumptions were:

		6202	6212	Difference for 6202
Coal	lb/mile	41.5	41.5	—
	lb/sq ft grate/hr	49.8	49.3	+0.9%
	lb/DBHP hr	2.93	3.12	−6.1%
Water	gal/mile	34.2	35.0	−2.3%
Water	lb/DBHP hr	24.1	25.9	−7.0%
Evaporation	lb/lb coal	8.16	8.44	−3.3%

All was not well, however, on the footplates. Test Report No 61 notes that:

> 'The general steaming of engine No 6202 was not completely satisfactory, as it was found necessary to coast . . . on several occasions . . . to effect an improvement in the boiler pressure and also to create a working level of water in the boiler.
> . . . From observations while running it appeared that the combustion was at times incomplete',

while

> 'The steaming of engine 6212 was more satisfactory, but . . . when working heavily . . . a satisfactory boiler pressure was only effected by maintaining a minimum level of water . . .'.

The superheat temperatures recorded were substantially lower than those of No 6202 in the previous July, on the heavier sections they varied from 566°F-585°F, as compared with 556-580°F for No 6212. No explanation was offered for the difference. The running was not detailed in the report, but a good example of No 6202's performance as between Symington and Carlisle is available and is shown in Table 9. The aim was, of course, to stick closely to booked times after a slight late start.

Table 9

10.00 Glasgow Central-Euston, The 'Royal Scot'

Dynamometer Car Test Run, 5 May 1936

Locomotive:	Class 7P 4-6-2 No 6202
	(Turbomotive)
Load, coaches:	16
tons tare/gross	499/525
Enginemen:	Dvr Wardle (Crewe N)

Distance miles		Sched min	Actual Time min sec	Speeds
0.0	SYMINGTON	0	0.00	—
			pws	
3.7	Lamington		—	55/50
11.6	Crawford		—	54½
14.3	Elvanfoot		—	47/55
17.2	Beattock Summit	22	22.20	39
27.2	BEATTOCK	32	31.25	77½ max
32.4	Wamphray		—	72½
38.2	Nethercleugh		—	66/72½
41.1	LOCKERBIE	45	43.25	65
44.2	Castlemilk		—	53 min
50.2	Kirtlebridge		—	70/63½
56.7	Quintinshill		—	72½
58.3	Gretna	62	59.20	eased
66.9	CARLISLE	71	68.25	—
	Net Time		68	

the differences being more marked when working through to and from Glasgow. The report concluded:

> '. . . that for general economical operation the loading for the Class 7 4-6-2 engines running in Special Limit timings between Euston and Crewe should be 500 tons, and that (between) Crewe-Carlisle and Glasgow in limit (sic) timings the loading should be 475 tons'.

Whatever the operators thought of that recommendation, both the 'Princesses' and the later 'Duchesses' were to shoot holes in it.

In July 1936 the 'Turbomotive' was fitted with new boiler No 9236, with 40-element superheater using 1in diameter bifurcated elements, and on 5 October that year further comparative dynamometer car tests started between Euston and Glasgow. The 'Princess' used this time was No 6210, fresh from Service Repair and having run 98,977 miles from new 13 months earlier. This time each engine worked the current diagram, involving the 10.00 down 'Royal Scot', the 22.45 sleeper back, the 14.00 down 'Mid-day Scot' and 10.00 up 'Royal Scot' back. However, a disastrous start was made, the first week's runs being cancelled when, on the first day, No 6210 developed trouble with the LH crosshead, and the tests with No 6202 in the second week were abandoned due to poor steaming. It was not until 19 October that satisfactory tests could begin. Both engines were worked by four selected drivers and firemen in view of the intensive utilisation, and Grimethorpe Grade 1 coal fired. The loadings south of Symington ranged from 454 to 560 tons, and sectional running times were little changed from the previous year. The engines were thus worked in similar fashion to the April/May tests.

The Report[45] on these tests notes that:

> 'The steaming of engine No 6210 was very satisfactory throughout . . . full boiler pressure was maintained under the severest working conditions, and a working level of water in the boiler could be also maintained without difficulty. After the tests on 12, 13, 14 October, engine No 6202 was examined and modifications were made which resulted in the steaming being very satisfactory for the remainder of the test'.

This may well have been when the blastpipe cones were fixed in the minimum-orifice position. Now the superheat began to look more like the design intentions; on the heavier sections temperatures varied between 670°F and 692°F average on No 6202, and peaked as high as 720°F.

The coal and water consumptions omitted the figures for the 22.45 train on 26 October (engine No 6202) due to gale conditions; the remainder were:

		6202	6210	Difference for 6202
Coal	lb/mile	45.1	45.0	+0.4%
	lb/sq ft grate/hr	54.6	52.2	+4.5%
	lb/DBHP hr	2.85	2.98	−4.1%
Water	gal/mile	35.0	37.3	−6.2%
	lb/DBHP hr	22.1	24.7	−10.4%
Evaporation	lb/lb coal	7.74	8.30	−6.6%

No recommendations were made.

One final series of tests was made with No 6202, after she had been fitted with 1in diameter trifurcated elements in place of the bifurcated type. These tests were run on 22-25 June 1937, on the 'Royal Scot' train in each direction, with crew change at Carlisle.[46] Loads each day were between 483 and 489 tons. Performance was generally similar to that in the previous October, though not helped by a plethora of speed restrictions. Steam temperatures were a little higher than with the bifurcated elements (which were too small for the flue size), averaging 682°F throughout with a maximum of 740°F with all six valves open. Steaming was 'completely satisfactory', full pressure being maintained under the 'severest working conditions'. However, the exhaust steam injector was not reliable when the engine was worked hard and extensive use of the live steam injector was necessary, increasing the water consumption. The outcome was:

Coal	lb/mile	41.6
	lb/sq ft grate/hr	50.7
	lb/DBHP hr	2.78
Water	gal/mile	37.1
	lb/DBHP hr	24.8
Evaporation	lb/lb coal	8.93

Thus on similar work, successive changes to the 'Turbomotive' had improved the specific coal consumption figures, always good, to really excellent ones:

Standard 'Princess':	2.98lb/DBHP hr
No 6202:	
with 32 elements	2.94lb/DBHP hr
with 32 elements	2.93lb/DBHP hr
With 40 elements, bifurcated	2.85lb/DBHP hr
With 40 elements, trifurcated	2.78lb/DBHP hr

Table 10:
17.25 Liverpool (Lime Street)-Euston

Locomotive: Class 7P 4-6-2 No 6202

Year: Load, coaches: tons tare/gross Enginemen:				10 September 1935 11 331/345 Dvr L. Earl		1939 14 429/455 Not recorded		1945 15 455/485 Dvr L. Earl	
Distance miles		Sched min	Actual Time min sec	Speeds	Actual Time min sec	Speeds	Sched mins	Actual Time min sec	Speeds
0.0	CREWE	0	0†	—	0.00	—	0	0.00	—
4.8	Betley Road				8.05	—		8.46	47
8.0	Madeley				11.53	—		12.52	47
10.5	Whitmore				14.38	—	17	16.00	51
19.2	Norton Bridge				22.17	72	27	24.31	62
24.5	STAFFORD	26	24	30*	27.10	55*	35	29.55	50*
33.8	Rugeley	36	34		36.50	75	14	39.21	65
41.8	LICHFIELD	42	41.30		43.38	68/78	53	pws	
48.1	TAMWORTH				48.35	—	60	and	
			pws	30	pws	30		sig delays	
61.0	NUNEATON	60	59		62.37	70	75	69.20	64
66.7	Shilton				—	66/75		—	59/62
75.5	RUGBY	73	71.30	40*	75.30	40*	92	83.58	45*
					sigs	20			
88.4	Weedon			88	90.30	81½		97.25	68
95.3	BLISWORTH	91			95.48	—	116	104.05	60
								sig stop	
98.2	Roade	94	90		98.15	70	120	111.23	—
105.7	Wolverton				103.53	83½		119.00	63
111.4	BLETCHLEY	105	99.30		108.23	76½	134	124.31	63
117.9	Leighton Buzzard				113.37	72.75		130.14	68
122.0	Cheddington				116.59	71½		133.47	70
								sigs	
126.4	Tring	119	110.30		120.48	68	152	140.11	52
140.7	WATFORD JN			90	131.17	86½	167	153.53	67
150.0	Wembley				138.08	78/86		sigs	
								sigs	
152.7	WILLESDEN JN	142	131		141.23	—	179	168.08	
								sig stop	
158.1	EUSTON						189	182.30	—
	Net Time		131		136¼			160	

giving a saving of 6.7% against the 'Princess'. Similarly the specific water consumption (discounting the last test series because of injector trouble) showed a reduction of 10.5%. This was not as high as Stanier expected; but then the standard 'Princess' with 32-element superheater was a highly economical locomotive.

Performance in Traffic

It is to the published records of No 6202's performances on the fast 17.25 Liverpool-Euston train that one looks for evidence of her capabilities. She quickly made a name for herself, in the hands of Camden and Edge Hill men, as complete master of this hard job, and the 420-ton limit was often waived if traffic called for strengthening of the train. In Table 10 are brought together details of three runs on this working over a period from 1935 to the end of World War 2; remarkably the 17.25 departure time was maintained through the war years, although suffering deceleration. The first, by Camden Driver Laurie Earl,[47] is the fastest recorded with No 6202, though six weeks earlier, with the dynamometer car as a special effort, 'Princess' No 6200 had made a time of 129½min (see Table 4, Chapter 3).[48] The times as far as Rugeley are probably understated by at least ½min, being guard's journal figures, but would have involved making something like 60mph up the 1 in 177 to Madeley; this means around 1,600EDBHP and using all six valves. That this was no flash in the pan was confirmed by another run with 315 tons tare, when Driver Fryer passed Whitmore in 12min 47sec from the Crewe start, accelerating to 61mph to Madeley and turning out about 1,570EDBHP in the process. The rise to Tring must have been surmounted at over 70mph.

The 1939 run[49] was made with a heavy 14-coach load marginally over the weight limit. All six valves were evidently used to Madeley — the average speed from Betley Road to Madeley was just over 50mph, so that about 1,560EDBHP was being applied. To Rugby, downhill speeds were moderate, but the severe signal check at Welton seemed to put the unnamed driver on his mettle, with 81½mph at Weedon, the Roade hump rushed at 70 minimum, 83½ at Castlethorpe, and a fine climb to Tring with power output as high as 1,590EDBHP. The average speed from Weedon to Wembley with this slightly excessive load was 77.6mph.

Finally, a 1945[50] run on easier timings with the redoubtable Earl again. To sustain 47mph on the 1 in 177 to Madeley with 15 coaches required 1,520EDBHP. Downhill speeds were moderate, and any gain in time only led to a succession of signal checks, culminating in a dead stand at Roade for the 19.05 Euston-Birmingham to cross in front on to the Northampton line. This seemed to spur Earl to make one of his energetic climbs to Tring, speed being worked up from 63mph at Bletchley to an excellent 70 approaching Cheddington and the prospect of topping the 1 in 335 at well over 60. Alas, it was ruined by a serious signal check at Tring Cutting box, costing 3½min, but even then 52mph was regained by Tring.

In the down direction the morning Liverpool train attracted little attention, for it was a relatively easy job. Indeed, on a run in 1939 on the 10.40 from Euston, with a 400-ton load, Edward Livesey recorded the use of three valves on Camden bank and up to Tring, only one valve down to Cheddington, and after Rugby, no more than two for most of the way to Stafford, from where the driver positively dawdled to Crewe to spin out time.

But at about the time of the October 1936 tests — and probably on a familiarisation trip, for Driver Wardle to Crewe North was at the regulator — a run on the heavy down 'Royal Scot' was recorded[51] which showed some good work with a 17-coach train (Table 11). Up to Bushey a sustained 58mph required 1,590EDBHP, but it is likely that the engine

Table 11
10.00 Euston-Glasgow, The 'Royal Scot'
('Special Limit' timings)

Locomotive:				Class 7P 4-6-2 No 6202	
Load, coaches:				17	
tons tare/gross:				536/560	
Enginemen:				Dvr Wardle, Crewe N	

Distance miles		Sched min	Actual Time min sec	Speeds
0.0	EUSTON	0	0.00	—
1.0	mp1		3.15	—
5.4	WILLESDEN JN	10	9.10	
11.4	Harrow		15.10	60/58
17.4	WATFORD	23	21.13	66
24.5	Hemel Hempstead		28.10	—
31.7	Tring	38	35.57	53
40.2	Leighton Buzzard		43.47	71½
46.7	BLETCHLEY	51	49.25	69/66
			pws	
59.9	Roade	63	63.40	—
62.8	BLISWORTH	66	67.15	—
69.7	Weedon		73.30	65
75.3	Welton		79.00	56
82.6	RUGBY	87	87.00	—
5.5	Brinklow		8.05	—
14.5	NUNEATON	16	16.38	71
			pws(2)	
27.4	TAMWORTH	30	32.03	66
33.7	LICHFIELD	36	38.08	60
38.4	Armitage		42.41	—
			pws	
41.7	RUGELEY	43	46.58	—
51.0	STAFFORD	53	57.00	30*
56.3	Norton Bridge	60	63.08	
60.8	Standon Bridge		67.50	—
65.0	Whitmore	69	72.00	—
70.7	Betley Road		77.15	78
75.5	CREWE	81	82.35	—

| Net Times | | | 85+77¼ | |

* Permanent Speed Restriction

was not steaming well (as at the start of the tests) for speed fell off fairly sharply up to Tring. Wardle would no doubt have liked time in hand at that stage for the Castlethorpe slack. But after the Polesworth pitfall check a good recovery was made, with 66mph attained in five miles and nothing less than 60 on the 1 in 331 rise through Lichfield. After the Stafford slack there was a steady acceleration to over 60mph on the gently rising grades to Standon Bridge, and the average of 60.4 from there to Whitmore suggests 59-60 at the top, good with this load.

So a general picture emerges clearly; No 6202 was fully capable of taking her place alongside the 'Princesses', and even had the edge on them, while not being unduly perturbed by load limits laid down for the special timings of the 17.25 from Liverpool. One could hardly ask more of an experimental machine.

Mechanical Performance

The novel features built into No 6202 had to prove themselves in a traction environment, which is very different from a static application, and it was to be expected that problems would arise which could require modifications. Such problems were not slow to materialise, and were the cause of numerous special shoppings. These are listed in Appendix 5, which has been compiled mainly from information in a monumental paper read by R. C. Bond in January 1946 to the Institution of Locomotive Engineers.[52]

In the first 10 years of 'Turbomotive's' life, there were 13 occasions when the engine was taken to Crewe Works for attention resulting from faults or failures in traffic, together with two further occasions when she was shopped for normal wear and tear. The breakdown of the 13 fault incidents was:

● Reverse turbine engagement clutch	2
● Reverse turbine bearings	4
● Turbine oil leakage	4
● Failure of forward turbine	2
● Failure of flexible drive	1

and the following notes deal with the failures and resultant modifications where they were of relevance to traffic operations.

(a) Reverse turbine clutch, etc

Visit No 2 followed a failure after arrival at Liverpool, when reverse gear could not be engaged and rubbing noises were heard at the front end, associated with oil leakage from the reverse turbine. The two halves of the dog clutch were held in contact by the steam reversing cylinder but had not meshed, and the ends of the dogs had been distorted by rubbing when steam was given to the reverse turbine. Prior to this there had been complaints about the feebleness of the reverse turbine, and so this was redesigned to increase power. At the same time the clutch was interlocked with the turbine steam valves, the steam reversing cylinder was replaced by a manual device on the control box, a visual indicator of clutch engagement was fitted, and minor modifications made to the lubrication of the reverse turbine. But just under 3,500 miles later (visit No 3) a very similar failure occurred in Euston station when reversing the engine ready to back the train out after arrival from Liverpool, and the damage was similar. It was then found that slight steam valve leakage was sufficient to turn the reverse turbine as soon as the clutch spindle was released from the inching gear. The valves were therefore fitted with stronger springs, and careful attention given to their seating; in addition, drivers were instructed to close the main regulator and open the drain cocks before reversing. Later, the clutch shaft and inching gear were redesigned to prevent this trouble.

(b) Reverse turbine bearings

This was a recurrent problem, despite various palliatives; the fitting of the dedicated third steam-driven oil pump, in conjunction with previous modifications, eliminated this weakness.

(c) Forward turbine

The forward turbine was altogether more trouble-free than its reverse counterpart, but visit No 6 arose after a failure at Willesden during shunting operations, when forward power was lost and the coupled wheels locked as she was being towed away. The forward turbine had jammed due to movement of one of the stator diaphragms, which then stripped and damaged blading on the rotor. The locking arrangements for the diaphragms were revised, and blade clearances increased, as a result. Visit No 10 arose from a fracture of the turbine rotor spindle at the thrust collar while the engine was running at more than 60mph near Leighton Buzzard on the 17.25 from Liverpool. This allowed the rotor to move laterally, causing severe blading damage.

(d) Flexible drive failure

Visit No 13 arose from a serious failure on Camden shed after the engine's arrival from Liverpool, when the coupled wheels locked without warning during a shunting move. The engine had to be hauled dead to Crewe with the leading coupled wheels packed up clear of the rails and coupling rods removed. Stripping revealed that wear in the link pins and bushes between slow-speed gear wheel, yoke and axle arm had become serious, with a cumulative effect on the two pins in the axle arm, the securing arrangements of which had been seriously damaged.

The resultant shocks, particularly when reversing, had been sufficient to fracture one of the link-arm pins, and damage two pinions. Over a quarter of the plates in the multi-leaf buffer springs between the slow-speed gear rim and the yoke, provided as shock-absorbers, were broken. In the ensuing repair, the springs (32 in all) were each fitted with an additional leaf, and a 100,000-mile final drive examination was instituted.

(e) Oil leakage from turbines

This proved to be an intermittent problem and difficult to overcome. It was associated with oil contamination by condensed steam, but because of the small oil reservoir capacity, the oil was perpetually in a frothy condition; nothing short of a major redesign would have overcome this. Improved gland ejectors were fitted to both turbines in 1946 to give improved protection against steam leakage into the oil, and this went some way to get over the trouble.

To sum up, therefore, there were a number of recurrent teething problems with the turbines and transmission; the causes, and hence the modifications necessary, were not always easy to identify. The operators and shed staff must always have kept their fingers crossed, wondering what might happen next and in what traffic context. But R. C. Bond made a fair appraisal in his 1946 paper:

> 'Doubts have sometimes been expressed regarding the suitability of high speed geared turbines for the arduous conditions of locomotive service. The experience already gained with engine No 6202 has, it is submitted, effectively dispelled any doubts on this matter. The ahead turbine and gear transmission has, over 300,000 miles' running, exhibited a degree of mechanical reliability at least as great as that of the cylinders, valves and motion of a reciprocating engine. Since they were redesigned, the reverse turbine and reversing mechanism have given good service, and unsatisfactory features in the lubrication system have largely been overcome.

The remaining problem of oil leakage is certainly not insoluble'.

He went on:

'A cursory examination of the availability record and cost of repairs to date . . . might well excuse expressions of doubt of a sufficiently favourable outcome. Nevertheless, this engine has completed over 300,000 miles in revenue-earning service, which has never been done before in this country by any locomotive which departs so fundamentally from accepted standard practice . . . neither the availability record nor the cost of repairs should be regarded as a fair criterion of what will be achieved during the next 10 years'.

On this note of confidence No 6202 entered the postwar era, but Bond's view of another 10 years was not to be.

There were 12 further works visits in the next five years and over 161,487 miles, the last one resulting in the engine being rebuilt as a conventional one. The causes of these visits are no longer documented, and it is evident that the General Repair in 1946/7 (visit No 17) involved major work on turbines and transmission. But even after that the longest period that the engine was in service was 18 weeks, and by 1950 the spells at Camden were down to a month or less. Finally, in April 1950 there was a major transmission failure, the cost of rectifying which would have been very high. A

stage had been reached where there was really nothing further to learn from the experiment, and no further turbine locomotives would be built. The decision was therefore taken in 1951 to rebuild No 46202 as a normal four-cylinder reciprocating engine, though not quite in the 'Princess' mould.

To overcome the weaknesses in cylinder layout and eliminate the inside valve gears, Derby produced a hybrid design from the intermediate coupled axle forward. What was in effect a 'Duchess' front end, with 16½in diameter cylinders, 9in diameter piston valves and rocking levers was welded on. Roller bearings were kept, as was the 40-element boiler, but there was no attempt to provide rocking grate, hopper ashpan or self-cleaning smokebox. A normal single blastpipe and chimney were applied (Fig 18).

This might well have been a formula for the rebuilding of the remaining 'Princesses' had the future of steam been more assured. Back the engine went to Camden after running in, and entered service on 28 August 1952 on her old diagram, the 08.00 Euston-Liverpool and 17.25 return. This she did for six weeks. Very little is now known about her work in this form, but one of the Derby mechanical Inspectors rode on her and reported her a little shy for steam; slight blastpipe modifications would probably have put this right. But it was not to be. On 8 October 1952, on the 08.00 from Euston, she was involved in the appalling multiple collision at Harrow and Wealdstone, finishing on her side. She was so extensively damaged that she was condemned on the spot and cut up at Crewe. Only the boiler and tender were retained and put into the spares pool — a sad end to a life of great promise.

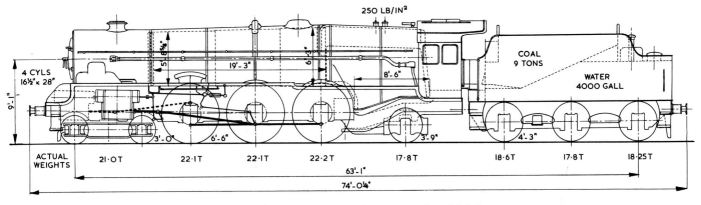

18 Rebuild of 'Turbomotive' as conventional 4-6-2 locomotive, 1952.

Left:
The frames of No 6202 in the Crewe erecting shop on 3 March 1935. This shows the forward 6-valve control unit (left side of the engine) and reverse 3-valve unit (right side of the engine) with shafting from the cab control unit (temporarily covered by a tin box). It also shows the vacuum pump driven by a connecting rod from the leading crankpin; this feature was quickly discarded. *W. L. Good*

Above left:
No 6202 in the erecting shop on 18 August 1935. This was her first visit for repair, caused by an oil leak from the turbine bearings and water in the leading coupled roller bearing axleboxes.
W. L. Good

Left:
On dynamometer car test with the up 'Royal Scot' in May 1936, No 6202 is on Brock troughs hauling 16 coaches. This picture, though of indifferent quality, is the only known one of 'Turbomotive' north of Weaver Junction.
J. M. Thomlinson

Below left:
No 6202 on an up empty stock train on Bushey troughs. This was probably taken in September 1935 on a test of the power of the reserve turbine after complaints from drivers. There appears to be a motive power inspector in the cab.
E. R. Wethersett

Below:
Entering Euston on the 17.25 ex-Liverpool after fitting of the domed 40-element boiler in July 1936. The man on the fireman's seat is probably one of the travelling fitters who accompanied the engine at all times.
Photomatic

Above:
No 6202 as running in 1947. Smoke deflectors were added in 1939, and the RH casing lengthened in 1942 to accommodate an additional steam-driven oil pump. *Real Photos (W9305)*

Left:
'Turbomotive' breasts the top of Camden bank on the morning Euston-Liverpool express in BR days.
F. R. Hebron/ Rail Archive Stephenson

Below left:
Princess Anne on the up 'Red Rose' (17.25 ex-Liverpool) approaching Wavertree in September 1952. The classic Treacy picture, and judging by the interest of both enginemen, with smoke 'by arrangement'. *Eric Treacy/ P. B. Whitehouse collection*

5

The 'Coronation Scot'

As we have seen, the early Stanier Pacifics had, by 1936, established quite new standards of performance on the West Coast main line. Heavier trains were being handled without assistance, while speeds were increasing steadily. But the LMS, spurred on by what the LNER had already done with their 'Silver Jubilee' service between King's Cross and Leeds, and the publicity accorded to the successive high speed records of *Flying Scotsman* (100mph in 1934), *Papyrus* (108mph in 1935) and *Silver Link*, a streamlined 'A4' (112½mph also in 1935) saw the desirability of putting on a fast prestige train. Something was needed to bring back the laurels to the West Coast, and the obvious answer was a high-speed service over the 401.4 miles between London and Glasgow. A nice round figure of 6hr might be a suitable target to aim at, one which would dictate a fairly moderate train formation if the daily reliability essential to such an up-market service was to be upheld. The introduction of the new service was planned for July 1937.

Before the question of the locomotive to work such a train was considered, the important aspect of brake performance had to be considered, for there could be no wholesale resiting of distant signals to give greater braking distances. This aspect was particularly important with a heavy locomotive having little over 50% brake power, attached to a light train with over 90% brake power. Stopping tests were run on 3 May 1936 with No 6203 on a seven-coach train,[53] in the course of which 102½mph was reached at Milepost 39 (south of Leighton Buzzard) in the down direction. One outcome was the adoption of direct admission vacuum valves for the brakes of the coaches for the new train.

If the first engines were to be ready in time to work this high-speed train, it was clear that the outlines of the design had to be frozen by the autumn of 1936 at the latest, in order

that working drawings could be made, material ordered and supplied, and the first locomotive completed in May 1937. This design finalisation has to be seen against the background of Stanier's commitment to a non-LMS activity in the role of eminent consultant; the Wedgwood Committee of Inquiry into Indian Railway finances took him to India from November 1936 until March 1937, and the Committee Report was not completed until early June. Much of the detailed design approval on the new engine thus had to be delegated to Tom Coleman, the recently-appointed Chief Draughtsman at Derby. Stanier had complete confidence in Coleman in his absence.

An order was placed for five new 4-6-2s in the 1937 Building Programme, to be numbered 6213-7. They were envisaged as developments of the 'Princess' design, and two schemes were prepared for Stanier's consideration. The first was essentially a 'Princess' with the coupled wheelbase shortened by 9in (Fig 19), resulting in a weight saving of 0.5 tons, but retaining four sets of valve gear. The second scheme used a similar chassis to the first, but with a boiler enlarged at the firebox end from 6ft 3in to about 6ft 5in dia; it is not now clear whether the grate area had been increased at this stage. In both schemes 6ft 6in diameter coupled wheels and 16¼in diameter cylinders were kept. In the meantime the drawing office was busy marking up 'Princess' drawings for Nos 6213-7 and ordering material on this basis.

Coleman, however, was not very happy with the 'Princess' design, particularly at the front end, and the coupled axleloads were still unsatisfactory. Eric Langridge has recorded[54] how:

'. . . Coleman came out asking for a diagram of a
4-6-2 with 6ft 9in wheels and as big a diameter

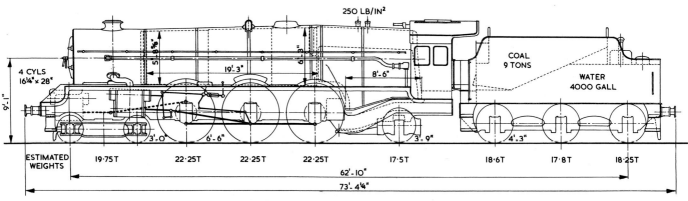

**19 Preliminary scheme for new Stanier 4-6-2, with
'Princess' boiler and 6ft 6in wheels.**

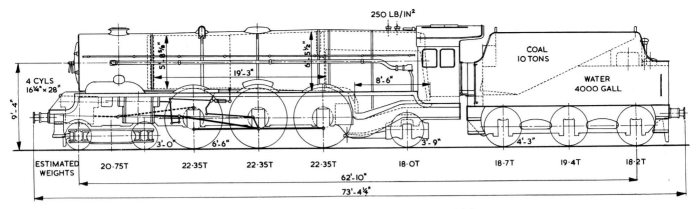

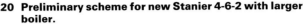

20 Preliminary scheme for new Stanier 4-6-2 with larger boiler.

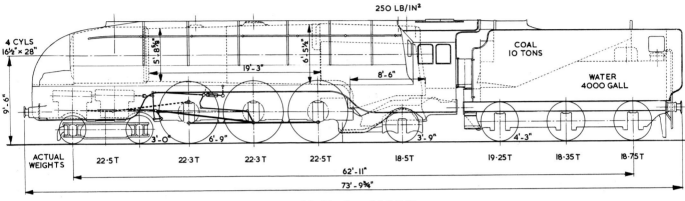

21 'Duchess' 4-6-2 Nos 6220-9 as built.

boiler as we could get in the loading gauge. He asked me to get rid of the inside motion. . . . The drawing of the L&Y Class 8 appealed to me as the thing, so I got out a scheme along these lines'.

The larger boiler was also schemed out, with the barrel increased to 6ft 5½in diameter at the firebox end and the grate increased to 50sq ft (Fig 20). One can deduce that Stanier was thinking beyond the high-speed service to the new design taking over from the 'Princesses' on the harder turns; after all, the dynamometer car tests on Pacifics had shown no higher combustion rate than a modest 55lb/sq ft/hr. By increasing the corner radii of the Belpaire firebox, this great boiler could be carried above 6ft 9in diameter wheels, but clearances were so tight that small rubbing plates were provided on the barrel over the trailing coupled wheels so that, with full wear and maximum axlebox rise, the wheel flanges should not rub on the barrel itself! These two schemes were taken by Coleman to Euston for discussion with Stanier, and it is perhaps a sign of Stanier's final break with those items of Swindon practice which had not translated well to LMS conditions that both were accepted there and then. The fundamentals of the new engine design thus settled (Fig 21), detail design could proceed.

Both these early schemes omitted any form of streamlining; no doubt it was thought that this would complicate the evaluation of the new design and could be applied as an add-on extra. In fact, wind-tunnel tests were under way at Derby, using a 'Princess' model to which alternative front ends could be added together with various valances. In

addition to measuring air resistances, smoke was provided at the chimney and its subsequent movement photographed. The final form of the streamlining was determined by these tests, though with minor compromises.

Simulating a High Speed Schedule
Perhaps as important as the locomotive, the civil engineering implications of running a high speed train on existing tracks needed examination, and arrangements were therefore made for dynamometer car simulation of the new train, on a non-stop 6hr schedule in both directions, on 16 and 17 November 1936. In the train a continuous Hallade record of the movement of the train relative to the track was made, particularly important on curves for comfort; as a result some of the plethora of speed restrictions below the blanket 90mph limit were abolished or eased after attention to cant and transitions.

The engine selected for the tests was No 6201 *Princess Elizabeth* fitted with long-tube (20ft 9in) boiler No 6049, by now fitted with 32-element superheater, 2⅜in diameter small tubes and separate dome. She had at this time run just over 77,000 miles since General Repair and 1,612 miles since last Service Repair, and had the standard Stanier 4,000gal tender with 9-ton coal capacity. She was specially fitted with a Hasler self-recording speed indicator. The enginemen were from Crewe North — the only depot with throughout route knowledge — and comprised Driver T. J. Clarke, Fireman C. Fleet and relief Fireman A. Shaw. R. A. Riddles also rode on the engine. In passing, it is not clear why the test trains were worked non-stop; for regular service such an arrangement

Table 12
Dynamometer Car Test Run: Euston-Glasgow, 16 November 1936

Locomotive: Class 7P 4-6-2 No 6201 *Princess Elizabeth*

Load, coaches: 7
  tons tare/gross: 225/230

Enginemen: Dvr T. J. Clarke, Fmn C. Fleet, Rlf Fmn A. Shaw
(Crewe North)

Distance miles		Sched min	Actual Times min sec	Speeds
0.0	EUSTON	0	0.00	—
1.0	mp1		2.23	32
5.4	WILLESDEN JN	8	7.24	66
			2xpws	35
8.1	Wembley		10.38	—
13.3	Hatch End		15.42	73½
17.4	WATFORD JN	18	18.55	80½
24.5	Hemel Hempstead		24.20	78½
31.7	Tring	30	29.55	77
40.2	Leighton Buzzard		35.49	95½/76*
46.7	BLETCHLEY	41	40.23	85/79*
52.4	Wolverton		44.53	85½/70*
59.9	Roade	51	50.53	79/77½
62.8	BLISWORTH	53½	53.02	87/73*
69.7	Weedon		58.19	82/68*
75.3	Welton		62.46	77½
82.6	RUGBY	70	68.33	86½/35*
88.1	Brinklow		74.17	77½/68*
97.1	NUNEATON	82	81.08	90/83*
102.3	Atherstone		84.56	86/64*
			pws†	
106.5	Polesworth		88.22	82/30
110.0	TAMWORTH	95	92.53	67
116.3	LICHFIELD	100	97.38	85/74*
124.3	Rugeley	106	103.36	90/71*
127.2	Colwich		105.58	75/62*
133.6	STAFFORD	114	111.52	78½/30*
138.9	Norton Bridge		116.50	75/60*
147.6	Whitmore		123.47	82/60*
153.3	Betley Road		128.15	93½
158.1	CREWE	136	132.52	20*
165.5	Winsford		139.53	88
174.3	Weaver Jn	149	146.00	90/50*
179.3	Moore		150.30	82/65*
182.1	WARRINGTON	156	153.30	45*
185.6	Winwick Jn	160	157.03	55*/51*
193.9	WIGAN	168	164.55	75/50*
196.1	Boars Head		167.22	56½/54
199.7	Coppull		170.41	66/90
203.6	Euxton Jn	177	173.36	60*
209.0	PRESTON	183	179.15	80/20*
213.8	Barton		184.29	75
218.5	Garstang	191½	188.05	88
225.7	Galgate		193.08	86½
230.0	LANCASTER	200	196.35	57*

Distance miles		Sched min	Actual Times min sec	Speeds
236.3	CARNFORTH	205	201.28	83½
239.5	mp9½		—	74
243.6	Milnthorpe		206.45	85½
245.5	Hincaster Jn		208.18	62*
249.1	OXENHOLME	215	211.38	68/60*
252.6	Hay Fell		214.51	65½
254.0	mp24		—	68
256.2	Grayrigg		218.04	66½
262.2	TEBAY	227	223.05	65*/78½
266.0	mp36		226.28	61
267.7	Shap Summit	233	228.12	57
272.9	Thrimby Grange		232.37	82/75*
277.0	Clifton		236.12	65*
282.2	Penrith	245	240.05	79/53*
286.0	Plumpton	249	243.45	88
288.3	Calthwaite		245.25	75*
294.2	Wreay		250.00	85½/60*
299.1	CARLISLE	260	255.24	81/20*
301.1	Kingmoor		258.15	63½
307.7	Gretna	268	263.27	85½/58*
312.1	Kirkpatrick		267.39	70½
315.8	Kirtlebridge		270.38	82
321.8	Castlemilk Sdg		275.15	75
324.9	LOCKERBIE	282	277.40	80
327.8	Nethercleugh		279.50	85½
333.6	Wamphray		284.58	82/90
338.6	BEATTOCK	293	287.35	80
341.4	Auchencastle		289.34	68
344.5	Greskine		292.30	57½/56
346.9	Harthope		294.59	57
348.8	Summit	306	297.06	56
354.4	Crawford		301.40	81
356.9	Abington		303.49	65
			pws	
362.3	Lamington		309.25	83½/20
366.0	Symington		313.15	69
369.1	Leggatfoot		316.05	77½/66
372.6	CARSTAIRS	328	319.30	35*
377.6	Craigenhill		324.44	75
383.1	Law Jn	338	329.38	79/40*
			pws	30
388.5	MOTHERWELL	344	336.34	—
			slacks	
401.4	GLASGOW CEN	360	353.38	—

Net Time   345

Calculated Average Equivalent DBHPs:
  Hemel Hempstead-Tring   1,150
  Norton Bridge-Whitmore   1,290
  Oxenholme-mp24   1,770
  mp24-Grayrigg   1,720
  Tebay-Shap Summit   1,820
  Gretna-Kirkpatrick   1,420
  Kirtlebridge-Castlemilk   1,230
  Beattock-Greskine   1,820
  Greskine-Summit   1,970

* Permanent Speed Restriction
† Polesworth pitfall slack, allowed for in schedule

would almost certainly have failed to get trade union acceptance.

Tables 12 and 13 show the two days' running in some detail.[55] Full regulator was generally used, and except on starting, recovery from speed restrictions and on the steep climbs, cutoffs of 15-18% proved adequate. South of Crewe this gave some distinctly unusual speeds — 73½mph at Hatch End, 77 over Tring, 77½ at Roade and again at Kilsby Tunnel, and 82 before *slowing* (!) for Whitmore northbound, and 81 before Whitmore, 80 at Bulkington, 75 at Kilsby

Tunnel following the Rugby slack, and 77½ at Tring next day. With the exception of the climb to Whitmore on the up run, where the EDBHP was over 1,800, all these climbs required power outputs only in the 1,150-1,300EDBHP range, while the overall average for the 401 miles was no more than 870DBHP down and 906DBHP up. But it was a very different story in the fell country and on Beattock. A furious timing of 28min was given for the 31.4 miles from Carnforth to Shap Summit (by comparison the accelerated 'Mid-Day Scot' had 37min), but this was improved on by

Table 13
Dynamometer Car Test Run: Glasgow-Euston, 17 November 1936

Locomotive: Class 7P 4-6-2 No 6201 *Princess Elizabeth*

Load, coaches: 8
    tons tare/gross: 255/260

Enginemen: Dvr T. J. Clarke, Fmn C. Fleet, Rlf Fmn A. Shaw
(Crewe North)

Distance miles		Sched min	Actual Times min sec	Speeds
0.0	GLASGOW CENTRAL	0	0.00	—
4.0	Rutherglen Jn		6.21	62½
6.6	Newton		9.05	50*
			pws	25
9.5	Fallside		12.58	55
			pws	30
12.9	MOTHERWELL	16	16.50	55
15.9	Wishaw South		21.24	48½
			pws	40
18.3	Law Jn	22	24.30	48
23.8	Craigenhill		30.16	62½
28.8	CARSTAIRS	33	34.30	83½/45*
32.3	Leggatfoot		38.01	64-77½
35.4	Symington		40.35	71½
39.1	Lamington		43.17	86½/65*
44.5	Abington		47.49	74
47.0	Crawford		49.49	77½
49.7	Elvanfoot		51.57	72½/80
52.6	Beattock Summit	57	54.20	66½
62.6	BEATTOCK	66	62.29	75
67.8	Wamphray		66.20	88/77½
73.6	Nethercleugh		70.33	89/75*
76.5	LOCKERBIE	77	72.49	77½
79.6	Castlemilk Sdg		75.15	72½
85.6	Kirtlebridge		79.55	86½/75*
89.3	Kirkpatrick		82.45	86½
93.7	Gretna	90	86.10	75*
100.3	Kingmoor		90.55	85/79/86
102.3	CARLISLE	97	93.20	20*
103.7	Carlisle No 13		95.31	51
107.2	Wreay		99.12	65
109.7	Southwaite		101.18	72½
113.1	Calthwaite		103.57	78/74
115.4	Plumpton	110	105.45	83½/80
120.2	PENRITH	114	109.15	85/75*
124.2	Clifton		113.00	55*
128.5	Thrimby Grange		117.05	63
131.7	Shap		120.03	64/67
133.7	Shap Summit	127	121.50	66
139.2	TEBAY	132	126.15	82/68*
145.2	Grayrigg		131.22	76/65*
152.3	OXENHOLME	143	137.18	80/65*
155.9	Hincaster Jn		140.15	84/65*
157.8	Milnthorpe		141.45	88
161.9	mp9½		—	72½

Distance miles		Sched min	Actual Times min sec	Speeds
165.1	CARNFORTH	153	147.12	86½/65*
171.4	LANCASTER	158	152.07	80/66*
182.9	Garstang	167	161.00	87
187.9	Barton		164.18	83½
192.4	PRESTON	175	168.55	25*
194.7	Farington		171.53	69
197.8	Euxton Jn		174.42	62*
201.7	Coppull		178.00	71½
207.5	WIGAN	190	182.42	82/50*
213.5	Golborne Jn		187.03	77½/50*
215.8	Winwick Jn	198	190.14	68/53*
219.3	WARRINGTON	202	193.34	66/55*
227.1	Weaver Jn	209	200.37	77/50*
235.9	Winsford		207.26	87
240.6	Coppenhall Jn		210.32	95
243.3	CREWE	223	213.17	25*
248.1	Betley Road		218.25	—
251.3	Madeley		—	77½
253.8	Whitmore	233	222.53	81/70*
262.5	North Bridge		229.37	84/67*
267.8	STAFFORD	245	233.46	83/30*
277.1	Rugeley	253	242.25	82/70*
285.1	LICHFIELD	259	249.37	91
291.4	TAMWORTH	264	252.58	80
			pws†	30
299.1	Atherstone		260.48	79
304.3	NUNEATON	277	264.33	87
310.0	Shilton		268.45	80
318.8	RUGBY	289	276.05	87/35*
	Kilsby Tunnel North		—	75
331.7	Weedon		287.08	88/73*
338.6	BLISWORTH	305½	292.24	82
341.5	Roade	308	294.33	78½
349.0	Wolverton		299.50	80/70*
354.7	BLETCHLEY	318	304.27	81
361.2	Leighton		309.14	85
365.3	Cheddington		312.10	81
369.7	Tring	331	315.30	77½
376.9	Hemel Hempstead		320.38	91
384.0	WATFORD JN	342	325.38	78
393.3	Wembley		332.38	84
			pws	42
396.0	WILLESDEN JN	352	335.45	—
401.4	EUSTON	360	344.15	—

Net Time   339

Calculated Average Equivalent DBHPs:
Law Jc-Craigenhill	1,740
Lamington-Crawford	1,520
Crawford-Elvanfoot	1,590
Carlisle No 13-mp57	1,860
Clifton-mp40	1,770
Shap-Shap Summit	1,640
Crewe-Whitmore	1,830
Nuneaton-Shilton	1,060
Cheddington-Tring	1,190

* Permanent Speed Restriction
† Polesworth pitfall slack, allowed for in schedule

1¼min. Grayrigg was surmounted at the remarkable speed of 66½mph *after slowing to 60 through Oxenholme*, representing EDBHPs in excess of 1,700, while Shap was tackled with cutoffs from 25% to a maximum of 32%, producing an average of over 1,800EDBHP and a minimum speed at the Summit of 57mph. As if this were not sufficient, a major assault was made on Beattock bank with cutoffs of 30-37½%, as a result of which the 10.0 miles from Beattock to Summit were actually run in under 'even time' — 9min 31sec to be precise — and 56-57mph was sustained all

the way from Greskine box (the dynamometer car record quoted a speed of 58mph at Summit). The calculated EDBHPs on the bank lay between 1,800 and 2,000, with boiler pressure steady at 240lb/sq in. So the down run was completed in 353min 38sec, despite four pw slacks (the Polesworth slack is excluded as being allowed for in the timing) and a miserable run into Glasgow from Motherwell; the net time would be about 345min. Maximum speed was 95½mph below Cheddington.

We know[56] that Riddles's evening in Glasgow was

enlivened by the news that No 6201 had run the whitemetal from the top slipper of one of the crossheads, and arrangements had to be made to hurriedly take the engine round to St Rollox Works for attention during the night, so that she could take up the return working at 13.20 from Glasgow. Also it was on Riddles's instructions that the return load was increased by one coach. With this loading some very fine work was done, despite a start as far as Law Junction broken up by three permanent way slacks. From 48mph on the curve there, the train accelerated in 5½ miles of hard climbing to 62½ at Craigenhill box, requiring over 1,700EDBHP, while on the second stage from the 65mph bridge slowing at Lamington to Beattock Summit the train accelerated to 77½ at Crawford, fell only to 72½ before Elvanfoot, and cleared the summit to 66½mph, using cutoffs between 20% and 28% and exerting nearly 1,600EDBHP on the latter section.

From Carlisle up to Shap Summit a remarkably uniform 1,640-1,860EDBHP was produced, the engine cutting off at between 30% and 35% from Clifton onwards. Speeds such as 74mph after Calthwaite, and 85 before Penrith were never really equalled until the 'multiple Class 50' era of the 1960s. Boiler pressure was held in the 220-240lb/sq in range. To hold 63-64mph on the 1 in 125 from Clifton up to Shap was also quite remarkable. Thereafter it became a case of sprinting between speed restrictions, with a maximum speed of 95mph at Coppenhall Junction, on level road; there were two more 90s before Euston. The overall time for the up journey was 344min 15sec, or about 339min net.

The Dynamometer Car Report[57] on these tests records that:

> 'The steaming of the engine was completely satisfactory . . . practically full boiler pressure being maintained throughout'.

The consumption figures, as compared with those of No 6210 working the heavier but slower 'Royal Scot' the previous month were:

	6201		6210	
	Nov 16	Nov 17	Oct 19	Oct 21
Train Weight, tons	225	255	552/482*	534*
Average Speed, mph	66.1†	70.0†	52.0	54.0
Work Done, HP hr	5,134.6	5,197.5	6,685.3	5,691.6
Coal: Total burned, tons	8.41	8.07	8.54	7.39
lb/mile	46.8	44.8	47.6	41.2
lb/DBHP hr	3.68	3.48	2.86	2.91
lb/sq ft grate/hr	70.8	69.9	55.0	50.6
Water: Total used, gal	13,860	12,105	15,925	13,935
gal/mile	34.5	30.2	39.6	34.7
lb/DBHP hr	27.0	23.3	23.8	24.5
Evaporation: lb/lb coal	7.36	6.70	8.32	8.43

* South of Symington.
† Slightly different figures given in official report.

The report concluded:

> '. . . the coal consumption on the DBHP hr basis is higher than in the case of . . . normal "Royal Scot" train . . . as in the case of the high speed train with its lighter load a greater proportion of

the total power . . . is absorbed by the engine . . .'.

The lower evaporation rates were attributed to the much higher rate of combustion. Finally it opined that:

> 'From all the data obtained from this test, it would appear that a 6hr schedule with loads comparable with those of the test trains is quite practicable, and is within the capacity, without undue stress, of the Class 7 4-6-2 passenger engine'.

In the author's view this final opinion was a little optimistic for the everyday world. The *average* steam rates throughout the journey (making no allowance for running without steam through speed restrictions, of which there were between 30 and 40 in each direction) were around 25,000lb/hr northbound and 22,500lb/hr in the easier up direction; while the regulator was open these were probably of the order of 30,000 and 27,000lb/hr respectively — tremendous rates to maintain over six hours. The coal rates, likewise, averaged 3,197lb/hr down and 3,151lb/hr up, which must be regarded as right at the upper limit of continuous firing for a man. Any deterioration in coal quality, engine condition or weather would have increased these rates markedly, with the fireman scratching about in the back of the bunker for coal towards journey's end. But the *coup de grace* was given by the decision to increase the new trains to nine-coach formations, weighing 297 tons, which would step up consumptions still further. So the operating authorities did not buy this option, and settled for an overall journey time of 6½hr with a 2min Carlisle stop.

The 'Duchess' design
Meanwhile the design of the new locomotives was being completed at Derby and Crewe. Many features introduced with the 'Princesses' were continued, but some important changes were made in the light of experience under the guiding hand of Tom Coleman, who had very firm ideas about how to make the new engine a crowning glory (Fig 21).

1 Frames
These were of 1⅛in high tensile steel; there was a change in philosophy in that horizontal stretchers were provided extending from the inside motion plate almost continuously to the trailing axle (Fig 23). This, together with the inside cylinder casting and stretchers for bogie centre pin and truck pivot pin, gave a very stiff frame structure, enabling axlebox guide cross-stays to be dispensed with. This chassis proved extremely satisfactory and very free from frame fractures.

2 Cylinders
With the larger coupled wheels, cylinder diameter was increased to 16½in to maintain tractive effort. The piston valves were enlarged to 9in nominal diameter. The outside cylinders moved forward to a position 12in behind the bogie centre, the exhaust passages being brought together into the smokebox saddle. The exhaust from the inside cylinders was taken back between the valve chests and led up via a large elbow casting behind the cylinders into the blastpipe base, giving freer flow and less vulnerable joints. Again the valves were given 1¾in lap and ¼in lead, but exhaust clearance of 1/16in was provided. Liner ports were the usual 1¾in wide.

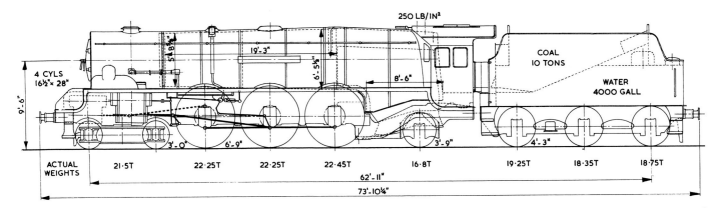

**22 'Duchess' 4-6-2 Nos
6230-4 as built, 1938.**

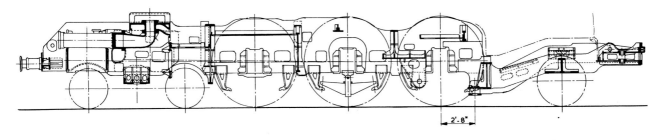

23 Frame arrangement, Nos 6220-4 as built.

From No 6234 the ports were cast with guide vanes to improve steam flow, and replacement outside cylinders had easier bends in the exhaust passages.

3 Valve Gear and Motion

The valves of the inside cylinders were driven from the outside Walschaerts gear by rocking levers behind the outside cylinders (Fig 24). These were connected via short links to the outside valve spindle crossheads, thus neatly avoiding any transfer of thermal expansion to the inside valves. All motion pins were originally fitted with needle roller bearings. Wartime supply difficulties led to these being replaced by bronze or steel bushes, with grease lubrication retained. Return crank pins had self-aligning ball bearings.

The rather complex reversing gear arrangement of the 'Princesses' was discarded in favour of a rocking lever on the reversing gear stand, coupled to a straight supported reversing rod below platform level.

High-tensile 'Vibrac' alloy steel was used for coupling and connecting rods; these were of much lighter section, and the 11ft outside connecting rods were actually 7lb lighter than the corresponding 9ft rods of the 'Princesses'. The coupling rods were fluted (Stanier's previous practice had been to use a plain rectangular section which could better whip in a slip without permanent set).

4 Balancing

Again 50% of the reciprocating masses was balanced, equally divided between the three coupled axles, and the

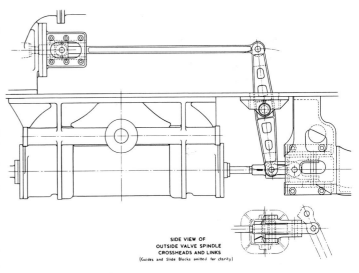

SIDE VIEW OF
OUTSIDE VALVE SPINDLE
CROSSHEADS AND LINKS
(Guides and Slide Blocks omitted for clarity)

24 Arrangement of rocking levers for driving inside valves, Nos 6220-57.

hammerblow figures were virtually identical with those of the earlier Pacifics, namely:

Per wheel	1.31 tons	
Per axle	Nil	at 5rps
Per rail	3.47 tons	
Whole engine	0.24 tons	

5 Brake Gear

The first five engines (Nos 6220-4) were built with single brake blocks to each coupled wheel. This was soon found to result in heavy block wear and inadequate braking efficiency at high speeds, and from No 6225 onwards, twin blocks mounted on equalising beams on the brake hangers were fitted; the first five engines were never brought into line, however.

6 Trailing Truck

While this generally followed the 'Princess' design, the position of the side bolsters was changed to one outside the wheels, at 6ft 4in centres. The male portion was bolted to the underside of stretchers between inner and outer rear frames, the female portion (the 'spittoon') sliding on pads carried on brackets attached to the top of the truck outer frame in a more accessible position.

7 Boiler and Firebox

The increase in barrel diameter at the firebox end, together with the raising of the firebox crown by 2in from the hitherto-sacrosanct 2ft 0in dimension below the outer wrapper, gave more space on the firebox tubeplate, allowing 129 small tubes 2⅜in diameter along with 40 superheater flues, as compared with 101+40 on the special 'Turbomotive' boiler No 9236. The firebox was widened by some 8-9in to get the additional 5sq ft of grate, making the back corners a little more remote from the firehole. The contemporary change on Stanier boilers from copper to monel metal stays outside the breaking zones was also followed in these boilers. The dome was moved forward and the topfeed re-designed, using the standard caged clacks set directly in a manhole casting to save height; this also reduced the number of joints with potential for leakage.

The boiler ratios now began to look almost as good as it was reasonable to get without departing from the traditional A-type superheater. The 2⅜in diameter small tubes had an A/S ratio of 1/435, but the superheater flues with 1in diameter trifurcated elements had a ratio of 1/550; the 5⅛in diameter flues were a constricting feature, and the 5½in flues later used on the BR Standard Pacifics would have been preferable. The total free gas area through the tube bank climbed to 6.89sq ft, or 13.8% of the grate area. It proved to be a remarkably free-steaming boiler, as results in the following chapters will confirm; its one weakness was the very moderate degree of superheat obtained.

From No 6229 onwards, two drop grate sections were provided on the front slope of the grate to aid fire-dropping at disposal, but from No 6253 this was superseded by a full rocking grate. The safety valves had an annoying habit of blowing off at progressively lower pressure after a period, down to about 235lb/sq in, and it seemed rare to find an engine that could maintain any higher pressure without at least one of the four valves blowing.

8 Regulator

This was of Stanier's usual horizontal pattern in the dome. The main valve ports were large, as befitted entrance to a 7in diameter main steam pipe, and the original design of valve lacked adequate stiffness. This occasionally resulted in inability to close the regulator, with embarrassing and spectacular results, as will be seen in Chapter 11. The valves were therefore beefed up and the problem largely ceased.

9 Smokebox

Internal deflector plates were not provided on the 'Duchesses', and since jumper blastpipes had fallen into disfavour, a plain 5¾in diameter blastpipe cap was fitted (Fig 25). After the first five engines the blastpipe was lowered by 3in and the internal profile of the chimney improved. As the next chapter shows, this arrangement, while satisfactory for most duties, could not sustain very high steaming rates, and from 1939 all new engines were built with plain double

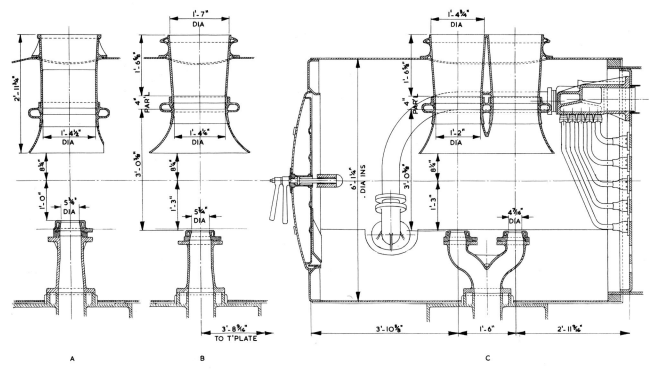

25 Smokebox arrangement and alternative draughting arrangements.

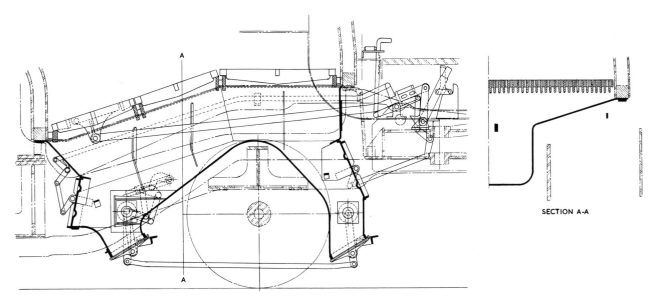

26 Hopper Ashpan arrangement, Nos 6229, 6234-52.

SECTION A-A

blastpipes and chimneys, the earlier engines being converted between 1940 and 1944. The blastpipe caps were initially $4^5/_{16}$in diameter but were finalised at $4^7/_{16}$in. This arrangement was so eminently effective that postwar testing was unable to establish a 'front end limit' for the engine with Grade 1 coal before other factors intervened.

For a short period from new in 1943, No 6245 was fitted with a '1K/1C' Kylchap double blastpipe and chimney, with caps 5½in diameter (less the size of the knife-edged blocks in the orifices). It could be readily identified by the characteristic thin rasping sound of the exhaust. Little is now known of the performance of this application, but the Motive Power Department complained[58] that the cowls above the blastpipes seriously interfered with tube cleaning, and it was not persevered with.

It was announced early in 1947[59] that 33 'Duchesses' were to be fitted with self-cleaning smokeboxes — Nos 6220-52, as Nos 6253-7 had been fitted when built — but so far as can be traced, this work was never carried out.

10 Ashpan
The complex ashpan of the 'Princesses', with its multiplicity of dampers, was discarded in favour of a simpler pan with front and back dampers only. Constrained by the rear end frames and truck, the side slopes of this pan could not be made to fall sufficiently to be self-cleaning; build-ups of ash occurred, particularly in the front corners, which if ignored could lead to burning of the grate bars. Nos 6229 and 6234 were built in 1938 with an experimental hopper ashpan with drop grate, and a similar pan was used on new production from No 6235 to 6252 (Fig 26). The two drop sections in the front of the grate concentrated all clinker into the front hopper during disposal, and the narrow rear hopper tended to take ash only. The side slopes were unchanged, and water jets were provided on them to sluice ash away, but in practice these dribbled after disposal, causing further ash to set like concrete, thus further obstructing the slopes; they were soon removed. To give clear hopper openings, the bottom doors were suspended on external links (Fig 26) to swing clear, but

the operating gear had so many pin joints that there was little positive hold on the doors, which tended to gape open.

11 Streamlining
This was borne on a light framing carried partly on the side platforms and partly on profile frames fitted over the usual boiler clothing. Access to the smokebox door was provided by half-doors in the streamlined nose which opened outwards on vertical hinges, revealing a horizontal platform on which staff could stand while cleaning out the smokebox or sweeping tubes. The cab front was veed at 45° to eliminate reflections in the front windows. Rubber sheeting stretched between cab roof and tender front bulkhead, though this was somewhat vulnerable to damage during coaling.

In mid-1946 removal of the streamlining commenced, its value being less than the nuisance caused by more difficult access for servicing and examinations. This revealed the misshapen smokebox, and led to the separate and unlinked platforms in front of the cylinders, which enabled piston valves to be withdrawn without dismantling platform fallplates. For some reason No 46242 when thus 'unfrocked' was given the vertical fallplates as on the 6230-4 batch.

The non-streamlined engines, after getting double chimneys, were particularly prone to drifting smoke and steam obscuring the driver's forward vision. O. S. Nock described[60] a run northwards from Carlisle:

> 'The soft blast . . . did nothing to lift the exhaust steam, and for mile after mile . . . it was drifting down and completely blanketing our lookout . . . as each interlocking area was neared (the driver) shut off steam so as to get a clear view of the distant signal . . .'.

This brought many complaints (and may even have contributed to one or two accidents involving passing signals at danger) and in 1945 No 6252 was fitted with large smoke deflectors. These were successful and became standard on the 'Duchesses'.

49

12 Tender

This was based on the final 'Princess' 10-ton tender, but to match the streamlined locomotive a number of them had a cowl extending from the front bulkhead some 3ft 9in over the front of the bunker. (Nos 6220-4 did not have this as built; it was added soon after.) It prevented air being sucked from the bunker into the cab, but seriously interfered with coaling to capacity and was removed during World War 2. The tank sides were extended back at full height behind the back of the tank to close some of the gap to the front coach; this made it necessary to provide large apertures in the sides to enable water column bags to be hauled into the twin tank fillers, and these apertures were covered (usually) by sliding doors. It was not a happy arrangement through which to pull a heavy wet bag by chain, and its removal along with the streamlining was unmourned. The bottom valance largely hid the tender springs and made inspection more difficult. The usual large frame openings between the wheels were not initially provided on Nos 6220-52, but this made brake block inspection and replacement more difficult and they were subsequently cut. The tenders for Nos 6249-52 were built in streamlined form though the engines were not streamlined. When locomotives were de-streamlined the tender sides were cut down to a similar profile to those on Nos 6230-4.

A feature of these tenders was the steam-operated coal pusher, known by some as the 'chucker'. A 10½in diameter cylinder fitted just in front of the rear bulkhead pushed two linked triangular section crossbeams down the slope sheet on guide rails. Control was by a regulator handle on the fireman's side of the tender front, and the steam from the pusher originally exhausted into the tank. This was soon altered to exhaust to atmosphere vertically, giving the characteristic plume of steam above the tender back when in use. When the pusher was working well it was a great boon to firemen, pushing coal down to the shovelling plate in a few strokes. It was, however, far from reliable, living in a highly corrosive environment of wet coal, and the guides could jam with accumulations of small coal. The design of the control piston valve was also poor, but Camden shed made it reliable by machining 'blank' valves to take several standard Austin 7 piston rings each end with suitably positioned ring stops; this made it very reliable and after one engine inadvertently went to shops with a modified valve, all were eventually so treated. In later years the lower pusher beam was removed, but this had little effect.

13 Preparation and Disposal

From the driver's point of view, preparation was not difficult, in that only the inside big ends, and axlebox underkeeps needed oilcan attention between the frames. Access to the little ends, etc, was more restricted than on the 'Princesses', since the frame access hole in front of the outside cylinder was necessarily smaller, but by judicious setting of the engine it *could* be achieved from outside. In streamlined form the filling of mechanical lubricators and sandboxes called for ladders, but with de-streamlining this was avoided.

In making up the fire, the same technique as for a 'Princess' was used. It has been graphically described by P. G. Johnson:[62]

> 'First of all, with a shout of "Mind ye feet!" he undid the catches which held the tender doors shut, and the coal . . . cascaded down on to the footplate. . . . When the avalanche had stopped, he cleared the tender doorway and closed and clasped them. . . . Grabbing hold of the biggest lumps of coal, the fireman proceeded to sling them into the box, adding "If they'll go through yon hole, they're all reet". Gradually the pile went down, all the lumps being thrown in first with the cobbles and slack shovelled in after them . . .'.

Practical, if not ideal! If the run was to be a long one, after putting at least two tons on to that 50sq ft of grate, it was common to go back under the coaling plant to top up. It has been alleged that at Polmadie after refilling, firemen used the underside of Polmadie Road bridge to trim the top of the coal on the tender, but photographs hardly bear this out and it would have been highly dangerous for the enginemen!

Disposal could be very heavy work on that large grate, but the use of drop grate sections on many engines, and of rocking grates on No 46253 onwards, in conjunction with hopper ashpans, did much to ease it. But to do the job properly, it was necessary to have a good look round the ashpan after clearing the bulk of the clinker and ash, to see that the slope sheets were reasonably clear.

14 Firing

Everything depended on the fireman having the knack to get coal into the back corners and keep them well filled. If this was done, then a 'Duchess' would steam its head off and the firing of the rest of the grate could be varied within reasonable limits without trouble. A fairly thick saucer-shaped fire, well thickened up under the door and fed regularly with 12-15 shovelsful at a time, was very successful and gave good superheat. Some men had different ideas, and would put a great mound of coal in the box which would take the engine 30 miles or more between firings. It was usual to run with the back damper only open, unless the engine was working hard, but there was much to be said for partial opening of front and back dampers to get a better and more even air distribution to the fire.

Most firemen ran with the water at the very top of the gauge; it was a long boiler, and in changing from 1 in 100 rising to the same grade falling, the water could drop the length of the glass. If the water was carried too high, however, carry-over could occur, and if there was a slip it could be impossible to close the regulator.

The 'Coronation Scot' Demonstration Runs

The new trains, on a fairly fast 6½hr schedule with a Carlisle stop, were introduced with the 1937 summer timetable in July, departure being at 13.30 from each terminus. The point-to-point timings were special to these trains, giving 283min for 299.1 miles between Euston and Carlisle, and 105min for the 102.3 miles between Carlisle and Glasgow. Nine-coach formations of 293-297 tons were provided.

In order to show off the new market leader to the press, both popular and technical, a demonstration run was made to Crewe and back on 29 June 1937; the train was one of the dedicated sets but reduced by omitting one of the two kitchen cars, leaving eight coaches of 263 tons tare. Engine No 6220 was in charge of Driver T. J. Clarke (who had done such magnificent work with No 6201 seven months earlier) and Fireman J. Lewis of Crewe North shed. Their experience of

Table 14
Euston-Crewe 'Coronation Scot' press run. 29 June 1937

Locomotive: Class 7P 4-6-2 No 6220 *Coronation*
Load, coaches: 8
      tons tare/gross: 263.270
Enginemen: Dvr T. J. Clarke, Fmn J. Lewis (Crewe North)

Distance miles		Sched min	Actual Times min sec	Speeds
0.0	EUSTON	0	0.00	—
1.0	mp1		2.39	32
5.4	WILLESDEN JN	8	7.53	68
8.1	Wembley		10.05	76
13.3	Hatch End		14.04	82
17.4	WATFORD JN	18	17.02	86½
20.9	Kings Langley		19.40	82
24.5	Hemel Hempstead		22.20	80½
31.7	Tring	30	27.45	80½
40.2	Leighton Buzzard		33.56	87½/75*
46.7	BLETCHLEY	41	38.57	82
52.4	Wolverton		43.08	86/77½*
59.9	Roade	51	48.56	79/76½
62.8	BLISWORTH	53½	51.09	86
69.7	Weedon		56.20	77*
75.3	Welton		60.38	82/78
82.6	RUGBY	70	66.28	85/39*
88.1	Brinklow		72.20	79
93.5	Bulkington		76.27	82/79
97.1	NUNEATON	82	79.05	83
102.3	Atherstone		83.08	72*
110.0	TAMWORTH	94	89.24	77/73*
116.3	LICHFIELD	99	94.25	76½/72*
124.3	Rugeley	106	100.46	80½/71*
127.2	Colwich		103.20	60*
129.5	Milford		105.29	70½
133.6	STAFFORD	115	109.56	30*
138.9	Norton Bridge	120	115.45	60
143.4	Standon Bridge		119.44	75½
147.6	Whitmore	127	122.48	85
150.1	Madeley		124.27	94½
153.3	Betley Road		126.25	108
156.0	mp156		127.53	113
158.1	CREWE	135	129.46	—

Calculated Average Equivalent DBHPs:
Wembley-Hatch End	1,590
Hemel Hempstead-Tring	1,450
Castlethorpe-Roade	1,240
Weedon-Kilsby Tunnel	1,290
Standon Bridge-Whitmore	1,760

* Permanent Speed Restriction

Detailed Timings: Whitmore-Crewe

	Actual Times min sec	Time for ½-mile sec	Average speed over ½-mile mph
Whitmore (147.6)			
mp148	123.16.8		86.5
		20.8	
mp148½	123.37.6		88.2
		20.4	
mp149	123.58.0		90.9
		19.8	
mp149½	124.7.8		93.7
		19.2	
mp150	124.27.0		94.7
		19.0	
Madeley (150.1)			
mp150½	124.46.0		96.8
		18.6	
mp151	125.4.6		98.9
		19.2	
mp151½	125.22.8		102.3
		17.6	
mp152	125.40.4		103.4
		17.4	
mp152½	125.57.8		105.9
		17.0	
mp153	126.14.8		107.1
		16.8	
Betley Road (153.3)	126.8		108.4
mp153½	126.31.4		
		16.6	
mp154	126.48.0		109.8
		16.4	
mp154½	127.4.4		111.1
		16.2	
mp155	127.20.6		112.5
		16.0	
mp155½			112.5
		16.0	
mp156	127.52.6		
Basford Hall Jn (156.3)			
mp157	128.27		

hard up to Roade or Kilsby, but time-saving continued until the train was 5min early by Stafford. Now the engine was eased severely, to get the boiler into perfect shape for the record attempt and also to ensure that the promised clear road was not jeopardised. The finale started from no more than 60mph at Norton Bridge.

Now 'Coronation' was really put hard at it, steaming at over 35,000lb/hr and no doubt mortgaging the boiler a little to sustain this furious rate, for cutoff must have been between 25% and 30%. The detailed timings over the last stretch are shown at the foot of Table 14, and these have been plotted as a speed curve in Fig 27. Surprisingly, C. J. Allen appears to have used a ⅕sec stop watch at this sensitive time, and this has introduced some minor hiccups in the curve. However, there is little doubt that the claimed 114mph maximum just before Basford Hall Junction (on the basis of the Hasler recorder on the locomotive) was not fully justified, and that 113mph would be more accurate. On a longer down grade the engine could have reached 118-120mph without difficulty. However, by this time

the new engine must have been very limited, for after running-in she had only worked her first trains on 1 June, an unexciting circuit of stopping and express trains between Crewe, Liverpool and Shrewsbury. R. A. Riddles was in overall charge on the footplate, complete with his roll of route data on speed restrictions, gradients, etc. A general speed limit of 90mph was laid down as far as Norton Bridge; from there a determined effort was to be made to beat the LNER's speed record of 112½mph.[63]

An extremely brisk start was made (it was unheard of to get through Willesden in under 8min) and the train was accelerated up the first long 1 in 339 bank from 76 to 86½mph, involving some 1,590EDBHP. On the second stage, up to Tring on 1 in 335, a steady 80½mph was maintained, with a slightly lower output of 1,450EDBPH, requiring steam rates in the 30-32,000lb/hr band. By now the train was 2min before time, and the engine was not pushed so

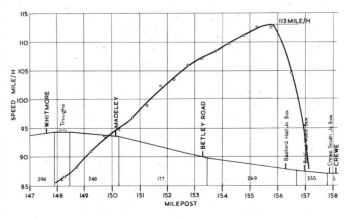

27 Speed diagram of 'Coronation Scot' demonstration run, 29 June 1937.

51

No 6220 was rapidly running out of rail, and stopping was the top priority.

The story of the train's spectacular entry into Platform 3 at Crewe station was only hinted at at the time; the first mile of braking, from milepost 156 to milepost 157, was covered in 34sec, at an average of 105.9mph, and Fig 27 suggests that speed at milepost 157 must have been 92-94mph. The full story was not revealed until Riddles gave his Presidential Address to the Junior Institution of Engineers in 1947.[64] It was perhaps not the occasion to go into detail, but he said:

'Basford Hall Sidings 1½ miles away now . . . and the train still hurtling along at 114mph! On went the brakes, off the regulator; but on we sailed, with flames streaming from the tortured brake blocks. The signals for Platform No 3 at Crewe, entered by a reverse curve with a 20mph speed restriction, came into sight. We were still doing 60 to 70mph when we spotted the platform signal. The crockery in the dining car crashed. Down we came to 52mph through the curve, with the engine riding like the great lady she is. There was nothing we could do but hold on and let her take it . . .'.

In fact, it was something of a miracle that the train did not spread itself all over Crewe South Junction. H. A. V. Bulleid tells[65] how, immediately after the train's arrival, C. R. Byrom (Chief Operating Manager) remonstrated in restrained manner with Stanier on the platform: 'How foolish to come in so fast', to which Stanier riposted, 'How foolish to turn a high-speed test train into a reverse curve, merely to bring it alongside a platform'. It was a not wholly informed reply, for *two* reverse curves were unavoidable; the approach to Platform 3 then, and until 1985, comprised not *one* reverse curve, but no less than *three* crossover roads — fast to slow at about 157.6 miles, slow to through at 157.75 miles, and through to platform soon after — and Allen recorded[66] that they hit the first crossover at 57mph. As he wrote:

'The condition of the track itself must have been superlative to sustain such terrific thrusts . . . with no worse damage than one or two fractured chairs'.

It was also a remarkable tribute to the design of the locomotive. As a footnote, it is worth recording that the 10.5 miles from Whitmore to Crewe, pass-to-stop, was run in 6min 58sec, at an average speed of 90.4mph!

None the worse for her exploits, 'Coronation' took the train back to Euston in the afternoon, and while not providing another speed record, the running in this direction was perhaps even more remarkable (Table 15). The train went out to Crewe like a rocket, and actually passed Whitmore in only 12sec over 'even time', breasting the bank at 80½mph. This effort needed over 1,800EDBHP (about 34,000lb/hr of steam) and no cutoff less than about 25%. Before Rugby no less than six separate 90s had been recorded, and another six were notched up between there and Euston. The recovery from the Rugby slack up to Kilsby Tunnel was fine work indeed at over 2,000EDBHP. Roade hump was rushed with nothing less than 88½mph, and the magic 100 was reached at Castlethorpe and maintained

Table 15
Crewe-Euston. 'Coronation Scot' press run. 29 June 1937

Locomotive: Class 7P 4-6-2 No 6220 *Coronation*
Load, coaches: 8
    tons tare/gross: 263/270
Enginemen: Dvr T. J. Clarke, Fmn J. Lewis (Crewe North)

Distance miles		Sched min	Actual Times min sec	Speeds
0.0	CREWE	0	0.00	—
2.1	mp156		3.34	56
4.8	Betley Road		6.06	71½
8.0	Madeley		8.44	74
10.5	Whitmore	11	10.42	80½
19.2	Norton Bridge	18	16.51	90/74*
24.5	STAFFORD	23	20.58	82/30*
31.0	Colwich		27.05	80/71*
37.1	Armitage		31.02	90/88
41.8	LICHFIELD	37	34.44	92
48.1	TAMWORTH	42	38.55	89/90
51.6	Polesworth		41.27	78*
55.7	Atherstone		44.41	83/71*
61.0	NUNEATON	54	48.29	90
64.6	Bulkington		50.58	86/93½
75.5	RUGBY	66	59.27	85/88½/40*
	Kilsby Tunnel North End		—	75
88.4	Weedon		69.41	92/79*
95.3	BLISWORTH	82	74.24	92
98.2	Roade	84	76.22	88½
103.3	Castlethorpe		79.36	100
111.4	BLETCHLEY	93	85.10	83*/89
117.9	Leighton Buzzard		89.32	93/85*
122.0	Cheddington		92.21	89
126.4	Tring	107	95.23	86½
137.1	Kings Langley		102.30	99
140.6	WATFORD JN	117½	104.59	84*/85
146.7	Harrow		109.00	96
152.7	WILLESDEN JN	127	112.50	85*
157.1	mp1		116.57	—
158.1	EUSTON	135	119.00	—

Calculated Average Equivalent DBHPs:
Betley Road-Madeley	1,840
Nuneaton-Bulkington	1,320
Rugby-Kilsby Tunnel	2,050
Blisworth-Roade	1,330
Cheddington-Tring	1,520

between mileposts 55½ and 54 (did the fireman attempt to take water from Castlethorpe troughs at this speed, one wonders?). The 15.0 miles from Bletchley to Tring were run in 10min 13sec, with a minimum of 86½mph at the top (1,520EDBHP) and 100mph was almost reached again before Watford. So the 158.1 miles from Crewe to Euston were reeled off in 119min exactly, an average of 79.7mph; from Betley Road to Kilburn the average was 93.3mph, and from Welton to Kilburn 89.0mph. With such magnificent running the 'Coronation Scot' was well and truly launched. However, running such as this, spectacular in its own right, was not the stuff of everyday performance.

Service Performance
The 6½hr schedule was not difficult with a nine-coach load; between Euston and Carlisle, at an average of 63.4mph start-to-stop it was well within the capacity of a large Pacific. Calculations have been made for an engine working at 24,000lb/hr steam rate on the principal uphill stretches, with 20,000lb/hr on the easy sections, and as Table 16 shows, these rates were adequate for timekeeping with some margin,

Table 16
The 'Coronation Scot'

Calculated times at 24,000/20,000lb/hr steam rate

Distance miles		Sched min	Calculated Times min sec
0.0	EUSTON	0	0.00
5.4	WILLESDEN JN	9	8.05
17.4	WATFORD JN	20	19.35
31.7	Tring	33	31.55
46.7	BLETCHLEY	45	43.33
59.9	Roade	56	54.18
62.8	BLISWORTH	59	56.47
82.6	RUGBY	76	73.32
97.1	NUNEATON	90	86.43
116.3	LICHFIELD	107	102.04
124.3	Rugeley	113	108.44
133.6	STAFFORD	122	*117.19
138.9	Norton Bridge	127	121.59
147.6	Whitmore	135	129.27
158.1	CREWE	144	139.16
		pass	pass
209.0	PRESTON	194/0	0.00
		pass	pass
218.5	Garstang	10	9.47
230.0	LANCASTER	20	19.51
236.3	CARNFORTH	25	25.28
249.1	OXENHOLME	37	37.14
262.2	Tebay	52	51.37
267.7	Shap Summit	60	59.04
		pass	pass
0.0	CARLISLE	0	0.00
8.6	Gretna	9	9.13
25.8	LOCKERBIE	23	25.05
39.7	BEATTOCK	35	37.02
49.7	Beattock Summit	50	52.48
		pass	pass

No allowance included for recovery.

* Based on 55mph limit at Queensville curve, Stafford, introduced in spring 1938.

Table 17
The 'Coronation Scot'

Locomotive: Class 7P 4-6-2 No 6220 *Coronation*
Load, coaches: 9
    tons tare/gross: 297/310
Enginemen: Not recorded

Distance miles		Sched min	Actual Times min sec	Speeds	Calculated Speeds‡
209.0	PRESTON	194	197.17	25*	25*
		pass	pass		
213.8	Barton		203.16	73†	72½†
218.5	Garstang	204	207.16	72½/75½	69½/70½
230.0	LANCASTER	214	217.06	59*	60*
236.3	CARNFORTH	219	222.37	77½	71½
243.6	Milnthorpe		228.34	67½/80	59/73½
249.1	OXENHOLME	231	233.22	62½	55
256.2	Grayrigg		241.02	49½	44
262.2	Tebay	246	246.22	74½	69
267.7	Shap Summit	254	253.02	36	34

Calculated Average Equivalent DBHPs:
Oxenholme-Grayrigg		1,490	1,330
Dillicar-Shap Summit		1,430	1,350

* Permanent Speed Restriction
† At Brock troughs
‡ At 24,000/20,000lb/hr steam rate

particularly between Blisworth and Crewe. But north of Carlisle, after 300 miles of running, the task of getting the train over Beattock Summit became harder; a timetable demanding an average of 73.7mph from Gretna to Lockerbie, with its 65mph restriction at Gretna Junction and long stretches rising at 1 in 200, was tough to say the least. The same levels of output result in over 2¾min loss to the Summit, most of it before Lockerbie. To keep time required 28,000lb/hr as far as the crest before Castlemilk box, after which the same 24,000 and 20,000lb/hr rates were just adequate but with nothing in hand. The Polmadie crew working from Carlisle were, of course, quite fresh, and good coal could be relied on, so in practice the men generally rose to the occasion by dropping a little time to Lockerbie and going harder at Beattock bank to recover it.

In the up direction the same overall timings represented somewhat easier work, but the timing of 18min from Law Junction to Symington (57.0mph average) was very difficult in view of the 40mph slack at the start and the heavy climb to Craigenhill box.

To illustrate the work of the streamlined Pacifics on this train some out-of-the-ordinary snippets will thus suffice. In the Fell Country, a run in 1938[67] produced the excellent work recorded in Table 17. The train had made a 1½min out-of-course stop at Rugby to rectify a defect with the

engine's sanding gear, and further delays and some easy running had made the train 3¼min late through Preston; by Carnforth this had become 3½min. But the engine was then opened out to produce a sparkling performance on the main banks; no greater drop took place than from 77½mph after Carnforth to 67½ over the Yealand hump, indicative of first-rate footplate work, and by Tebay all but 1¼min had been recovered. The ascent to Shap Summit, with the engine putting out 1,430EDBHP average, had the train past that point a minute early. All this was done without cutoff exceeding 25%. The net time to Carlisle was 273min instead of the 283min allowed.

North of the Border, the run in Table 18 with the same engine[68] showed a real determination to be on time despite the schedule and a permanent way slack through Lockerbie station. For once the limit through Gretna Junction, more honoured in the breach than the observance by many drivers, was scrupulously obeyed; to then *accelerate* up 1 in 200 to 70mph beyond Kirkpatrick was somewhat unusual, to say the least. The 1 in 200 to Castlemilk was run at a similar power output and a minimum of no less than 75mph. The assault — no other word seems adequate — on Beattock bank was fairly spectacular, and shows the effect of dropping the reverser down early. From Beattock station the calculated average EDBHP as far as Greskine was as much as 1,720, with cutoffs in the 25-28% range assuming use of full regulator. The published details recorded an acceleration from a minimum of 37mph to 39½ at the summit, but this does not tally with the times and a minimum of 35½mph immediately before Beattock Summit is more probable. On this basis there was a tailing-off in the output from Greskine to Summit consistent with an unchanged cutoff while speed gradually fell.

In the up direction, Table 19 shows part of a 'Coronation Scot' run[69] in 1939 when, despite a subsidence slack at Newton (a long-standing affair, this), permanent way slack at

53

Table 18
The 'Coronation Scot'

Locomotive: Class 7P 4-6-2 No 6220 *Coronation*
Load, coaches: 9
    tons tare/gross: 297/310
Enginemen: Not recorded (Polmadie)

Distance miles		Sched min	Actual Times min sec	Speeds	Calculated Speeds†
0.0	CARLISLE	0	0.00	—	
8.6	Gretna		9.33	75/65*	75½/65*
13.0	Kirkpatrick		13.29	70	58¼
16.7	Kirtlebridge		16.34	81½	72½
22.7	Castlemilk		—	75	61¾
			pws		
25.8	LOCKERBIE	23	23.52	—	78½
34.5	Wamphray		31.45	85½	66½/70½
39.7	BEATTOCK	35	35.38	75½	61
42.3	Auchencastle		37.53	55½	42
45.4	Greskine		41.42	42½	34
47.8	Harthope		45.20	37	33
49.7	Beattock Summit	50 pass	48.29	39½‡	33¼

Calculated Average Equivalent DBHPs:
Mossband-Kirkpatrick	1,730	1,230
Kirtlebridge-Castlemilk	1,610	1,130
Wamphray-Beattock	1,490	1,150
Beattock-Auchencastle	1,450	1,210
Auchencastle-Greskine	1,720	1,400
Greskine-Harthope	1,560	1,370
Harthope-Summit	1,420	1,300

* Permanent Speed Restriction
† At 24,000/20,000lb/hr steam rate
‡ See text

Table 19
The 'Coronation Scot'

Locomotive: Class 7P 4-6-2 No 6224 *Princess Alexandra*
Load, coaches: 9
    tons tare/gross: 297/310
Enginemen: Not recorded (Polmadie)

Distance miles		Sched min	Actual Times min sec	Speeds
0.0	GLASGOW CENTRAL	0	0.00	—
			pws	
12.9	MOTHERWELL	18	17.50	—
			pws	30
18.3	Law Junction	26	25.51	45*
20.4	Carluke		28.22	53
23.8	Craigenhill		32.15	57
28.8	CARSTAIRS	38	37.10	*
35.4	Symington	44	44.02	—
39.1	Lamington		47.14	74
44.5	Abington		51.40	75
49.7	Elvanfoot		56.04	68/72
52.6	Beattock Summit	62 pass	58.44 pass	58

Calculated Average Equivalent DBHPs:
Law Jn-Craigenhill	1,700
Lamington-Elvanfoot	1,450
Elvanfoot-Beattock Summit	1,540

* Permanent Speed Restriction

Flemington and a checked approach to Carlisle, the 105min booking was improved on by 2min, after passing Beattock Summit 3¼min early. Again cutoffs of around 25% are indicated.

Finally, as a piece of sheer *joie de vivre*, a morsel from early 1939[70] reproduced fairly closely the press demonstration run in 1937. The 'Coronation Scot' made a US tour in that year, with engine No 6229 taking No 6220's identity for the purpose, and with a somewhat hybrid train which actually included a first class sleeping car. Following an official inspection at Euston on 9 January, the train returned to Derby Works to be prepared for shipment, and during the journey tests were made of the riding qualities of the stock at high speeds. The train made a special stop at Blisworth to set down guests, and details of the ensuing sprint to Rugby are shown in Table 20. The finish to the Rugby stop was slow, but not far out of line with normal running. Calculated EDBHP from Weedon up to Kilsby was no more than 1,280 with the light formation.

The outbreak of World War 2 in September 1939 put an immediate stop to the 'Coronation Scot'. Passenger train speeds were initially limited to 60mph, though this was soon raised to 75mph when the expected widespread air raids failed to materialise. The 'Duchess' Pacifics, augmented by further batches until 1943, now took up the haulage of very heavy trains at speeds more modest than prewar, in order to save on coal and maintenance. Not until 1957, with the introduction of the new 'Caledonian' service, did they again get a regular high-speed, medium-weight service on the West Coast, and even then on a 6hr 40min timing.

Table 20
The 'Coronation Scot' US Tour train

Locomotive: Class 7P 4-6-2 No 6220 *Coronation*
Load, coaches: 8
    tons tare/gross: 262/270
Enginemen: Dvr C. Langdale, Fmn W. Pointer (Camden)

Distance miles		Actual Times min sec	Speeds
0.0	BLISWORTH	0.00	—
4.5	Heyford	6.00	68
6.9	Weedon	8.00	79*
12.5	Welton	12.15	77½
13.8	mp76½	13.12	80
17.5	Hillmorton	15.58	86½
19.8	RUGBY	19.05	—

* Permanent Speed Restriction

Left:
**The open smokebox of a
streamlined 'Duchess'. The
outer doors opened to reveal
a level platform on which to
work. The single blastpipe
and petticoat are visible,
together with the battery of
superheater elements.**
*Crown Copyright,
National Railway Museum*

Below:
**The 'Duchess' bogie. The
side bolster spherical cups
through which weight is
transferred are sitting on the
slides and one of the bogie
side control springs shows
beneath the centre casting.**
*Crown Copyright,
National Railway Museum*

Left:
Valve gear of a 'Duchess'. Also visible (extreme left) is the operating stub for the hopper ashpan doors.
J. R. Carter

Below left:
Cab of a non-streamlined 'Duchess'. The regulator is fully open. On the left the geared reversing handle is visible. The fitting directly above the firehole doors is the sandgun for cleaning the tubeplate; it was removed in the 1940s. *Ian Allan Library*

Below:
The tender front. Through the coal doors can be seen the coal pusher, controlled by the vertical handle on the left of the fireiron tunnel. The open coal doors hide the water pickup handle and tank gauge.
Crown Copyright, National Railway Museum

Left:
The coal pusher as modified in the 1950s. Compare with the previous picture; the bottom pusher beam has been removed and the guides for the main beam set further apart to minimise jamming. Note the heavy corrosion inherent in an environment of wet coal.
J. R. Carter

Below left:
Publicity stunt! Early on the morning of Sunday 13 June 1937 all four tracks between Colwyn Bay and Llandudno Junction were blocked for the making of a film of the blue-and-silver 'Coronation Scot' train alongside 'George the Fifth' No 25348 *Coronation* of 1911 on a period train and *Lion* hauling a replica Liverpool and Manchester Railway train.
Ian Allan Library

Below:
The 'Coronation Scot' press demonstration run of 29 June 1937. No 6220 *Coronation* on a slightly reduced formation passes Kilburn No 1 at close on 60mph on the down train. Just over 2 hours later she was running at 113mph.
Ian Allan Library

The 'Coronation Scot' in service

Above left:
The south approach to Crewe station. This circa-1950 picture shows the first two crossovers which led to the down platforms. No 6220 on the demonstration run took the first one at 57mph!
Eric Treacy/P. B. Whitehouse collection

Above:
No 6224 *Princess Alexandra* on the down train passing through Rugby. In the background are the ex-GCR line bridge and the famous 44-arm signal gantry. The signalman in Rugby No 1 box has replaced the down through line signal very smartly! While the bridge survives, disused, the gantry came down in 1939 when colour-light signals were installed. *T. G. Hepburn/ Rail Archive Stephenson*

The 'Coronation Scot' 1939 visit to the USA

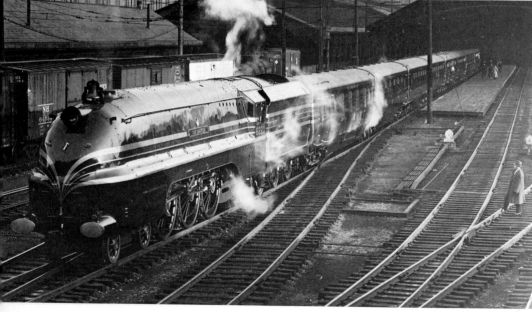

Above left:
No 6220 (actually No 6229 renumbered and named for the trip) sets her train back into the platform at Hartford, Conn (New Haven RR) for public inspection. The man leaning from the cab behind the driver appears to be R. A. Riddles.
Photomatic

Left:
The train leaves another stop on the tour. The bell and headlight were specially fitted for the visit. The seventh coach was a 12-wheeled first-class sleeper inserted for crew use.
Ian Allan Library

The 'Duchesses' begin to take over

Left:
No 6225 *Duchess of Gloucester* takes a down express through Rugby in 1938. The train is on the down line passing Rugby No 4 box. The five engines Nos 6225-9 were painted crimson lake with gold striping and lining.
Eric Treacy/P. B. Whitehouse collection

Left:
This purports to be the down 'Mid-day Scot' picking up water on Whitmore troughs. The first seven coaches of the 15 are of ex-LNWR and Midland stock, some of them vintage examples, hardly appropriate to such a prestige train.
Real Photos (R5308)

Below:
No 6227 *Duchess of Devonshire* with through GWR coach from the West of England waits on the down through line at Crewe to take over the down 'Mid-day Scot', probably in 1938.
Real Photos (R4918)

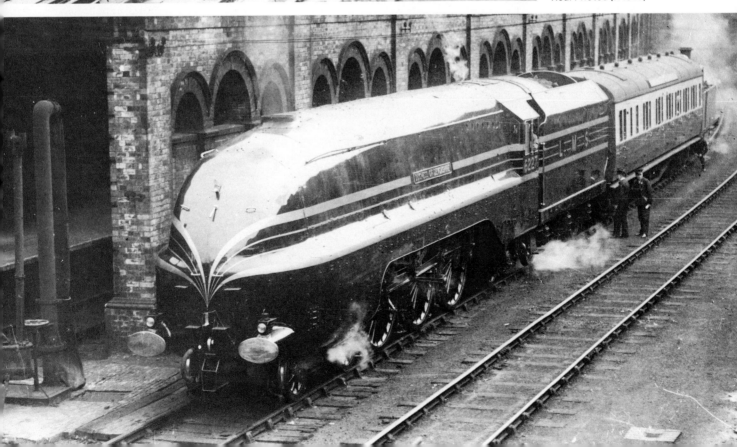

Above left:
No 6225 *Duchess of Gloucester* storms through Edge Hill on an up Euston train. *Eric Treacy/ P. B. Whitehouse collection*

Above:
No 6231 *Duchess of Atholl* passes Kilburn No 1 box with a down express in 1938/9. As built these five engines were painted crimson lake with gold lining, and commode handles, lamp brackets, smokebox door handles, etc were chrome plated. *E. R. Wethersett*

Left:
No 6232 *Duchess of Montrose* has 16 coaches in tow as she hammers through Penrith on an up train in 1938. *Eric Treacy/ P. B. Whitehouse collection*

Below:
No 6231 blows off as she coasts into Oxenholme on an up express. *Real Photos (R5306)*

6
Pushing the 'Duchesses' to the Limit

As Stanier's magnum opus settled down in service, and numbers grew (18 were in service by the outbreak of World War 2) they increasingly took over the hardest duties which had developed round the 'Princesses'. In this work, as on the sustained fast running of the 'Coronation Scot', they showed that they were complete masters. Typical, perhaps, of their work at that time was a trip[71] on the down 'Royal Scot' on its winter 1938 timings, calling at Rugby and Crewe, and with a 13-coach train grossing 435 tons. Driver F. Bishop (Camden) with No 6228 got the train into Rugby in 81min 9sec (net 77min, schedule 80min) despite a signal check to walking pace at Bushey and a severe signal check approaching Rugby. Hatch End was breasted at 62½mph (1,390EDBHP) and Tring at 65mph (1,480EDBHP), Roade at about 63 (the claimed 67 does not match the times), or 1,150EDBHP on the basis of the lower speed, and Welton at 65 (1,210EDBHP). After Rugby, there was a signal check to a long crawl at Colwich, and another at Basford Hall, but the net time to Crewe was only 72min (75 allowed). The working was easy — from Stafford slack on the rising grades to Whitmore full regulator and no more than 18% cutoff were used, taking the train over Whitmore at 70mph minimum (1,540EDBHP) — and there were no very high speeds; 80 before Leighton, 83 past Nuneaton and 80 at Betley Road were the maxima. Clearly the work was well within the engine's capabilities.

But traffic departments are ever wanting to capitalise on the assets provided for them, and for the 'Duchesses' they made no exception. The 'Princesses' had given a taste of what could be expected; they were performing finely on heavy trains; even so C. J. Allen had been forced to admit[72] in 1936 that:

'. . . the LMS Pacifics become a little uncertain in their performances when the loads near the 600-ton mark, and timekeeping, as yet, proves to be a matter of some difficulty with 17- and 18-coach trains . . .'.

on 'Special Limit' timings. So did the new engines offer scope for working even heavier trains on fast schedules? At that time there was only one sure way to find out — to use the dynamometer car on a test run.

The *Duchess of Abercorn* Tests, 1939

On Sunday, 12 February 1939, at 08.10, therefore, No 6234 *Duchess of Abercorn*, six months old and having run about 50,000 miles, pulled out of Crewe for Glasgow with an empty coaching stock train of 604 tons tare, including dynamometer car, on 'Special Limit' timings corresponding to an overall

7hr timing between Euston and Glasgow. The engine was as built, with standard single blastpipe and chimney, and Crewe North men worked her to Carlisle.

Things did not go well.[73] Northwards, there was a proliferation of signal checks and a permanent way slack before Preston, where some 6¾min had been dropped, and thenceforward sectional times were exceeded on the level and climbing sections to Carlisle. Steaming with such hard working was not good; between Carnforth and Shap Summit pressure was not above 220lb/sq in, with a minimum of 202lb/sq in. The Polmadie men who took over at Carlisle did even less well, not appreciating for some time that they were expected to push the engine right to the limit. They dropped more than 9min to Beattock station, the engine steaming poorly due largely to the fireman's work not being up to standard. The train was assisted in rear to Beattock Summit, as booked, after which time was kept to Motherwell; here it was diverted via Bellshill due to engineering work. Coming back, matters were little better. While the new Polmadie men managed to sustain 220-230lb/sq in on the heavy climb to Craigenhill, and from Lamington to Beattock Summit, the fire was not in good shape; 2¼min were dropped on the hard slog up to Shap Summit, with pressure down as low as 200lb/sq in. This was no formula for running heavier trains on fast timings.

The engine was now taken into Crewe Works to be fitted with a plain double blastpipe and chimney, the design for which must have been prepared some weeks previously. (At this time LMS experience with double blastpipes had been confined to the unfortunate and short-lived application on 'Princess' No 6201[73a] and the double Kylchap exhaust tried on 'Jubilee' No 5684, which had proved unsatisfactory.[74]) The design was perfectly simple — 4⁵⁄₁₆in diameter plain blastpipe caps and normal chimney petticoats, with no cowls in between. Two weeks later, on 26 February, the tests were repeated. The enginemen were Driver C. Garrett and Fireman S. Farrington (Crewe North) as far as Carlisle and back, with two sets of Polmadie men between Carlisle and Glasgow.

There seems to have been little co-ordination within the operating department, for the start was a shambles; single line working was in force between Minshull Vernon and Winsford Junction, and by the time the test special cleared the latter point it was 22½min late. After a signal check through Lancaster, lateness increased to 23min at Carnforth. Then followed a remarkable climb to Shap Summit, the 31.4 miles being run at an average speed of 56.5mph with this great train and recovering over 5½min on this section alone. The timetable allowed for a water stop at Beattock station, but in the event there was sufficient in the tank to get through to Symington before stopping at a column; it must have been tight by then, however, for another six miles, coasting much of the way, would have got the engine on to Pettinain troughs!

The turnround time was only about 2hr in Glasgow, and the engine did not go to Polmadie shed; the rocking grate was used to clean the fire, and the engine and dynamometer car were turned via Strathbungo Junction. Then, as C. J. Allen commented:[75]

'Perhaps the most amazing performance put up by the engine was the one that immediately followed, for Driver N. McLean and Fireman A. Smith of Polmadie worked this train, more

than double the weight of the "Coronation Scot", down (sic) to Carlisle in 106½min, or only a minute more than the "Coronation Scot" schedule'.

But the performance from Carlisle up to Shap Summit was in no way over-shadowed by what had gone before. Penrith was passed in just 21½min, only ½min outside the 'Coronation Scot' timing and despite a slight signal check, while Shap Summit was cleared in 40¼min, as against the 'Coronation Scot' timing of 36min.

Figures 28 and 29 show the speeds and actual DBHPs (making no allowance for the power to get the 161.6 tons of

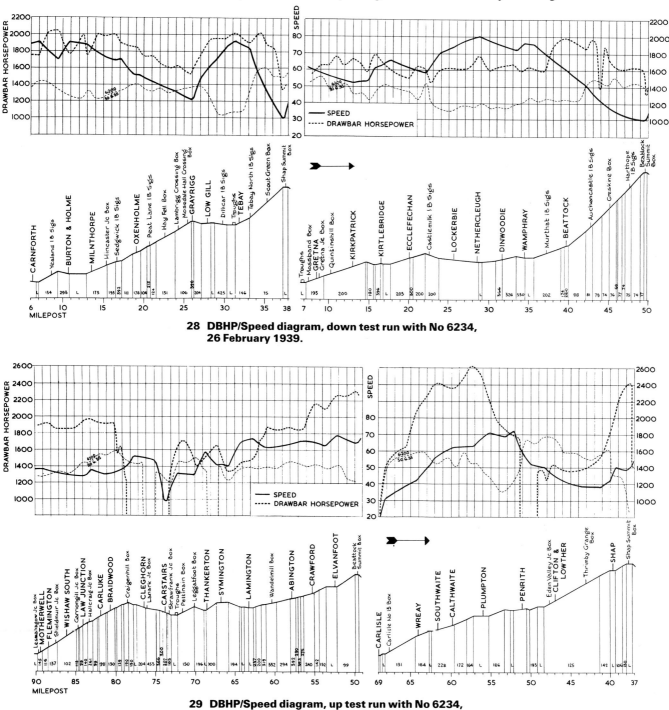

28 DBHP/Speed diagram, down test run with No 6234, 26 February 1939.

29 DBHP/Speed diagram, up test run with No 6234, 26 February 1939.

62

Table 21
Performance of No 6234 *Duchess of Abercorn*, 26 February 1939

| | DBHP | | IHP | Av | Cutoff | Boiler |
	Average	Maximum	max	Speed	Range	Press
Down Direction:						
Carnforth-Oxenholme	1,870	2,120	3,209	68.0	20-25%	250
Oxenholme-Tebay	1,668	1,934	2,806	53.0	25%	245
Tebay-Shap Summit	1,830	2,065	2,963	47.9	25-35%	240
Gretna-Lockerbie	1,598	1,733	2,236	59.3	20-25%	250
Lockerbie-Beattock	1,609	1,823	2,556	72.5	20-25%	245
Beattock-Summit	1,724	2,081	2,761	36.8	30-40%	245
Up Direction:						
Motherwell-Law Jn	1,923	1,998	2,584	46.7	20-30%	250
Law Jn-Carstairs	*	1,978	2,567	49.4	30-35%	250
Carstairs-Symington	1,520	1,638	2,138	46.1	20-25%	245
Symington-Beattock Summit	1,860	2,282	3,333	63.4	30-35%	245
Carlisle-Plumpton	1,822	2,511	3,248	43.9	30-35%	245
Plumpton-Penrith	2,000	2,394	3,241	71.4	20-30%	230
Penrith-Shap Summit	1,560	2,331	3,021	44.4	30-40%	245

* Not shown: engine coasting part way for Carstairs restriction

engine and tender up the hills) over the main climbs, while Table 21 summarises the dynamometer car records for those sections together with cutoffs and boiler pressures. The IHP figures are calculated values from the DBHP peaks, since the engine was not indicated. The thinner lines show the power exerted by No 6200 in 1935.

Highlights of the day's running were almost too numerous to mention, but it is worth noting that, northbound, the maximum DBHP was not exerted on the main climbs to Grayrigg, Shap or Beattock, but on the short rise to Yealand, the engine being immediately opened out to 25% cutoff with speed still in the 70s. To the DBHP figure can be added about 350 to give the Equivalent DBHP on level road — nearly 2,500 in all. Cutoff was set at 25% in the vicinity of Milnthorpe at 74mph and was unchanged to Grayrigg, passed at 41mph; DBHP steadily fell from about 2,000 to just over 1,500. On Shap, 35% was used from before Scout Green box but was not increased further, so that DBHP declined from 2,065 to only about 1,350 in passing Summit at 30mph.

The engine was not unduly pressed from Carlisle to Castlemilk; sectional times were kept with nothing over 25% cutoff, probably with water saving in mind. Beattock station was passed in exactly 'even time' — 39.7 miles in 39min 40sec — and the 10.0 miles thence to Summit were run in the fine time of 16½min, at an average speed of 36.4mph and with an absolute minimum of 30. Cutoff was set at 30% at Beattock station, and advanced by stages to 40% on the climb — how the sound must have echoed round those Lowther Hills — but there was a brief but marked fall in power before Greskine box, with corresponding loss of speed, suggesting an incipient slip which was quickly mastered.

Southbound, the use of 30% cutoff appears to have started at Garriongill Junction, to counter the effect of the sharp curve from there towards Law Junction, with 35% from Hallcraig Junction on the punishing stretch to Braidwood. Speed there was down to 44mph, but rallied to 50 on the easier stretch (a relative term for 1 in 129/130!) to the summit at Craigenhill box. Throughout the 11 miles from Motherwell, the engine had been turning out around 1,900DBHP, peaking to about 2,000, for a quarter of an hour. After the Carstairs slack, again the engine was not pressed; not until after Wandelmill box was the engine opened out with 30% cutoff, and further to 35% before

Crawford. This was sufficient to get this enormous train over the final 1 in 99 to Beattock Summit at no less than 63mph, with DBHP reaching over 2,250 from Elvanfoot. Pressure was maintained at almost blowing-off point throughout.

From Carlisle an all-out effort was made; the maximum DBHP of 2,511, or about 2,870EDBHP, was exerted near Calthwaite. Even on the 1 in 131 up to Wreay, using 35% cutoff, the DBHP reached 2,000 as speed rose to 42mph. After 73mph before Penrith, where speed was reduced to 53mph for a slight signal check, the long 1 in 125 past Thrimby Grange was tackled on cutoffs up to 40%, with speed slowly falling to a minimum of 38mph. On the last part of the bank, from Shap station to the Summit box, DBHP reached a peak of 2,331.

On the face of it, the cost in fuel and water of this spectacular running was heavy:

Coal,	lb/mile	68.7
	lb/DBHP hr	3.12
	lb/sq ft/hr	75.7
Water,	gal/mile	52.1
	lb/DBHP hr	24.1
Evaporation,	lb/lb	7.58

though in relation to the work done the engine had proved very economical. But for a hand-fired locomotive one can only say 'C'est magnifique, mais ce n'est pas la guerre'. On the 268min schedule this rate of working needed an overall coal consumption of almost 7.5 tons, at an average coal rate of 3,750lb/hr, so that allowing for the lengthy coasting down from Shap and Beattock the fireman was having to fire well over 2tons/hr for much of the distance. This brought the working firmly into mechanical stoker range, not that of two arms. However, the spin-off from the tests was the double blastpipe and chimney, which had given impeccable steaming at the highest outputs. Fitting on existing engines started 15 months later, and was applied to new engines from No 6235 onwards.

Tests on No 46225 in 1955/6
The onset of World War 2 put an immediate end to thoughts

of heavy high-speed workings, and the speed revival did not begin until the early 1950s. Along with this revival came a growing interest in the more 'scientific' production of train schedules, and an appreciation that data from the stationary testing plants showing the most economical working range of a locomotive could be applied to scheduling and bring, at least theoretically, fuel economy. (In practice, enginemen became fairly adept at 'adjusting' the schedule for their own working comfort within overall timings!) In view of the key role of the 'Duchesses' in West Coast passenger operation, No 46225 was put through her paces on the Rugby Testing Plant during the spring of 1955, following a General Repair, at speeds up to 100mph. Unusually, she was then put back into traffic for the busy summer workings, and did not resume test running until March 1956, following an Intermediate Repair. The new tests were run on the Skipton-Carlisle line, usually with the dynamometer car controlling the ex-LMS Mobile Test Units for load simulation, but some with a 640-ton train; speeds up to 80mph were run. The time-lapse led to some discrepancies between the two sets of test results, due to various differences including valve setting, and some adjustment of the line test results in the light of new information was needed to get fair agreement.

Report R13 of July 1958 on these tests notes that:

'Steaming rates, using the live steam injector, range from 14,640 up to 41,500lb/hr on the test plant and from 15,000 to 40,000lb/hr on the line, the upper limits being set by the liability to slipping, but also, on the line, by the limited water capacity of the tender, which was designed for . . . a route exceptionally well equipped with water troughs, and by the difficulty of handling bagged coal at a sufficient rate in the confined space of a coal bunker'.

Indicator cards were taken during the line tests only. On the Rugby plant, tests were made both with South Kirkby Grade 1 and Blidworth Grade 2 coals; on the Skipton-Carlisle route only the Grade 1 coal was used. On maximum evaporation, the Report commented that no front end limit was established, but:

'. . . an actual steaming rate of 36,000lb/hr is very close to the limit with Blidworth coal. For the South Kirkby coal the limit is less clear: it is certainly appreciably above the maximum rate at which a test was completed without being prematurely ended by slipping, namely 41,500lb/hr . . .'.

From the many graphs included in the Report, four are reproduced here. Figure 30 shows the drawbar tractive effort between 20 and 80mph, with cutoff lines superimposed, while Fig 31 sets out the performance in terms of 'traction drawbar tractive effort' (ie drawbar tractive effort less the gravity component of the weight of engine and tender on rising grades) through the same speed range and steaming rates,

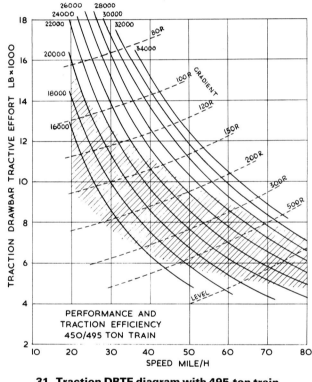

31 Traction DBTE diagram with 495-ton train.

and relates this to the haulage of a 495-ton gross train. In this latter diagram the shaded area is the working range over which the engine was working most efficiently — measured in terms of a coal/DBHP hr figure within 2% of the minimum — and it is perhaps not entirely surprising that this range is roughly defined by a 10% cutoff line at the bottom and a line approximating to 28% cutoff at the top.

Figure 32 shows the variation in gas and steam temperatures with firing rate. The steam temperatures were disappointing; even at a firing rate of 3,000lb/hr they were not above 640°F. But the gas emerging from the superheater flues was even cooler at only 585°F at this rate, a direct result of the unsatisfactory A/S ratio of 1/550 for the flues. With flues of this length, high steam temperatures could only be obtained by departing from the standard 5⅛in diameter flues, as was done with the 'Britannia' boilers. The author has

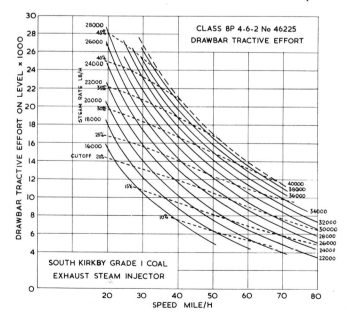

30 DBTE/Speed diagram, No 6225 on Rugby Testing station.

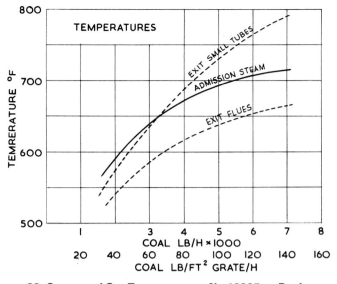

32 **Steam and Gas Temperatures, No 46225 on Rugby Testing Station.**

demonstrated in a previous book how this might have been done, using 5½in diameter flues, at the same time giving a 3% increase in total free gas area. The Report mentioned the possibility of getting higher superheat by the use of the French 'Houlet' or other special type of element, but made no specific mention of the '5P4' elements with which the last two 'Duchesses' had been built with this aim in mind. However, it is very doubtful whether in 'Duchess' flues they would have produced any great increase.

On the Skipton-Carlisle line the results of the confirmatory tests were remarkable, even after the BR Standard 'Britannias' and Class 5s had shown that they could maintain

'Limited Load' timings with nearly double the authorised loads under test conditions. The special test tender with through corridor and separate bunkers for loose and bagged coal was used, and at high powers two firemen were used. The tests culminated in working at a constant steam rate of 40,000lb/hr with a train of 442 tons tare, including the Mobile Test Units working against the engine to simulate a trailing load of approximately 900 tons. On the final climb from Appleby to Ais Gill, predominantly at 1 in 100, speed fell from 54mph at Ormside viaduct (punctuated by slipping in Helm Tunnel) to 37mph at Crosby Garrett, 31½ at Kirkby Stephen, and a sustained 30mph on the 1 in 100 from there to Mallerstang box; this performance required EDBHPs approaching 2,100 at these low speeds.

The main problem proved to be slipping at high outputs and low speeds; the adhesion limit was repeatedly reached under poor rail conditions, especially in tunnels. In addition, the safety valves tended to blow off below the correct pressure and had to be reset or replaced several times. The cylinder pressure relief valves, too, showed a propensity for blowing under heavy working conditions.

Indicating showed up discrepancies in the valve setting. With the valves set cold to drawing standards, ie equal leads, the mean effective pressure at the back ends of the cylinders was consistently less than at the front ends. For some reason the revised valve setting policy[76] applied to the two- and three-cylinder engines from the late 1940s, making proper allowance for thermal expansion, had not been applied to the Pacifics. The results, as shown in Fig 33, taken at about 59mph at about 24% cutoff, showed that 15-37% more work was being done at the front end than at the back. The somewhat 'rule-of-thumb' resetting by pulling the valve heads back ¹⁄₁₆in tended to over-compensate slightly, thus

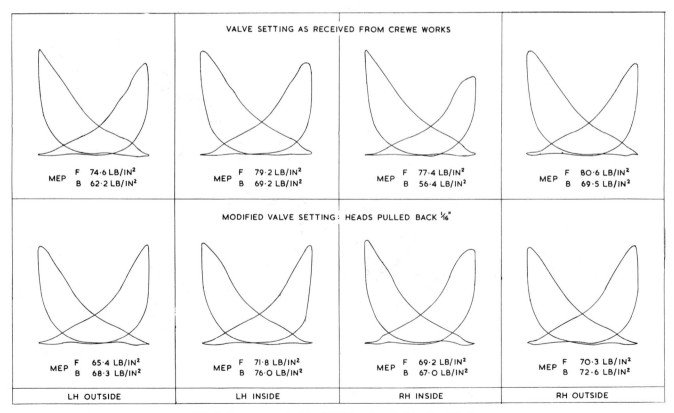

33 **Indicator cards, No 46225 on Rugby Testing Station.**

allowing for the area of the rod itself. The Report, however, considered that this 'probably had very little effect on the steam consumption'.

No experimental alterations were made to the draughting proportions, since none proved necessary, though it was felt that alteration of the internal chimney profile might have improved combustion and allowed the boiler to cope with lower grades of fuel, but this was never put to the test.

Left:
No 6234 *Duchess of Abercorn* on Crewe North shed. This is the condition in which she made the first 20-coach test run to Glasgow on 12 February 1939. *Real Photos (R2527)*

Below:
***Duchess of Abercorn* ready to leave Crewe on the test run on 26 February 1939 with double blastpipe and chimney. Driver Garrett leans from his cab. On the platform are (left to right) E. S. Cox (then Personal Assistant to Stanier), C. H. D. Read (then Mechanical Inspector) and Nicholson (Chief Draughtsman, Crewe).** *E. S. Cox collection*

7
Preparing for the Postwar Revival

The onset of World War 2 in September 1939 put an immediate stop to the enterprising running which had developed with the Pacifics. For the duration, timetables concentrated on haulage of increased loads at speeds downgraded to 'Full Load' category and a maximum of 75mph. In practice, loads did not increase on the principal West Coast trains to the same extent as on the GN main line; 17 or 18 coaches, say 560 tons tare, was rarely exceeded except on one or two night trains, when the load might reach 20 coaches. So a Pacific did not need to be hard pressed for punctuality when allowed 188min start-to-stop from Euston to Crewe, at an average speed of 50.5mph, or 182min from Crewe to Carlisle start-to-stop at 46.5mph average. This schedule lethargy seemed to drain much of the spirit out of keen enginemen, and punctuality went to the winds under the influence of line congestion, blackout conditions at stations and air raid alerts.

The first 15 'Duchesses' (except for No 6229 at Crewe North) had started life at Camden, along with the 'Princesses'. But after the panic transfers of September 1939, and an interlude at Holyhead in 1940 for Nos 6203-5 for 'Irish Mail' working, a longer term resettlement took place. The 'Princesses' divided up, with five at Camden, four at Crewe North and three at Edge Hill, while by mid-1940 14 'Duchesses' were at Camden, six at Crewe North and five at Polmadie, covering all the principal Anglo-Scottish trains and many shorter workings.

Not all drivers, however, succumbed to the influence of easy timings, and where circumstances allowed there was some encouraging locomotive work. A run recorded by C. J. Allen in 1942[77] showed that enterprise was not entirely dead. On the 10.00 from Euston to Glasgow, engines were changed at Crewe and the train worked forward by Polmadie men on the 182min timing to Carlisle. On this instance the load was 16 coaches of 525 tons gross, and after leaving Crewe 21min late due to fog, suffered from a special stop at Preston. Table 22 gives details of the running on to Carlisle. Getting this train away up the bank towards Oxheys was a slow business, as witness the time of 5¼min to pass that point, but after that the running was fully up to prewar standards, with 74mph before Lancaster, 69 beyond Carnforth, 53½ minimum over Yealand and 67 again before Milnthorpe. An excellent climb was made to Grayrigg, with a minimum of 37mph, but better was to come on Shap where, after a strong acceleration to 67mph at Dillicar troughs, the bank was surmounted with no lower speed than 30mph and the engine turning out 1,840EDBHP average. Maximum cutoff must have been about 40%. It is of interest to note that the pass-to-pass time from Lancaster to Penrith was 56min 24sec, exactly the same as that achieved start-to-stop by

Table 22
10.00 Euston-Glasgow, 1942

Locomotive: No 6221 *Queen Elizabeth*
Load, coaches: 16
      tons tare/gross: 480/525
Enginemen: Not recorded

Distance miles		Sched min	Actual Times min sec	Speeds
0.0	PRESTON	0 pass	0.00 start	—
1.3	Oxheys	3	5.18	—
9.5	Garstang	13	14.34	68
13.3	Bay Horse		19.36	71½
21.0	LANCASTER	26	24.27	74/*
27.3	CARNFORTH	33	30.15	69
34.6	Milnthorpe		37.19	53½/67
40.1	OXENHOLME	50	43.23	49½
	Lambrigg		—	43½
47.2	Grayrigg		53.18	37
53.2	Tebay	69	59.41	67
56.2	Scout Green		64.14	41
58.7	Shap Summit	81	67.54	30
72.2	PENRITH	96	80.51	79/55*
			sigs	
90.1	CARLISLE	116	102.42	—

Net Times	98½

Calculated Average Equivalent DBHPs:
Carnforth-mp9½	1,540
Milnthorpe-Oxenholme	1,600
Oxenholme-Grayrigg	1,710
Tebay-Shap Summit	1,840

* Permanent Speed Restriction

No 6209 in 1936 with 55 tons less, so that the gruelling prewar 'Mid-day Scot' timing was in fact being kept.

In 1944 another engine, No 6244, demonstrated the remarkable power of a 'Duchess' when really opened out.[78] She was working the 10.05 from Euston, a relatively light train (for then) grossing 474 tons, and was stopped by signals at Oxenholme South. Restarting speed was then worked up to 59mph above Hay Fell, on the 1 in 131, and on the last two miles of 1 in 106 to Grayrigg fell only to 57mph. As O. S. Nock wrote:

'. . . for about 8min . . . they steamed the engine at a considerably higher rate than could be sustained indefinitely . . . the two stalwarts got 2,600EDBHP out of her . . .'.

This must have required use of at least 40% cutoff — at

nearly a mile a minute — and a steam rate well over 45,000lb/hr!

Surprisingly, perhaps, in view of wartime restrictions on building new locomotives of other than mixed traffic or freight types, the construction of 'Duchesses' continued on a rather piecemeal basis. An outstanding eight engines from the 1939 Building Programme were put in hand late in 1942 (two more had been authorised but later concelled) and the first, No 6245, was completed at the end of June 1943; the remainder followed at intervals until No 6252 emerged in June 1944. No changes of any significance were made from the preceding batch, and the first four even came out complete with streamlined casing; the decision was taken that engines from No 6249 would be built without streamlining.

With the arrival of these engines, all the 'Princesses' at Camden were replaced by 'Duchesses' and moved to Crewe North; however, this did not suit traffic requirements, and within 12 months the division of the 'Princesses' was made between Crewe North and Edge Hill which broadly lasted until withdrawal. The proportion varied a little over the years, depending on availability and summer traffic, but was usually seven at Crewe North and five at Edge Hill (though for nearly two years from September 1951 Nos 6200 and 6203 lived at Polmadie). The new 'Duchesses' went to no new depots, but weighted the allocation towards Polmadie.

Looking to the Future

Meanwhile, the CME Department, in the uncertain years when the war seldom went right, was giving some thought to postwar needs. Just before Christmas 1942, E. S. Cox (by now the CME's Chief Technical Assistant) produced a report headed 'Postwar Developments: Steam Traction Policy and Development'. This looked critically at the current state-of-the-art and made a series of 17 proposals covering the fields of research, development, detail design, financial appraisal and availability. These make extremely interesting reading, the more so since about half of them either came to fruition or were the subject of partial trial. It was felt that the existing range of modern LMS locomotives, given some 'tune-up' in performance, would meet all foreseen traffic requirements *except* for the heaviest express passenger and fast freight duties, for which super-power 4-6-4 and 4-8-4 designs were outlined. Mention was made of the virtues of bar frames, wide steel fireboxes and roller bearings.

A further report by Cox[79] was completed in June 1944, looking at current shopping mileages and steps to improve them. It said:

'. . . increasing engine repair mileage is the most profitable line of development which it is possible to undertake, and 100,000 miles is a practical goal to aim at'.

How far short of this goal even modern classes were falling was illustrated by an analysis of General and Service Repairs to 372 such locomotives in 1943, when only 2% bettered 80,000 miles and as many as 25.5% failed to reach 40,000 miles between repairs, the average being 49,830. However, substantial progress *had* been made; since 1930, for instance, the average mileage between boiler lifts had risen from about 65,000 (a remarkably low figure), to 111,960 in 1943. At this time the US-built austerity 2-8-0s had only recently arrived, and it was perhaps too early to mention the servicing aids built into them which so delighted the Motive Power Department. The emphasis was on refining the breed by careful analysis to identify weaknesses in mechanical performance and develop improvements. In addition, the flange force testing concept, in abeyance during the war, was to be taken up again. An intensive role was envisaged for the incomplete Rugby Testing Station (opened late in 1948) with particular reference to cylinder performance and draughting. While the application of such a programme to LMS power was restricted by nationalisation in 1948, with its production of new designs and central control of locomotive testing, several aspects of the report began to materialise and find limited application on the 4-6-2s.

The remaining five 'Duchesses' were authorised as part of the 1946 Building Programme. By this time the LMS, as a result of experience of modifications to Class 5 4-6-0s, had adopted a revised policy on frame design; Horwich-type hornstays, bolted direct to frame extension legs, and manganese steel liners on axleboxes and horn faces to reduce wear,[80] became the new norm. Commencing with No 6253, three engines incorporated these features, while the drop grate and hopper ashpan design which had served since Nos 6229/34 was discarded in favour of a full rocking grate and a modified hopper ashpan with centre-hinged bottom doors. The standard back end frame arrangement under the firebox, and the plate frame trailing truck, were retained. In addition the smokebox was fitted with deflector plates and mesh screens to make it self-cleaning. All these modifications were designed to reduce servicing requirements and thus increase utilisation and mileage between shoppings. In the event, as will be seen in Chapter 9, this did not happen, though more for reasons of depot allocation than from

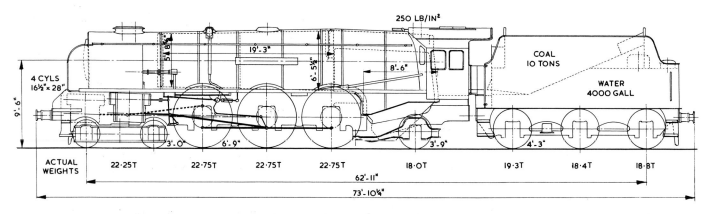

34 'Duchess' Nos 6256/7 as built, 1947/8.

engineering causes. All three spent long periods at Upperby, and to a much lesser extent at Crewe North, where opportunities to amass mileage were less than at Camden.

Just over 12 months elapsed before the final development, No 6256, appeared (just in time to wear LMS livery), followed five months later by No 46257. In these two engines (Fig 34) five new developments were incorporated:

1   The four-plate structure spliced to the main frames behind the trailing coupled wheels was replaced by two bar frame extensions, 2in thick (Fig 35). These slabs made it possible to reduce frame depth while retaining vertical stiffness, and by setting them inwards over the trailing truck gave greater freedom in the ashpan design.

2   The plate-frame trailing truck was replaced by a

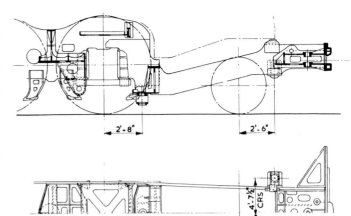

35   Rear end frame arrangement, Nos 6256/7.

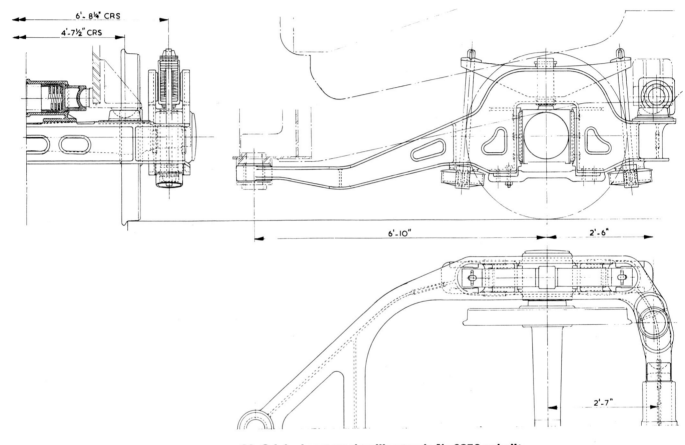

36   Original cast steel trailing truck, No 6256 as built.

one-piece steel casting (Fig 36). The weight was transferred to the truck by side bolsters positioned behind the wheels on the rear crossmember straddling the side control springs. While neat and simple, this truck was not a success, suffering cracking due to defective casting, and it was replaced during 1948 by a revised frame made up by welding smaller cast sections.

3   The ashpan was redesigned with a single commodious hopper (Fig 37); even with the new rear-end frames the side slopes could not be inclined sufficiently to be self-cleaning, however, and so raking doors were re-adopted. It was surprising in an engine of this size to have only one (front) damper.

4   Roller bearings were fitted on all axles. Except for those on the crank axle where, to accommodate flexing of the axle SKF separate boxes with grease lubrication were fitted, they were of Timken manufacture, oil lubricated, the coupled boxes being of cannon type. The bogie, trailing truck and tender bearings were of the same size as those of the 'Turbomotive'.

5   The unsatisfactory superheat temperatures of the 'Duchesses' led to the use of the Superheater Co's '5P4' type elements; these consisted of four 1in diameter finned tubes from the downcomer pipe towards the firebox, the return being via a single 1½in diameter pipe. There was a marked increase in superheater surface, to 979sq ft.

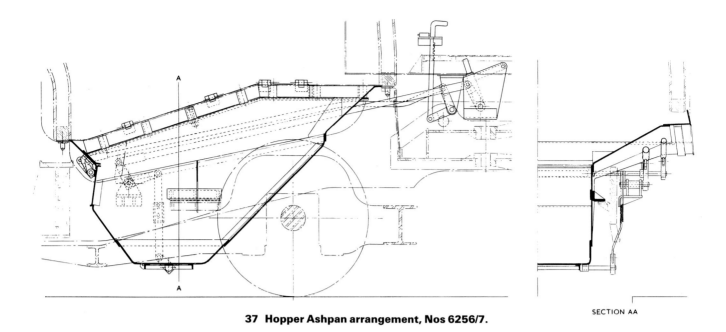

37 Hopper Ashpan arrangement, Nos 6256/7.

SECTION AA

There were also changes in the reversing gear and other details; the servicing aids of Nos 6253-5 were also included.

A dynamometer car test was made on 16 March 1948 with No 6256, to assess the changes in steam temperature resulting from the '5P4' elements. The arrangements were odd, for a secondary train was used, the 13.00 Euston-Carlisle, loading to 14 coaches to Crewe but only nine onwards. Pressure was allowed to fluctuate widely as far as Crewe, falling to 203lb/sq in at Cheddington and 200 at Kilsby Tunnel. The main valve of the regulator was barely opened at any stage, but a maximum temperature of 668°F was recorded at Tamworth, probably 30° higher than could be expected with a standard engine. No 46256 was remanned at Crewe, but while the new fireman kept pressure at 230-250lb/sq in, temperatures were generally lower, with a maximum of 628°F before Preston and generally 605-620° beyond. Brief maxima of 637° at Hincaster Junction and 663° below Scout Green were recorded. The test was relatively inconclusive, however.

On entering service it was officially stated that these two Pacifics were to compete with the two new 1,600hp diesel-electric locomotives Nos 10000/1 in the fields of availability and maintenance costs, and instructions were given to Camden depot, where they were allocated, to work them intensively to get 100,000 miles a year; this was never achieved in practice by any 'Duchess', the highest being 95,917 miles by No 6230 in 1939, while the highest figure for Nos 46256/7 was 88,441 miles by the latter in 1949.

The 1948 Interchange Trials

Recovery from the depressing conditions of wartime were abysmally slow; there were numerous delays due to permanent way work as the engineers struggled to catch up with deferred maintenance, while the competitive position *vis-à-vis* other transport modes had not hotted up to demand improvement on the easy 'Limited Load' schedules. It was under these conditions, following nationalisation in January 1948, that the newly-formed Railway Executive determined to carry out comparative trials of selected locomotives from the four railway companies, covering express passenger, mixed traffic and freight types. In the express passenger

category the 'Duchess' was the automatic choice to run tests against two other Class 7P (then) Pacific classes, the Gresley 'A4' and the Bulleid 'Merchant Navy', as well as two 4-6-0s, the rebuilt 'Royal Scot' (only in Class 6P) and the GWR 'King'.

The selected routes and agreed loadings for the express passenger types were:

Dates of 'Duchess' tests	Reg	Route	Agreed loading, tons		
			Section	Down	Up
20-23 April	LM	Euston-Carlisle	Euston-Crewe	500	474
			Crewe-Carlisle	500	500
4-7 May	E	King's Cross-Leeds	—	512	512
18-21 May	W	Paddington-Plymouth	Paddington-Newton Abbot	485	500
			N Abbot-Plymouth	360	360
22-25 June	S	Waterloo-Exeter	—	470	470

The WR 'King' was prohibited from working over the LM and Southern Regions due to clearance problems.

A Crewe North 'Duchess', No 46236, was selected to represent the class, having run the specified 15-20,000 miles since General Repair. For the duration of the tests she was transferred to Camden, and handled throughout by Driver Byford and Fireman Saint from that depot. Because the tender water capacity was insufficient for the Southern Region route, which had no troughs, No 46236 was fitted with an eight-wheel 5,000gal tender from a WD 2-8-0 for the tests there. Byford with his Pacific was the only combination to cover all four routes unchanged; no less than three different 'A4s' and three 'Merchant Navy' Pacifics were used, partly by choice and partly due to defects and failure.

These trials raised plenty of enthusiast interest, seeing locomotives on strange routes for the first (and usually last) time, but as a technical fact-finding exercise they were almost completely useless. The schedules and loads seldom used the capacity of the engines, and the drivers received no consistent briefing on what was expected of them — not even, apparently, on keeping time! Engines working over 'foreign' routes handled the selected trains during four days of the previous week — two days in each direction — the driver being given a conductor. But the combination of a driver on a strange route (one learns very little on such brief acquaintance) and a conductor on a strange engine could never produce expert train handling, and so it proved. Again, certain routes were beset with temporary speed restrictions and delays, which made punctuality difficult. Byford's performances with *City of Bradford* were mostly rather mediocre, and characterised by gentle starts, leisurely uphill work and very fast (for 1948) downhill running in an attempt to recover lost time. The limited information in the Report[81] (selected examples from which are reproduced in Table 23) is plentifully strewn with EDBHP figures of 1,200-1,350, and it

Table 23
Interchange Trials, 1948

Power Outputs: 'Duchess' 4-6-2 No 46236

Date	Location	Grade	Speed	DBHP	EDBHP	Cutoff	Boiler Press
LM Region: Euston-Carlisle							
20 April	Northchurch	335R	52.9	986	1,130	19	245
(Down)	Norton Bridge	509R	50.5	1,229	1,416	26	232
21 April							
(Up)	Calthwaite	164R	44.1	1,287	1,496	30	240
22 April	Shap Bank,	75R	42.4	1,252	1,506	36	233
(Down)	mp34¾						
	Shap Bank,	75R	23	1,000	1,250	40	233
	mp37						
23 April							
(Up)	Shap Summit	130R	32	990	1,203	30	230
E Region: King's Cross-Leeds							
4 May							
(Down)	New Southgate	200R	48.2	1,172	1,332	27	230
5 May							
(Up)	Stoke Tunnel	200R	41.4	1,128	1,344	35	240
6 May							
(Down)	Wrenthorpe Jn	91R	35.5	1,348	1,775	40	230
W Region: Paddington-Plymouth							
19 May							
(Up)	Savernake	162R	48.5	913	1,227	25	230
20 May	Stoneycombe	57R	44	1,261	1,865	30	235
(Down)	Tigley	54R	32	1,320	1,817	35	235
21 May	Hemerdon	42R	18.5	962	1,376	50	233
(Up)	Bruton	140R	53.5	1,662	1,825	35	232
S Reg: Waterloo-Exeter							
22 June	Semley	145R	38.5	922	1,385	25	224
(Down)	Honiton Bank	80R	51	—	*	40	230
23 June							
(Up)	Hewish	120R	50	1,196	1,600	25	230
24 June	Honiton Bank,	80R	33.5	1,100	1,450	30	225
Down)	mp151						
	Honiton Bank,						
	mp152¾	132R	31	1,185	1,475	35	228
25 June	mp142	165R	39.5	1,109	1,400	30	233
(Up)	mp80½	169R	46.5	1,306	1,575	35	228

* Transitory EDBHP of 2,400 with main regulator valve just open, and with falling water and boiler pressure.

is apparent that he regarded his duty as working the trains with minimum coal consumption, almost regardless of the consequences. Only on the Western Region, however, did he succeed in undercutting the 'A4's' consumption in absolute terms. Full regulator was very rarely used, even on the heavier banks, and most of the running was with either the first valve only, or the main valve just a little open, with cutoffs of 20% or more.

As examples of No 46236's work, selected portions of published runs are shown in Tables 24 and 25. First, on her home ground on 22 April,[82] is the climb of Grayrigg and Shap banks following a permanent way slack at the very foot of the gradient. Even though the train was already running late, the

recovery produced nothing higher than 40mph on the ¾ mile of 1 in 392 above Hincaster Junction, and then there was a gradual fall to 34½ on the 1 in 131 and to only 31mph topping the 1 in 106. But the engine was in no way 'puffed', for she

Table 24
Interchange Trials, Euston-Carlisle, 22 April 1948

Locomotive:			No 46236 *City of Bradford*	
Load, coaches				16
tons tare/gross				500/530
Distance miles		Sched min	Actual Times min sec	Speeds
0.0	CARNFORTH	0 pass	0.00 pass	70½
3.2	mp9½	—	pws	53 17
7.3	Milnthorpe		9.21	—
9.2	Hincaster Jn		13.45	34/40
12.8	OXENHOLME	17	19.37	36/39
16.3	Hay Fell		25.26	34½
19.9	Grayrigg		31.35	31
25.9	Tebay	37	38.18	69
28.9	Scout Green		41.44	39
31.4	Shap Summit	49	47.16	22½

Calculated Average Equivalent DBHPs:
Oxenholme-Grayrigg   1,380
Tebay-Scout Green   1,840
Scout Green-Shap Summit   1,350

Table 25
Interchange Trials, Paddington-Plymouth, 20 May 1948

Locomotive:			No 46236 *City of Bradford*	
Load, coaches			10	
tons tare/gross			329/350	
Distance miles		Sched min	Actual Times min sec	Speeds
0.0	NEWTON ABBOT	0	0.00	—
1.1	Aller Jn		3.00	—
1.9	mp216		4.03	51
2.9	mp217		5.26	39
3.9	Dainton	8	7.22	28
8.8	Totnes	15½	14.25	45*
9.9	mp224		16.05	—
11.4	Tigley		18.40	31½
12.4	mp226½		20.23	37
13.3	Rattery	25	21.55	36
15.6	Brent	28	25.05	47
17.8	Wrangaton		27.59	47½
			2xpws	
31.9	PLYMOUTH	50	50.04	—

Net time   46

* Permanent Speed Restriction

Calculated Average Equivalent DBHPs:
Aller Jn-Dainton   1,480
Totnes-Tigley   1,910
Tigley-Rattery   1,560

swept over Dillicar troughs at 69. The effort on Shap was rather greater than a first glance suggests; for once Byford appears to have dropped the reverser down early, resulting in a comparatively slow fall in speed to Scout Green (where cutoff was 36%) and a high average EDBHP. But little further was done to push the engine as speed fell on the 1 in

75, the EDBHP tailed off to 1,350 on the last stage to the Summit.

On the Eastern Region the performances were dismal. But for a whim of fortune it might have been even more so, for on one of the familiarisation trips with the 07.50 Leeds-King's Cross the conductor failed to advise Byford adequately about the 20mph restriction entering Peterborough station, and the Pacific hit the crossover at close on 60mph. Shades of 1937! But on the Western Region things began to look up, even if the vicious South Devon banks took a toll of the inexperienced enginemen. Between Paddington and Taunton the running was seldom good and sometimes downright dilatory, but the second down test run shows that skill *was* increasing and that on the steepest sections EDBHPs approaching 2,000 were being generated briefly.

The Southern Region route timings were easier than prewar, and there was little of interest. West of Salisbury the switchback route called for sweeping down the banks at high speed to rush the climbs; Byford certainly got the downhill speeds right, but was insufficiently energetic on the climbs, and on the fairly tight timings of the up train making several station stops, this led to time being dropped on some sections. Mostly Driver Brooker with 'Royal Scot' No 46154 beat Byford hands down.

The coal and water consumptions for the test series brought no great surprises. They were:

| | Coal | | Water | |
	lb/mile	lb/DBHP hr	gal/mile	lb/DBHP hr
LMR 'Duchess':				
Euston-Carlisle	44.1	3.07	37.9	26.4
King's Cross-Leeds	44.1	3.04	37.2	25.7
Paddington-Plymouth	41.7	3.24	37.6	29.3
Waterloo-Exeter	42.7	3.17	36.8	27.3
Overall		3.12		27.1
ER 'A4':		3.06		24.3
SR 'Merchant Navy':		3.60		30.4
WR 'King':		3.57*		28.6*
LMR 'Royal Scot'		3.38		25.8
*On two routes only.				

On specific coal consumption the 'A4' was marginally more efficient than the 'Duchess', and notably more so on water consumption, due to higher superheat temperatures. But there was little to be learned from the results, and the decision had already been taken to develop a new BR range of standard locomotives using design criteria identified long before the Interchange Trials.

Those immediate postwar years were a time of relaxed attitudes and sometimes rather casual working practices. The standards of disciplined duty had been eroded during the war and were only slowly being rebuilt. In 1947 the author, then a CME Mechanical Inspector, was going to Watford one day to ride down on a rebuilt 'Scot', and was waiting for a train from Rugby at 09.31, when in came a very late-running overnight express headed by a 'Princess'. On climbing aboard the engine, the driver happened to mention a Bletchley stop. The platform signal cleared, and we were just about to start when a Rugby crew hurried down the platform and said, 'Do you want relief?' This was gratefully accepted, and there was a very hurried changeover. We were getting up towards Kilsby Tunnel when the new driver turned to the author and said, 'D'you know what train this is?' 'Not sure, but I think it's the Stranraer'. 'Oh. Where do we stop?' 'Well, the previous driver did say something about Bletchley'. 'That's all right, then, that's what we'll do!' One was left wondering what some irate passengers would have said if the author had not happened to be on the engine that day!

Preparing for the Post-war Revival

Below:
'Duchess' No 6249, built in 1944, had quickly gained a coating of grime when she was caught by the camera climbing to Shap Summit. *Eric Treacy/P. B. Whitehouse collection*

Above left:
The fascination of the steam locomotive was undoubtedly the visual and aural evidence of being hard at work. No 6230 *Duchess of Buccleugh* is working on something like 50% cutoff as she drags 16 coaches up the 1 to 75 approaching Scout Green box.
Eric Treacy/P. B. Whitehouse collection

Centre left:
No 6204 *Princess Louise* heads the down West Coast Postal past the lineside apparatus at Harrow in 1946. This is a 14-coach train; the net is extended on the eighth vehicle to collect the three suspended pouches. *Real Photos (24196)*

Left:
No 6208 *Princess Helena Victoria* will be making a mile-a-minute as she approaches Brent Junction box with a 13-coach down Liverpool train in 1947.
Real Photos (24122)

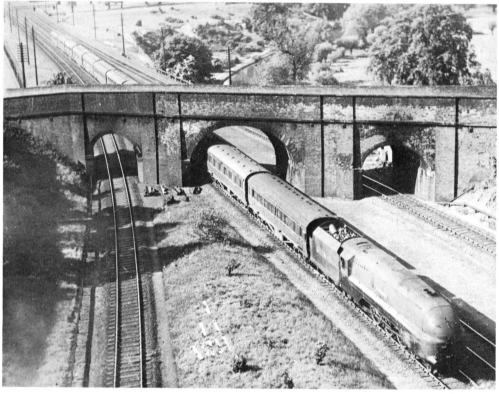

Above left:
Looking distinctly grimed, No 6230 *Duchess of Buccleugh*, a Polmadie engine, is on very mundane work, an Edinburgh Princes Street to Glasgow Central stopping train, passing Kingsknowe on 29 August 1945. While the Scottish Duchesses were used widely on fill-in turns, No 6230's external appearance suggests that she may be confined to local work due to some defect.
J. L. Stevenson

Left:
Up Perth-London express approaches Linslade Tunnel in June 1947, hauled by No 6243 *City of Lancaster*.
W. S. Garth

Below:
Accelerating away from the Preston slowing in 1948, No 6254 *City of Stoke-on-Trent* has about 14 coaches on her drawbar. *Eric Treacy/ P. B. Whitehouse collection*

Left:
**No 6256 *Sir William
A. Stanier FRS* as built in
December 1947. She was
completed just in time to
carry LMS livery. The cast
steel trailing truck is the
original (readily identified
by the H-section yoke arms
and the lightening holes),
which was replaced by a
modified design within a
matter of months.**
Real Photos (13090)

Below left:
**No 46256 repainted in LNWR
black livery and displayed at
the opening of the Rugby
Testing Station on
19 October 1948. She was
now fitted with the modified
trailing truck; the yoke arms
are of box section and there
is a single circular lightening
hole in the side. This design
of truck was fitted to
No 46257 from new.**
J. M. Jarvis

The 1948
Interchange Trials

Below:
**On a familiarisation run
from King's Cross to Leeds,
No 46236 *City of Bradford*
climbs through the northern
suburbs of the capital at the
end of April.**
P. Ransome-Wallis

Above:
During the following week *City of Bradford* makes a run to Leeds with the venerable-looking Eastern Region dynamometer car. She is here approaching Finsbury Park. *E. R. Wethersett*

Left:
The runs to Plymouth were made in May 1948. Here No 46236 gets her train rolling out of Paddington on the 11th of that month on a familiarisation run.
C. C. B. Herbert

Above right:
On the 18th, *City of Bradford* is on a dynamometer car run to Plymouth, here seen in Sonning Cutting.
M. W. Earley

Right:
For tests over the Southern Region from Waterloo to Exeter, where there were no water troughs, No 46236 was coupled to an ex-WD eight-wheeled tender holding 5,000 gallons. She is seen here at Surbiton on 24 June on a down test run, also with the Western Region dynamometer car.
D. A. Dant

8

The Last Years of Pacific Supremacy

In the early 1950s, British Railways stuck doggedly to steam. On its formation in 1948 only one main line diesel locomotive and a handful of diesel shunters had been taken over, and with continued modest construction programmes — as capital was tight and main line diesel reliability not good — only six more main line and 258 more shunting locomotives had been built by the end of 1954. It was not a very firm base on which to build the planned modernisation of the motive power fleet, and the initial orders for diesel locomotives under the 1955 Modernisation Plan clearly envisaged cautious progress; 174 main line locomotives were authorised at the end of 1954, of which no more than 28 were in the 2,000-2,300hp category which would pose any sort of threat to the Stanier Pacifics. None of these 'Type 4' diesels appeared until 1958. The intention was to gain three years' experience with main line diesel traction and to get the 'bugs' out of it before placing further large-scale orders to start eliminating steam. But such an orderly approach was not allowed to continue for very long, and from 1957 onwards further large orders were placed, with the very wasteful results which are well known.

The Timetables

While diesel policy was being thrashed out, the big Stanier engines took in their stride the changes which were wrought in the West Coast timetables. In 1953 a serious start was made in bringing the expresses on to 'Special Limit' timings south of Crewe, while in 1954 'XL Limit' timings appeared there. The Loads Book laid down the following permitted tonnages (tare) for the Pacifics, which since 1951 had been reclassified to '8P' under the unified BR system:

Timings	Full Load	Limited Load	Special Limit	XL Limit
Euston-Carnforth Shap Summit-Euston	—	655	600	510
Carnforth-Shap Summit Carlisle-Shap Summit	570	500	450	—

It was normal practice to derate the trains on the climbs to Shap Summit, so that, say, a down train would run on 'Special Limit' timings to Carnforth and 'Limited Load' timings on to Shap Summit, thus allowing a through load of 500 tons, with 100 tons in hand for strengthening on the more level (and busier) sections.

Now it is a curious, and most valuable, trait of human nature that the great majority rise to a challenge with improved morale, provided that what they are asked to do is realistic and practicable. After the dilatory wartime schedules and the easy postwar 'Limited Load' timings, which had eroded footplate enterprise and allowed signalmen to indulge in much dubious regulation of trains, the accelerations produced a keen response from enginemen, who knew that in the 'Duchesses' particularly they had a matchless machine. Indeed, C. J. Allen could comment[83] in 1955 that the improvement in LM timekeeping had been 'revolutionary'. Not every LM driver matched up to this general standard, however. The following year Allen encountered a driver on a 'Duchess' on the 'Royal Scot' at Euston[84] who

> '. . . expressed the opinion that we should not keep time, owing to engineering slacks, and proved his words by not even attempting to do so'.

North of the Border, the picture was more varied. In the early 1950s some very hard running was called for, thanks to heavy loads and tight timings; the weighty 'Mid-day Scot' was allowed 86min from Carlisle to Carstairs, 73.5 miles against the grade, and only 75min southbound. But in the winter of 1953/4 something happened to upset the Polmadie crews, though the timings were largely unchanged; C. J. Allen was constrained to write:[85]

> '. . . the position today as between the LM and Scottish Regions seems to be completely reversed, in comparison with that of the years immediately after the war. Then the Scottish Region drivers often busied themselves in trying to make good late arrivals at Carlisle from the south; nowadays it is between Glasgow and Carlisle that most of the time is being lost, in both directions, whereas Carlisle Upperby, Crewe North and Camden crews have been vying with one another in the commendable art of time recovery. While much of the time lost north of Carlisle appears to be due to operation rather than to locomotive, the Scottish driving over this route seems to be falling below its one-time standard, as is witnessed by the frequency with which drivers will now stop at Beattock to take assistance up to Summit, which they would have spurned to do with corresponding loads in days gone by'.

As important as assistance may well have been water consumption — always on the high side on the 'Duchesses' — which needed watching on the troughless 65½ miles between

Mossband and Pettinain, particularly when out-of-course delays occurred. Matters improved, however, and by the winter of 1955/6 the two named trains were on a 111min timing from Glasgow to Carlisle; this held until overtaken by the faster bookings consequent on the introduction of the 'Caledonian' in 1957.

But along with the accelerations came two significant trends to meet changing environment. The first was a move away from very heavy Anglo-Scottish trains à la 'Mid-day Scot' with its splitting and joining up at Crewe, Carlisle and Symington. Such moves were time-consuming, and gave too much potential for delay. More and more the Loads Book became of almost academic interest; now 12-14 coach formations taring up to 460 tons became the norm for the 'Royal Scot'. The 'Mid-day' continued as a heavyweight until the winter of 1954, when the down train ran as a straight Glasgow service on 'XL Limit' timings to Crewe and 'Special Limit' on to Carnforth. By contrast some Liverpool and Manchester trains continued to load up to 15 or more coaches and became some of the hardest workings ever scheduled.

The second trend was away from through Euston-Glasgow engine workings. In the postwar years, with a rapid increase in mechanised mining, the NCB was in growing difficulty in supplying the railways with sufficient coal of a quality suitable for long-distance work. The proportion of small coal increased, making the maintenance of a stable, porous firebed more difficult under the high combustion rates of the steam locomotive boiler. Gradually the high calorific value/low ash coals were supplanted by other sources with higher ash content and poorer clinkering characteristics. All this made through 400-mile working more chancy — especially northbound with the heavy Scottish banks to be surmounted after more than 300 miles' steaming — and engine changing at Crewe or Carlisle (matching the normal change of men) became usual.

These two trends also affected allocation; Carlisle (Upperby) increased its small allocation of 'Duchesses' at the expense of Polmadie, and more engines were based at Crewe North than Camden. Indeed, when Crewe's availability was good it was not unusual to find a Pacific (running-in or with defective coal pusher) working a three-return trip diagram[86] between Crewe and Manchester on stopping trains! Crewe North's Pacifics also regularly worked the West Coast Postal section to and from Aberdeen, and their appearance on fast fish trains out of that port were by no means rare.

In the summer of 1957 a new, faster service between Euston and Glasgow started under the name of the 'Caledonian', stopping only at Carlisle and with a 6hr 40min timing — rather faster than 'XL Limit', but not quite as fast as the prewar 'Coronation Scot'. The load was restricted to 280 tons, or eight BR standard coaches. It left Glasgow at 08.30 and Euston at 16.15, with a 2min Carlisle stop (not long enough to fill the tender tank!) and running times of 291min and 107min in both directions. The service was doubled in 1958, with morning and late-afternoon departures from each terminus, and the new trains made additional stops at Crewe (down) and Stafford (up). With the 1959 timetable an important shake-up brought the 'Royal Scot' and 'Mid-day Scot' on to similar fast timings and with the same restricted loads. The work entailed in running these trains was by no means hard, but since the engines worked right through, it was continuous.

But now a new and insidious influence arose; with

engineering work for 25kV electrification about to hit the West Coast line south of Weaver Junction, the winter 1958/9 timetable was drastically revised to allow for the many temporary speed restrictions anticipated. Large amounts of recovery time were built into the schedules, to the extent of *48 minutes* between Euston and Preston; the 'Royal Scot' started from Euston at 09.05 instead of its hallowed 10.00, and patronage suffered as a result. The effect of this recovery time was dire, for often it bore no resemblance to the actual delays. It was not unknown for trains to arrive in Euston half-an-hour early, their drivers unable to spin out the time; they were baffled to know what was expected of them when delays did not materialise. Some took it as an excuse for slovenly running. Allen noted[87] that:

'. . . on the majority of down runs that I made during the winter (of 1958/9) from Euston or Watford, time was dropped handsomely even by Tring, *well before the first permanent way check had been reached*',

and again, in 1960,[88] with the eight-coach up 'Mid-day Scot':

'. . . I joined at Crewe . . . at that time it was allowed 31min recovery to Euston, increasing the schedule from 145 to 176min. . . . The train . . . left Crewe 10min late. Up the 1 in 177 to Whitmore speed fell to 50½mph . . . and we had dropped the first minute . . . by Norton Bridge. After this came 40mph slowings at Great Bridgeford and Stafford, 30 at Colwich and Nuneaton, 28 at Rugby . . . 5 at Castlethorpe, 34 at Tring and 30 at Watford. Speed on almost dead level track at Bletchley was no more than 57½; at Roade it fell to 60; few of the tempting down grades produced more than 70mph, and at two points where speed reached 75mph (Lichfield and Hemel Hempstead) steam was promptly shut off. It is hardly surprising in these conditions that for fully one third of the distance up from Crewe the engine was blowing steam to waste through the safety valves. We even managed to drop a minute from Willesden into Euston and arrived 8min late . . . that 8min precisely equals the time lost by the Pacific over the point-to-point timings where the running was unchecked . . .'.

Thanks to a combination of poor timetabling (there is a long timelag between planning and execution), lack of clear objectives for the men at the sharp end, and an overwhelming sense of being 'messed about', standards of train running hit an all-time low, which remained until steam faded from this part of the main line. However, not *all* running was depressing, and some of the best will now be dealt with.

1 Euston-Crewe

Table 26 gives details of four runs in the down direction, covering the range of train weights that could be worked on 'XL Limit' or 'Caledonian' timings. (Incidentally, on this section these only differed by 9min, despite permitted loads of 510 and 280 tons respectively.) It is worth mentioning here that running times were traditionally much tighter to Rugby

Table 26
Euston-Crewe

Train:		'Mid-Day Scot', 1954					07.55 Euston-Liverpool, 1954			'Caledonian', 1957		
Locomotive:			46211		46255			46229			46232	
Load, coaches:			11		16			16			8	
tons tare/gross:			367/390		525/570			500/535			265/275	
Enginemen:			Dvr Crump, Fmn Rose (Crewe N)		Dvr Nicklin, Fmn Roberts (Crewe)			Dvr Aitchison, Fmn Corfield (E Hill)			Not recorded	
Distance miles		*XL Limit Sched min*	*Actual Times min sec*	*Speeds*	*Actual Times min sec*	*Speeds*	*XL Limit Sched min*	*Actual Times min sec*	*Speeds*	*Sched min*	*Actual Times min sec*	*Speeds*
0.0	EUSTON	0	0.00	—	0.00	—			—	0	0.00	—
5.4	WILLESDEN JN	9	9.25	—	10.45	56				9	8.25	63
8.1	Wembley		—	59	13.30	56					10.48	69
13.3	Hatch End		—	58	18.52	61/57					15.22	70
17.4	WATFORD JN	21	21.43	68	22.45	72	0	0.00	—	21	18.46	76
20.9	Kings Langley		—	—	26.00	64		5.58	57		21.44	72
24.5	Hemel Hempstead		—	—	29.10	65		9.34	62		24.27	74
28.0	Berkhamsted		—	—	32.20	63		12.52	64		27.26	72
31.7	Tring	35	35.23	60	35.45	67	16	16.20	64	34	30.37	72
			pws	55				pws	73/47			
36.1	Cheddington		—	—	39.15	84		—	—		34.08	78
40.2	Leighton Buzzard		—	—	42.21	78		24.16	71		37.14	75
					pws	36						
46.7	BLETCHLEY	47	48.39	80	49.10	48	28	29.40	74	46	42.15	75
52.4	Wolverton		—	85	54.54	74		34.17	78		47.00	73
54.8	Castlethorpe		—	—	56.51	73		—	—		48.58	71
59.9	Roade	58	59.05	71	61.05	72	39	40.45	62	57	53.23	67
62.8	BLISWORTH	61	—	—	63.30	81	42	43.25	71½	60	55.59	73
69.7	Weedon	67	66.50	83	68.27	88	48	49.06	73½	65	61.46	70
76.6	Kilsby Tunnel South		—	72/79	73.50	74/80		—	64½		—	60/64
								pws	37		—	—
82.6	RUGBY	80	78.35	—	80.00	—	60	62.47	32*	77	74.04	34*
5.5	Brinklow				—	—		69.03	64		80.00	60
								pws	76/15		sig stop	
14.5	NUNEATON	15			16.00	80	74	78.48	56	91	94.00	58
19.7	Atherstone				19.55	72		83.58	66		98.52	65
23.9	Polesworth				23.15	80		87.28	76½		102.19	74
27.5	TAMWORTH	28			25.54	74	87	90.12	80	103	105.07	73
33.7	LICHFIELD	34			31.10	64	93	95.07	68½	108	110.06	74
41.7	Rugeley	41			38.30	72	100	101.53	76½	114	116.40	76/73
46.9	Milford	46			43.10	64	105	106.10	70	118	121.02	74
51.0	STAFFORD	51			47.15	56*	110	110.01	54*	123	124.38	60*
56.3	Norton Bridge	57			53.07	56	116	115.02	66½	128	129.16	74
60.8	Standon Bridge				57.38	64		119.01	71½		132.54	75
65.0	Whitmore	66			61.35	64	125	122.36	74½	137	136.18	70
67.6	Madeley				—	—		124.35	79		138.27	72
					pws	28						
70.7	Betley Road				68.50	52		126.54	86		140.55	79
								sig stop			sigs	
75.5	CREWE	77			75.00	—	136	135.27	—	147	148.05	—
	Net Times		77½		77+72			125¼			140	
Calculated Average Equivalent DBHPs:												
	Wembley-Hatch End		1,150		1,630			—			1,140	
	Hemel Hempstead-Tring		—		1,920			1,820			1,150	
	Castlethorpe-Roade		—		2,210			1,320			1,020	
	Weedon-Kilsby Tunnel		1,250		1,780			1,490			720	
	Norton Bridge-Whitmore		—		1,660			1,990			980	

* Permanent speed restriction

than from there to Crewe, where the 13min time from Nuneaton to Tamworth [12min on the 'Caledonian'] still allowed for the long-standing Polesworth pitfall slack, abolished in 1938!)

The two 'Mid-day Scot' runs, made by Crewe North men, were with widely differing loads; the 'Princess' with her 11 coaches in 1954[89] was not pushed in the early stages, and barely kept time to Tring, after which a slight permanent way check at Cheddington put the train 1½min late. This seemed to be the spur the driver needed, for he then ran the 35.9 miles from Bletchley to Rugby in just under 30min, with excellent minima of 71mph at Roade and 72 at Kilsby Tunnel, to arrive 1½min before time. By contrast, that highly competent Crewe driver Harry Nicklin was faced with an unusually heavy 16-coach train[90] in 1958. He was banked up to Camden, but made a slow start to Willesden and then just kept sectional time to Watford. By now, though, he had the full measure of his Polmadie engine, and opened her out to some purpose; the climbs to Tring, Roade and Kilsby would have needed about 25% cutoff. Despite a permanent way slack at Stoke Hammond (Milepost 44¾), exact time was kept to Rugby. Onwards to Crewe, comfortable running had the train through Stafford with nearly 4min in hand, so that despite the impending slack at Madeley there was no need to press the engine. 1,660EDBHP sufficed for the gentle rise from Norton Bridge to Whitmore, and the train stopped at Crewe in 75min precisely. It was a very fine demonstration of what a 'Duchess' could take in her stride.

The next run[91] was on the 07.55 Euston-Liverpool during the first year of its 'XL Limit' schedule; this was the preserve of the Edge Hill top link, which contained some outstanding enginemen. No 46229 had a 16-coach train practically up to

Table 27
Crewe-Euston

Train:		Up Perth, 1953			17.25 Liverpool-Euston						'Caledonian', 1959		
Locomotive:			46237			46229			46209			46239	
Load, coaches:			14			16			14			8	
tons tare/gross			432/460			526/570			449/490			264/275	
Enginemen:			Not recorded		Dvr Trimenall (Camden)				Not recorded		Dvr Court, Fmn Virgo (Camden)		
Distance miles		Limited Load Sched min	Actual Times min sec	Speeds	Special Limit Sched min	Actual Times min sec	Speeds	Special Limit Sched min	Actual Times min sec	Speeds	Sched min	Actual Times min sec	Speeds
0.0	CREWE	0	0.00	—	0	0.00	—	0	0.00	—	0	0.00	20*
4.8	Betley Road		8.25	54		8.13	50				pass	5.31	63½
8.0	Madeley		11.52	57		—	49					8.28	65
10.5	Whitmore	16	14.22	64	15	14.54	58	15			12	10.42	71
19.2	Norton Bridge	24	21.24	82	23	22.35	77	23			19	17.00	90/79*
			sig stop								④		
24.5	STAFFORD	30	28.44	*	29	27.07	54*	29			28	21.00	85½/60*
												sigs	15
28.6	Milford	35	33.15	—	34	31.06	65	33			32	26.23	—
33.8	Rugeley	40	37.38	79/81	39	35.45	73	38			37	33.12	72
						sigs	43						
41.8	LICHFIELD	48	43.34	80/90	46	43.00	77	45			43	39.15	84½/94
48.1	TAMWORTH	54	47.48	82	52	48.23	72	51			49	43.30	84/85½
51.6	Polesworth		50.18	85		—	76					46.02	84/86½
55.8	Atherstone		53.21	78		54.39	67					49.05	69*
61.0	NUNEATON	68	57.10	82	66	58.55	72	63			61	53.03	84
64.6	Bulkington		60.00	72		—	67					—	76½
70.0	Brinklow		64.15	79		66.39	76					59.45	90
75.5	RUGBY	84	69.52	30*	82	71.55	36*	78	84.19	*	75	64.03	40*
79.3	Kilsby Tunnel North		75.40	56		—	52		—	54		—	73½
88.4	Weedon	98	83.46	81	95	85.50	76	90	97.50	82	86	74.46	91½/74*
						pws	24						
95.3	BLISWORTH	106	88.59	78	102	93.58	58	96	103.11	75	91	79.51	85
			pws	30									
98.2	Roade	109	92.00	—	105	96.55	61	99	105.38	70	94	81.55	82½
						pws	76/28				④		
105.7	Wolverton		99.46	74		104.45	—		—	90/75		86.56	95/79*
111.4	BLETCHLEY	125	104.35	70/73	117	111.37	62	110	115.22	80/77	109	91.10	82½
117.9	Leighton Buzzard		110.03	71		117.30	68/71		120.22	78		95.46	87½
122.0	Cheddington		113.41	65		121.07	67		—	—		98.42	83½
126.4	Tring	142	117.52	61	133	125.10	63	124	127.12	71	122	102.03	80
130.1	Berkhamsted		121.15	72		—	—		130.11	80		104.35	87½
133.6	Hemel Hempstead		—	—		134.45	70		132.38	96		106.58	91½
137.2	Kings Langley		126.41	80		—	—		—	—		109.15	95
140.7	WATFORD JN	155	129.21	77/70	146	137.45	67	136	137.22	85	133	111.36	86
146.7	Harrow		134.19	76		142.55	76		141.30	88		115.45	92½
150.0	Wembley		137.07	—		—	—		143.43	93	③	118.00	94½
												sigs	25
152.7	WILLESDEN JN	166	139.27	—	157	147.38	63	147	145.29	—	146	121.22	—
			sig stop										
158.1	EUSTON	175	162.00	—	165	155.45	—	155	152.09	—	154	129.50	—
	Net Times		141½			149½			—			123½	

Calculated Average Equivalent DBHPs:

Betley Road-Madeley	1,900		1,790		—		1,500
Nuneaton-Bulkington	1,360		1,790		—		1,000
Blisworth-Roade	—		1,910		1,440		1,340
Cheddington-Tring	1,340		1,700		1,710†		1,290

† Leighton-Tring
* Permanent speed restriction
④ Recovery time.

the 510-ton limit, and suffered three permanent way checks plus the indignity of a signal stop outside Crewe, yet dropped only ¾min. Time was nearly kept from the Watford restart on the tough 16min timing up to Tring (1,820EDBHP); the rises to Roade and Kilsby were taken rather more easily, using not more than 20% cutoff or so. From being 4¾min down at Nuneaton, Driver Aitchison fought back to being right time at Stafford, and put the engine hard at it to Whitmore, on about 25% cutoff and producing over 1,990EDBHP. From Nuneaton to Whitmore the engine substantially bettered the 45min allowance of the prewar 'Coronation Scot'.

The run selected to illustrate normal 'Caledonian' working[92] dates from 1958, and is mainly notable for the low EDBHPs which were all that was needed to run this light train with some minutes in hand. While speed was kept commendably uniform, almost entirely in the 70s, there was nothing higher than 79mph anywhere.

In the up direction, four runs are outlined in Table 27 which cover the whole range between very heavy 'Special Limit' trains and the lightweight 'Caledonian'. The first, on the day Perth train in 1953,[93] was noteworthy in that, although only booked on 'Limited Load' timings, the train was 32min late from Crewe with enginemen determined that it was going to be much less so in Euston. The climb to Whitmore was taken very hard, and the penalty for getting back 2½min by Norton Bridge was a dead stand for signals approaching Stafford. From there the 51.0 miles to Rugby were reeled off in 41min 8sec, at an average of 74.4mph with a maximum of 90mph at Hademore. After an unnecessarily slow passage of Rugby station, time recovery continued unabated, despite a permanent way slack through Roade, and by Willesden the train was no more than 5½min late. And the result? Euston was not ready, and a series of signal stops on Camden bank frittered away 14min of the hard-won gains. No doubt some hard words were said on *City of Bristol's* footplate that evening!

Two runs on the 'Red Rose' follows; the first was in 1954[94] with a 'Duchess'. One sometimes wondered whether the 600 tons permitted loading of 'Special Limit' timings was realistic, but certainly Driver Trimenall made it look as though it would not worry *him*. There were no tremendous speeds, the maximum of 77mph being very typical of West Coast running, but the power was really piled on on the banks, suggesting cut-offs lengthened before any loss of speed occurred. Notwithstanding a moderate signal check at Elmhurst and two permanent way slacks, Trimenall was 5½min to the good at Bletchley and could afford to take things very comfortably from there; he was fortunate to get a clear road into Euston and arrive over 9min early. The second run,[95] unusually, features a Crewe North 'Princess' on a 14-coach load a few years later (the train went on to 'XL Limit' timings in 1955), and this trip was delayed several times before Rugby, passed 6¼min late. Now by this time quite a few drivers and firemen, having been spoiled by the 'Duchesses', suffered some loss of confidence when given a 'Princess' on a demanding job, but evidently this unnamed crew were not of that ilk. They now got a completely clear road; the recovery to Kilsby Tunnel was fairly gentle, but from there the running was unrestrained, with 82mph at Weedon and nothing less than 70 over the Roade hump. From there they went like the wind — a maximum of 90mph before Castlethorpe, and the 15.0 miles from Bletchley up to

Tring run in 11min 50sec, at an average speed of 76.1mph and with a minimum of 70. The descent from the Chilterns was one of the fastest recorded in ordinary service with no less than 96mph below Hemel Hempstead and 93 before Wembley. From Weedon to Wembley the average speed was 80.6mph, the time being only 23sec outside that of *Princess Elizabeth* in November 1936 on her high speed test run — and with nearly twice her 260-ton load. Clearly there was still a lot of life in the 'Princesses', given sympathetic handling, as average EDBHPs over 1,700 showed!

Finally, a run on the 'Caledonian' during 1959;[96] the basic 143min timing had now stretched to 154min with electrification recovery time, yet on this occasion there was not a single permanent way slack! However, due to a derailment at Shap Summit the train had passed Tebay 50min late, and vigorous efforts to regain time had been frustrated by further delays to the point where Crewe was passed 46½min late. But the Camden crew were heading homewards, and now put up a splendid performance by extending the engine moderately but without exceeding 1,500EDBHP. No less than seven 90s were recorded, and the minimum of 80mph over Tring was pretty remarkable. Between Rugeley and Wembley the time of 84min 48sec for the 116.2 miles was just 3min longer than that of No 6220 on her 1937 demonstration run.

2 Crewe-Carlisle

However spritely the performance south of Crewe may be, there is always a special interest in the performance of steam locomotives on the northern banks, as they battled very audibly with gravity. The brief Yealand hump to Milepost 9½ just cried out to be rushed; the Grayrigg and Shap banks needed the use of longer cutoffs and an increased steam rate *right at the foot of the bank* which got the train farther up (and quicker) before the inevitable slog began. This paid dividends in reduced running times.

Table 28 gives details of four runs between Lancaster and Carlisle. The first, with 'Princess' No 46212 on the morning Birmingham-Glasgow train,[97] was a competent performance in relation to the 'Limited Load' timings, with something in hand on each section. The EDBHPs on the climbs, generally in the 1,250-1,500 range, indicate work rates well within the capacity of these engines, though on the lower part of Grayrigg the engine was allowed to make its own pace without opening up. But the second run,[98] when O. S. Nock was on the footplate, showed the better technique. The train had been 9min late from Crewe, and after further delays was still 6min late through Lancaster. The signal check approaching Carnforth was modest, and after reaching 72mph before the rise to Yealand the driver gave the engine 25% cutoff with the main regulator valve well open. This power, averaging 1,750EDBHP, kept the fall in speed on the 2½ miles of 1 in 134 to 10mph; the controls continued unchanged on the falling grades beyond, so that Grayrigg bank was started at 75½mph with the engine pouring out the power. Nock said that regulator and cutoff were unchanged to Grayrigg itself, but the increase in EDBHP above Oxenholme despite falling speed suggests that the regulator was nudged open farther — perhaps opened fully and the handle eased back, leaving a full opening — to produce this increase, something easily missed by an observer. The attack on Shap took the same technique to something like the ultimate, with the reverser set at 30% cutoff — at 65mph —

Table 28
Lancaster-Carlisle

Train:		10.55 B'ham-Glasgow			'Royal Scot'			'Caledonian'				
Locomotive:			46212			46237			46242			46221
Load, coaches:			11			11			8			8
tons tare/gross			383/405			385/415			264/280			264/280
Enginemen:			Not recorded		Dvr Hodgson, Fm Irving (Upperby)			Not recorded			Not recorded	
Distance miles		Limited Load Sched mins	Actual Times min sec	Speeds	Special Limit Sched min	Actual Times min sec	Speeds	Sched min	Actual Times min sec	Speeds	Actual Times min sec	Speeds
0.0	LANCASTER	0 pass	0.00 pass	60* pass	0 pass	0.00 pass	72*	0 pass	0.00 pass	65*	0.00 pass	2C
3.1	Hest Bank		2.58	67		2.42	74 / sigs 58		2.46	71	3.39	57 sigs
6.3	CARNFORTH	6	5.45	69	5	5.35	72	5	5.22	76	7.05 sig stop	60
9.5	mp9½		—	52		8.28	62		8.09	65	—	—
13.6	Milnthorpe		12.53	64		11.51	75½		11.33	76	17.32	75
15.5	Hincaster Jn		14.55	54		13.28	69		13.14	67/69	—	—
19.1	OXENHOLME	21	19.20	47	20	16.43	64	17	16.38	63	22.00	70
	Hay Fell		—	41/43½		20.10	56½		20.21	51	—	—
26.2	Grayrigg		29.12	42		23.58	50		24.32	53	28.10	66½
32.2	Tebay	38	35.17	64	36	30.11	65	32	29.34	80	32.47	83½
35.2	Scout Green		38.52	37½		33.21 sigs	50 39/15		34.22	53	35.21	—
37.7	Shap Summit	48	43.47 sigs pws	28½ 10	46	38.03	—	40	36.06	36½	38.05	51
51.2	PENRITH	61	59.55 sigs	*	59	52.23	*	52	47.23	82/63*	49.33 sigs	80/60*
69.1	CARLISLE	79	79.45	—	76	70.55	—	69	61.59	—	65.42	—
	Net Times		74¼			68			62		56½	

Calculated Average Equivalent DBHPs:

Carnforth-mp9½			1,160			1,750			1,240		—	
Milnthorpe-Oxenholme			1,240			1,870			1,240		1,700	
Oxenholme-Grayrigg			1,490			2,000			1,380		1,980	
Tebay-Shap Summit			1,480			2,140†			1,250		1,710	

* Permanent speed restriction
† Average to mp36¾

as the engine came off Dillicar troughs. This tremendous effort gave an average EDBHP of 2,140 up to Milepost 36¾, where steam had to be shut off for a signal check. From being 6min late at Lancaster, the train had been right time at Tebay and would have passed the Summit box in 37min from Lancaster but for this check.

Finally, two runs on the 'Caledonian'. The first, in 1957,[99] was fairly modest by the standards of the day; due to diversion via Northampton and other delays the train was nearly 10min late past Crewe, but by Lancaster this had been reduced to 3min. As far as Grayrigg the work appeared to involve no cutoff longer than 20%, but this was increased to about 25% on Shap. On the second run[100] No 46221 was worked much harder on the banks, no doubt reflecting the driver's frustration at the early delays, including a dead stand at Yealand IB signals. The engine was then driven quite hard to reach 75mph before Milnthorpe, in under five miles, and it was unusual, to say the least, to drop only 8½mph on Grayrigg to pass the summit at 66½; this would have needed 28-30% cutoff. The recovery to Dillicar, too, was very rapid, while the average of 1,710EDBHP up to Shap Summit resulted from cutoffs of 25-30%. When power of this order was applied to an eight-coach train, the results were distinctly exciting.

In the opposite direction, Table 29 sets out four runs between Carlisle and Lancaster during the 1954-7 period, surely the heyday of the 'Duchesses', even if the 'Princesses' were somewhat overshadowed. Here the problem was to accelerate out of Carlisle on the heavy gradients to a speed where the sheer boiler power of a Pacific could be brought into play, and similarly to maximise speed after the 60mph slack through Penrith to carry the train up the lower reaches of the 1 in 125 to Shap.

On the first run,[101] on the 'Royal Scot', No 46256 had come on fresh at Carlisle and left a few minutes behind time. The output on the climb past Wreay and Southwaite suggests about 25% cutoff, appropriate to warm up a 'cold' engine, but even by Penrith 2min had been pulled back on the 'Special Limit' timings, and a splendid climb was then made to Shap Summit, with a gradual fall to 44mph on the 1 in 125. The 1,680 average EDBHP implies up to 30% cutoff here. The next two runs reflect the heavy nature of the 'Mid-day Scot' in 1954/5. No 46243 with 15 on[102] made an energetic climb to Shap Summit after leaving Carlisle 10min late following delays in Scotland. To work speed up to 59mph by Milepost 59½ (on 1 in 128) and fall back to 55½ above Calthwaite on 1 in 172/164 needed an average of 1,810EDBHP, and this took the train through Penrith in

Table 29
Carlisle–Crewe

Train:		'Royal Scot', 1955			'Mid-day Scot', 1954/5					'Caledonian', 1957		
Locomotive:		46256			46243			46212		46242		
Load, coaches:		12			15			17		8		
tons tare/gross		413/445			471/510			542/580		264/275		
Enginemen:		Dvr Stuchbury, Fmn Kennedy (Camden)			Dvr Preece, Fmn Turner (Crewe N)			Dvr Betley, Fmn Fore (Crewe N)		Dvr Young, Fmn Rutter (Camden)		
Distance Miles		Special Limit Sched min	Actual Times min sec	Speeds	Limited Load Sched min	Actual Times min sec	Speeds	Actual Times min sec	Speeds	Sched min	Actual Times min sec	Speeds
0.0	CARLISLE	0	0.00	—	0	0.00	—	0.00	—	0	0.00	—
1.4	Carlisle No 13		—	—		3.30	33	—	—		—	—
4.9	Wreay		9.29	43		9.00	43	10.31	33		8.23	48
7.4	Southwaite		12.29	53		11.40	53	14.03	41		11.00	59
											pws	25
10.8	Calthwaite		16.10	56		15.33	59½/55	19.11	43½/40½		14.35	
13.1	Plumpton	20	18.35	61	21	17.52	64½	22.17	52	18	17.46	60
17.9	PENRITH	25	23.01	*	27	22.43	55*/60	28.15	47/56½	23	22.05	70½/75
21.1	Eden Valley Jn		25.33	70½		26.09	—	31.51	52		24.45	
23.6	mp45½		—	—		28.59	49	35.26	36		—	—
26.2	Thrimby Grange		31.21	48		—	43½	—	34		29.28	59½
29.5	Shap		35.26	44/48		36.49	44/50	45.04	38/44		32.46	58/64
31.5	Shap Summit	45	38.14	43	48	39.20	47½	48.04	38	39	34.44	64
37.0	Tebay	51	43.12	77½	54	44.10	86	52.58	82	45	38.57	88
						sig stop						
50.1	OXENHOLME	63	54.23	70*	66	61.25	72	63.47	66/77½	57	48.55	83½/75*
55.5	Milnthorpe		58.47	82		66.11	80½	68.20	71/78½		51.45	82½
59.6	mp9½		—	68		69.25	69	—	65½		—	75½
62.8	CARNFORTH	74	64.28	83½	78	72.01	79	74.16	76	68	58.40	90
66.0	Hest Bank		67.05	71½		74.36	72½/76	76.53	71/73		60.55	84
69.1	LANCASTER	79 pass	69.55 pass	64½*	85	78.26	—	80.21	—	73 pass	63.17 pass	74½
	Net Times		70			72		80¼			62	

Calculated Average Equivalent DBHPs:

Wreay–Calthwaite	1,690	1,810	1,390	1,260†
Eden Valley Jn–mp40	1,680	1,800	1,480	1,530

* Permanent speed restriction
† To mp59½

4¼min under the 'Limited Load' booking; the regulator was wide open and cutoff set at 25%. On the 1 in 125 from Eden Valley Junction successive mileposts from Milepost 46½ were passed at 52, 49, 47, 45, 42 and 41½mph, requiring 1,800EDBHP average. This was said to be done with regulator and cutoff unchanged, but this output would require 27-28% cutoff at these speeds. The result was that Tebay was passed on time, so unexpectedly that the train was stopped by signals at Low Gill while a preceding freight got itself into Grayrigg loop. The 'Mid-day' was thus 3½min late into Lancaster, but the net time was only 72min, 13min less than schedule.

In contrast, 'Princess' No 46212 had a tremendous load of 17 coaches,[103] 542 tons tare — just within the permitted load of 560 tons — to handle, and a late start of 8min as the stimulus. The pull up to Calthwaite was inevitably slow, and time was dropped to Penrith. There followed a long slog on the 1 in 125, at 34-35½mph, with the engine holding her own and even accelerating slightly; this won the train back to booked sectional time to Shap Summit. The 1,480 average EDBHP must have been very near the engine's continuous limit. After the Summit the running was lively and unchecked, thus recouping 4¾min to Lancaster with this enormous train.

The last run, with the 'Caledonian',[104] was actually made on the second day of the new train in 1957, with the departure 8½min late due to a derailment in Scotland. Bearing in mind the light train the start from Carlisle was quite relaxed — compare with column 2 with nearly twice the load — but a bad permanent way check before Calthwaite seemed to change Driver Young's perception of what was needed. C. J. Allen remarked, tongue in cheek, that 'Penrith station was taken at a speed which permitted the attainment of 75 by Eden Valley Junction', and there followed a remarkable climb to Shap Summit, with no lower speed than 58mph; the EDBHP of 1,530 would have needed about 22% cutoff at these speeds. So just half of the late start had been won back by Summit, and the rest by Carnforth. The average speeds look impressive, too — 64.5mph from Penrith up to Summit and 65.5mph from Carlisle start to pass Lancaster!

Slipping by Pacifics

This seems a suitable point at which to discuss the vexed question of adhesion. Both Pacific types had high tractive effort, amounting to 26.7% ('Princess') and 26.8% ('Duchess') of the diagram adhesion weight. With such high figures great care was needed in starting to avoid slipping, and sensitive handling of the regulator was essential. The volume of uncontrollable steam beyond the regulator valve — in the boiler main steam pipe, header, elements, smokebox steam pipes and steam chests — was very large, in the case of the 'Duchesses' being enough for about 1½ wheel revolutions in full gear, so that a raceaway slip could easily occur. Drivers adopted various methods to avoid a slip; some would open and close the regulator quickly several times when starting, until the train was on the move, while others would try to start on a restricted cutoff and, if the engine appeared 'blind', wind the reverser down just enough to bring movement. There was some weight transfer between axles, particularly on curves or through pointwork, which could reduce adhesion; the restart on the curve from Penrith station with the heavy prewar 'Mid-day Scot', for example, caused a certain amount of difficulty, especially if brakes were dragging at the rear of the long train. The very act of pulling on the train also brought forces into play which made the Pacifics, with their trailing trucks, less sure-footed than, say, a 4-6-0.[105] All this was more or less understood and allowed for by drivers, and help was usually near. Only rarely was there serious trouble when starting; in extremis O. S. Nock noted[106] a 'Duchess' attempting to start the 500-ton 'Red Rose' from Liverpool Lime Street station when, with no rear end assistance available, the driver struggled *for almost an hour* before finally getting the train out of the platform. By contrast, the author recalls travelling on a heavy 17-coach train to Glasgow in 1941 which was stopped by signal at Scout Green, on the 1 in 75 of Shap. The day was fine and clear, and when the signal came off the driver tried to restart, totally without success — *but the engine never once slipped.* It required one of the Tebay bank engines to get us away. Such were the extremes of rail conditions which could be experienced.

The real operating difficulties arose on the severe northern gradients, particularly Grayrigg and Beattock, and parts of the north approach to Shap, when pulling hard on a bad rail. With a clean, dry rail there was no problem, and likewise with a thoroughly wet rail in a downpour. But morning dew on the rail (Beattock could be bad for this), or frost, or the onset of a light drizzle, especially where external factors were present such as autumn leaves or the drippings from a Winsford salt train, could leave the rail head with a thin film of pseudo-lubricant. Work by the BR Research Department with their Tribometer Train in 1973 on Grayrigg bank showed[107] that while on one day the adhesion coefficient was in the range 0.25-0.3, with some slight lapses, the onset of light rain the next day immediately brought the figure down to about 0.1-0.12. In extreme cases coefficients well below 0.1 were recorded.

So in taking heavy sleeping car trains up Beattock in the early morning, or in November in the wooded Hay Fell area on Grayrigg, it was quite possible to slip to a standstill, and sanding gear was unable to cope; indeed, one could empty the sandboxes with prolonged slipping. This was the real weakness of a big Pacific for the line north of Carnforth, and there was little that the driver could do about it. Everything went well most days, but then came a damp day of low cloud and drizzle on the fells, and the Pacifics' Achilles heel became apparent.

O. S. Nock recorded a case in 1959[108] with a 430-ton train which was typical:

'. . . passed Beattock at full speed and started up

the bank. But as early as Auchencastle I felt an ominous surge in the train . . . and to cut a long and dismal story short we took no less than 28min to struggle up the 10 miles . . . to the Summit box. That was not all. The continuous slipping had so depleted the water supply that the driver felt constrained to stop at the summit to take water'.

Using the published indicator cards from No 46225 with valves set in Crewe's standard way (Fig 33) the actual wheel rim tractive effort has been calculated at 24% cutoff and 59mph — not untypical of work in the earlier stages of the banks. There is considerable cyclical variation (Fig 38), from 8,600 to 18,800lb under these conditions, but it is apparent that, using the diagram weights, momentary slipping could in theory occur with an adhesion coefficient of 0.12. In practice, inertia would not let this develop, but certainly at a

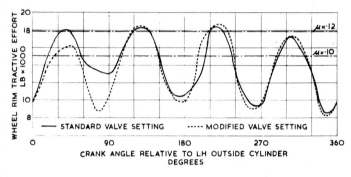

38 Cyclical wheelrim TE diagram, 'Duchess' 4-6-2.

coefficient of about 0.11, allowing for dynamic effects, it became a strong probability. The resetting of the valves for hot conditions gives no significant improvement in the evenness of the tractive effort.

3 Special Runs, Carlisle-Euston
During the 1950s, two fairly spectacular runs were made from Carlisle to Euston; neither, unfortunately, was recorded in detail by a competent observer. We are, therefore, dependent on guards' journals, plus in the second case the driver's comments. The first was made with a special charter train[109] in November 1953 with No 46241, and the second in September 1957 with No 46244 on the up 'Caledonian'.[110]

The first occasion was a train for guests returning from a Rolls-Royce factory opening near Glasgow, and loaded only to six coaches of 210 tons gross. There was considerable prestige attached to this train, and much anguish in consequence when it was severely delayed in Scotland and left Carlisle 31min late. Driver Pile and Fireman Wallis from Camden had no intention of suffering black looks from passengers on arrival at Euston; as a measure of their determination they started by passing Shap Summit in 33min for the 31.5 miles, regaining 13min! The fine work continued, interspersed with signal checks, permanent way slacks and a special set-down stop at Watford. By Tring the train was only 1min late, but with more delays the final arrival at Euston was 7min behind time.

The 'Caledonian' run was undoubtedly an LMR publicity 'stunt', with TV cameras at Euston for the 37min early arrival. The load was the normal eight coaches, 275 tons gross, with the engine in the sure hands of Driver W. Starvis

Table 30
Special runs from Carlisle to Euston

Train:		RR Special, 1953		'Caledonian' '57	
Locomotive:		46241		46244	
Load, coaches:		6		8	
tons tare/gross:		202/210		264/275	
Enginemen:		Dvr Pile (Camden)		Dvr Starvis, Fmn Wills (Camden)	
Distance miles		Sched min†	Recorded Time min	Sched min	Recorded Time min
0.0	CARLISLE	0	0	0	0
13.1	Plumpton	20	—	18	13 sig stop 3min
17.9	PENRITH	25	—	23	21
31.4	Shap Summit	45	33	39	35 sigs Scout Gn
36.9	Tebay	51	sigs — sigs Low Gill		40
50.0	OXENHOLME	63	—	57	52
62.8	CARNFORTH	74	—	68	61 pws
69.1	LANCASTER	79	65	73	68
90.1	PRESTON	101	83	93	86
105.2	WIGAN		—		102
117.0	WARRINGTON		—	126	113 sigs Norton C
124.8	Weaver Jn	145	120 sig stop Coppenhall	133	122
141.0	CREWE	162	142	148	134
10.5	Whitmore	15	11 pws Norton Br	160	—
24.5	STAFFORD	29	—	172	154
41.8	LICHFIELD	45	41	187	—
48.1	TAMWORTH	51	—	193	171½
75.5	RUGBY	78	68 pws Kilsby T	219	192
98.2	Roade	99	— pws C'thorpe	238	209½
111.4	BLETCHLEY	110	101	249	218½
126.4	Tring	124	112	262	228
140.7	WATFORD JN	136	131	273	238
158.1	EUSTON	155	149	291	253

† 'Special Limit' to Carnforth, 'XL Limit' forward

and Fireman A. Wills, again from Camden. The running was harder than that of No 46241, and the net time was no more than 242min for the 299.1 miles. C. J. Allen expressed doubts about the 9½min sectional time for the 15.0 miles from Bletchley up to Tring (average 94.7mph), though it was feasible, needing between 1,650 and 1,700EDBHP. Starvis, however, stuck to his guns,[111] writing that:

> '. . . this actually was the time taken from passing Bletchley No 1 box to Tring No 1, as recorded by two good watches. My old friend Laurie Earl always claimed to have done Bletchley to Tring in 9min; I have tried several times to equal this figure, but never got below 10min until the 9½min of our September 5 run . . .'.

But, apocryphal or not, there was no disguising the way that the enginemen rose to the challenge thrown down.

4 Carlisle-Glasgow

In Scotland, after the sticky period for punctuality referred to earlier, there was a total renaissance, and some of the work done over the 'Caledonian' main line in the late 1950s was of a standard never previously seen. The operating had been tightened up and the enginemen seemed to take on new enthusiasm. The four runs in Table 31 reflect this turnround.

The first,[112] on the 'Mid-day Scot' on Whit-Friday 1953 with the author on the footplate, left Carlisle 36min late after persistent delays south of Oxenholme. For this size of train the speeds and power outputs on the climbs to Kirkpatrick and Castlemilk were as high as any recorded there; on the first section cutoff was increased from 20% to 25% just beyond Quintinshill, with speed at 68mph. On the second it was put to 25% just after Kirtlebridge station and left there to the top. the regulator was wide open and pressure held at about 220lb/sq in. So we were through Lockerbie in less than 'even time' and started on Beattock bank, a mile after Wamphray, at 77mph. But the driver miscalculated his water consumption somewhat, with the tender gauge down to 2,250gal, and deemed it prudent to stop at Beattock for water, making it necessary to take a banker in rear. But there was no question of leaving the work to the other man; No 46255 was worked on 40% cutoff to the Harthope slack, and at 35% beyond, while the time of 18min 21sec from Beattock start to passing Summit, inclusive of a permanent way slack to 18mph, confirms hard work by both engines. In fact, we should have got through to Pettinain troughs with something like 1,000gal left. Water consumption was fairly high at 3,350gal, or 45.6gal/mile, but we had had our money's worth from it.

The second, on the 'Mid-day Scot' too,[113] appears to have been a piece of sheer exuberance, since there was no suggestion that the train was late. A fast getaway brought a signal check at Gretna from a train coming off the G&SW line, and the recovery up the 1 in 200 past Kirkpatrick was not unduly energetic — this was 20% cutoff stuff. But after that things really began to move; the rise to Castlemilk was taken at a minimum of 62mph (using about 24% cutoff) and the gentle falling grades through Lockerbie produced 80, with 78 beyond Wamphray. The high EDBHP to Greskine indicates an immediate lengthening of cutoff: this would have needed about 35% in the upper reaches.

The morning Birmingham-Glasgow run[114] was on the easier 87min timing; Carlisle was left 18min late due to gale conditions south of the border, but the running was such that without the signal delay approaching Carstairs the train would have been no more than 1½min late there! EDBHPs of over 1,700 on the 1 in 200 betoken 25% cutoff working at over 70mph, while on Beattock cutoff must have been up to 35% before Greskine and kept there to the Summit.

Finally, a run on the eight-coach 'Caledonian'[115] which was mainly notable for the Beattock climb. It was a cautious performance overall; the train was away from Carlisle *6min early* (it was a set-down stop only) and then the driver, anxious to get the last drop of water from Mossband troughs, actually *slowed* to 56mph for the purpose. One wonders whether he might have been better advised to use some of that 6min in taking water from the column at Carlisle and ignore the troughs! As it was, he frittered away one of the

Table 31
Carlisle-Glasgow

Train:		'Mid-day Scot', 1953, 1957						Birmingham-Glasgow			'Caledonian', 1957		
Locomotive:		46255			46246			46241			46229		
Load, coaches:		14			11			11			8		
tons tare/gross:		447/480			368/395			382/405			264/275		
Enginemen:		Not recorded (Crewe N)			Dvr Barnes (Crewe N)			Dvr Brown, Fmn Lightfoot (Polmadie)			Not recorded		
Distance miles		*Sched min*	*Actual Times min sec*	*Speeds*	*Sched min*	*Actual Times min sec*	*Speeds*	*Sched min*	*Actual Times min sec*	*Speeds*	*Sched min*	*Actual Times min sec*	*Speeds*
0.0	CARLISLE	0	0.00	—	0	0.00	—	0	0.00	—	0	0.00	—
6.1	Floriston		8.03	64		7.48 sigs	—		—	77		7.55	70/56
8.6	Gretna Jn	11	10.01	78	11	10.04	40	12	9.40	70	10	10.30	58
13.0	Kirkpatrick		13.58	62½		15.37	54		13.38	64½		14.49	65
16.7	Kirtlebridge		17.19	74½		19.29	70		16.54	76½		18.00	79
22.7	Castlemilk		—	66		24.54	62		21.49	68		22.41	71
25.8	LOCKERBIE	29	24.57	73½	28	27.27	78	30	24.27	76/66	24	25.05	80
28.7	Nethercleugh		27.19	74½		29.41	80		26.54	72		27.13	84
31.7	Dinwoodie		—	71		32.13	68		29.27	69		29.20	82
34.5	Wamphray		32.07	77		34.38	78		31.47	79		31.20	— sig stop
39.7	BEATTOCK	42	37.31 / 42.58†	—	40	39.01	65	43	35.56	71	36	40.28	63
43.0	mp43		—	41		—	—		39.03	56		—	—
45.4	Greskine		52.55 pws	43		45.33	44		—	43½		46.14	54
47.0	mp47		—	18		—	39		44.29	38½		—	—
49.7	Beattock Summit	62	61.19 pws	36 / 22	58	52.01	38	63	48.50	37	51	50.57	54 sigs
63.2	Lamington		75.35 sigs	69		63.34	82		60.55 sigs	77½		62.42	22
73.5	CARSTAIRS	86	86.05	—	81	73.12	—	87	74.13	—	73 pass	75.45	12*
	Net Times		74‡			71¼			70½			67¼	

Calculated Average Equivalent DBHPs:

	Mid-day Scot	Birmingham		Caledonian
Gretna-Kirkpatrick	1,870	1,340	1,690	1,420
Kirtlebridge-Castlemilk	1,910	1,500	1,740	1,340
Beattock-Greskine	—	2,110	2,150	2,030
Greskine-Beattock Summit	—	1,880	1,840	2,170

* Permanent speed restriction
† Assisted in rear from Beattock to Summit
‡ Assuming no water stop at Beattock

minutes to Lockerbie, but would have been through Beattock in 35½min, had it not been for a dead stand at Murthat IB signals for nearly 2min, while Beattock South was putting a returned bank engine across. This seemed to get the driver roused, for he then accelerated up 2½ miles of 1 in 202 in splendid style to no less than 63mph at Beattock station, and on the bank proper fell only to 54mph in the 5.7 miles to Greskine, and sustained this speed to Summit. The time for the 10.0 miles from Beattock to the top, climbing 653ft in the process, was no more than 10min 29sec, at an average speed of 57.2mph! Such was the result of applying 30-32% cutoff and over 2,100EDBHP to eight coaches!

Southbound over this route, there are the two long and dragging climbs, from Uddingston to Craigenhill box, beset with speed restrictions and usually with delays, and from the Clyde viaduct south of Lamington to Beattock Summit. The first demanded an engine that would slog and steam, the second one that would run hard and steam. From Beattock Summit a mixture of light steam and no steam would achieve respectable speeds; any more, and the results could make hay of timings and the overall 75mph limit in Scotland. Indeed, the latter was more honoured in the breach. . . . A regular observer of performance on this route[116] recorded regular high speed on this section, culminating in an instance of 96mph descending Beattock bank. The four runs in Table 32 all follow the impact of permanent way work or subsidence before Motherwell, and determined attempts by enginemen to recoup losses before reaching the inter-Regional boundary south of Gretna.

Three runs are on the 'Mid-day Scot', the first two on the hard 75min timing from a Carstairs stop after attaching a Perth portion, and the third in 1957 working non-stop from Glasgow and with a lighter load. On the first run,[117] No 46231 was 7min late from Carstairs, and made a spirited start to begin the main climb beyond Lamington at 76mph. From there to Elvanfoot the engine was putting out more than 1,800EDBHP; the final 1 in 99 from there to Beattock Summit must have been run on about 30% cutoff to sustain an average of 1,990EDBHP. From Symington to Beattock Summit No 46231 actually undercut the 16min 25sec of *Duchess of Abercorn* in February 1939 by no less than 47sec.

Table 32
Glasgow-Carlisle

Train:		'Mid-day Scot'. 1951, 1954, 1957					'Caledonian', 1957					
Locomotive:			46231		46201			46253			46242	
Load, coaches:			15		14			11			8	
tons tare/gross			488/530		448/490			365/380			264/275	
Enginemen:			Not recorded		Dvr Parish (Crewe N)			Not recorded			Not recorded	
Distance miles		Sched min	Actual Times min sec	Speeds	Actual Times min sec	Speeds	Sched min	Actual Times min sec	Speeds	Sched min	Actual Times min sec	Speeds
0.0	GLASGOW C						0	0.00 / pws	— / 20	0	0.00 / pws	— / 18
6.6	Newton						10	11.13 / pws	—	10	11.09 / sigs	— / 8
8.4	Uddingston							14.00 sig stop	—	13	15.13 sig stop‡	—
12.9	MOTHERWELL						18	26.10	—	18	27.37	—
15.9	Wishaw South							30.08	44		32.27	53
18.3	Law Jn						27	33.34	41/46	26	35.14	50*/56
20.4	Carluke							36.25	40		37.38	53/51
23.8	Craigenhill							41.23	45		41.32 / sigs	56
28.8	CARSTAIRS	0	0.00	—	0.00	—	41	47.15	61½/20†	39	46.30	61/49*
32.3	Leggatfoot		5.45	—	6.03	42		51.58	46½		49.59	60/59
33.8	Thankerton		—	64	—	58		53.34	61½		51.22	74
35.4	Symington	9	9.02	57	9.48	46	48	55.17	56	46	52.49	66
39.1	Lamington		12.18	76	13.39	67		58.32	75		55.45	80
44.5	Abington		16.47	—	18.50	59		62.58	72		59.58	72/75
47.0	Crawford		19.05	66	21.28	57½		65.07	70		62.03	74
49.7	Elvanfoot		21.36	59/65	24.24	53/60		67.26	65/70½		64.15	71/77
52.6	Beattock Summit	28	24.40	49½	27.48	44	65	70.08	54½	62	66.41	66
62.6	BEATTOCK	38	33.25	84/60	33.43	90/82	75	78.06	86	72	74.02	86
67.8	Wamphray		37.55	72/64	39.31	85/72½		81.54	79/76½		77.35	90
73.6	Nethercleugh		43.03	69	44.10	75		86.16	82/77		81.29	90/86
76.5	LOCKERBIE	50	45.37	—	46.42	69	87	88.34	73	84	82.32	82
79.6	Castlemilk		48.31	61	49.32 / pws	60 / 30		91.13	65		85.53	75
85.6	Kirtlebridge		53.30	78	56.36	62½/58		95.55	83/75		90.10	90/83
90.3	Kirkpatrick		56.26	80	60.11	72		98.45	82/80		93.41	87
94.7	Gretna Jn	65	59.53	eased	63.59	68/76	101	102.05	82	98	95.56	78/85
100.3	Kingmoor		65.40	—	— / sigs	—		107.30	70		100.58	75
102.3	CARLISLE	75	69.05	—	76.34	—	111	110.18	—	107	103.50	—

Net Times	69	70½	100	92

Calculated Average Equivalent DBHPs:

	46231	46201	46253	46242
Law Jn-Craigenhill	—	—	1,430	1,500
Lamington-Crawford	} 1,840	1,370	1,600	1,290
Crawford-Elvanfoot		—	1,680	1,600
Elvanfoot-Summit	1,990	1,530	1,670	1,730

* Permanent speed restriction
† Diverted via up slow line, Carstairs station
‡ Block failure, Motherwell Colliery

From there on the running was sparkling without requiring high power. The second run[118] saw an enterprising Crewe North team on one of their own depot's 'Princesses'. Getting away from Carstairs 6min late, they did well to keep sectional time to Summit, for on the 1 in 99 from Elvanfoot the boiler may have been mortgaged somewhat to sustain 1,530EDBHP. Beattock bank was taken fast, probably with just a breath of steam, and by Lockerbie 3¼min had been recovered; but a permanent way slack before Ecclefechan used up most of this, and even then Carlisle station had no platform for the train.

In the third column[119] No 46253 suffered an appalling start, with a signal stop after Uddingston and the indignity of being put through the up slow line at Carstairs, so that by Symington the train was 7¼min late. Now followed a vigorous and unchecked attack on the climb to Beattock Summit; from 75mph after Lamington speed fell only to 65 before Elvanfoot, and after recovering to 70½ on the level, dropped only to 54½ on the 1 in 99 to the Summit, pulling back 2min on this section. Thereafter speeds were kept as far as possible in the low 80s to Gretna, and the train ran into Carlisle ¾min early.

Lastly comes some spectacular running[119] on the 'Caledonian' in its first year of operation, again bedevilled by troubles on the Glasgow-Motherwell section in the shape of a block failure and reaction from other trains affected, so that Motherwell was passed more than 9min late. The climb to Craigenhill saw nearly 2min of that pulled back, and there followed a hard, high-speed climb to Beattock Summit, with 70mph or more sustained nearly to the top. The train was now only 4¾min down, and there followed a demonstration of sustained high speed that has probably not been equalled in commercial service here. From Beattock to Gretna the 32.1 miles were reeled off in 21min 54sec at an average speed of 87.9mph, and the train actually stopped in Carlisle 3¾min early, having regained 12¼min from Motherwell. Truly the running in Scotland had gone from strength to strength.

Running on the Western Region

The 1948 Interchange Trials were not the last occasion when Stanier Pacifics took a hand in working Western Region expresses. In April 1955 No 46237 was transferred on loan to Old Oak Common, for dynamometer car tests between Paddington and Plymouth on the 'Cornish Riviera', and on the Paddington-Wolverhampton route. For these tests she was manned by Old Oak and Laira men, who had had only limited opportunity to familiarise themselves with the engine. The loadings were moderate by West Coast standards — 12 coaches beyond Westbury, and similar size to Birmingham — but the Plymouth timings were fairly fast, the best being 190min for the 193.6 miles to Newton Abbot.

The performance[120] was closely geared to the demands of the timetable, and there were few high power outputs. Some of the running was patchy, partly because firemen were not accustomed to firing wide fireboxes and also because of concern about water consumption, which was higher than expected; on the down 'Riviera', for instance, drivers tended to run very gently from Reading until the water was in the scoop at Aldermaston troughs. This smacks of over-caution, however, with troughs at intervals of 45, 51, 42 and 41 miles. Such recorded details of the test runs as have been published show few outputs as high as 1,700EDBHP on the climbing sections, though in one case, in the up direction to Brewham Summit, calculations suggest an output of nearly 2,000EDBHP for a few minutes. Boiler pressure was well down at times, due to firing inexperience and incorrect air control.

In January 1956 came indications of bogie frame fractures on the 'Kings', and a special examination led to the majority being withdrawn until repairs had been made. To help with the resulting power shortage, the LM Region loaned two 'Princesses', Nos 46207/10, and two 'Duchesses', Nos 46254/7 to Old Oak Common for about a month until the 'Kings' came back into service. 'Princesses' were at first used on Wolverhampton trains, with the 'Duchesses' working to the West,[121] but on the diagram covering the 09.10 from Paddington and 14.35 from Wolverhampton there was insufficient time to dispose and reprepare such large engines at Stafford Road, because of the large grate, and so No 46210 also went West. The Western crews seemed to have very little feel for the engines, which went home with few regrets.

Finale

The last two 'Duchesses' had been built to run in some sort of competitive spirit against the two LMS/English Electric 1,600hp diesel-electric locomotives. Throughout the 1950s the competition was a little one-sided; the diesels did some fine work (though only in multiple could they out-perform a 'Duchess') but reliability left a great deal to be desired, though the facilities and organisation to maintain them were perhaps deficient. Meanwhile the Pacifics soldiered on to work the West Coast service largely unchallenged, save for being supplemented by a few East Coast 'A1s'. The 'Princesses' deputised for the 'Duchesses', and had their own handful of trains to work.

But the arrival in 1959 of numbers of Class 40 2,000hp diesel-electric locomotives brought the Pacifics up short. Suddenly the principal expresses were taken over by the big diesels, although with their dubious availability there were not enough of them to take over all the work. By September 1959 most of the Euston-Liverpool trains had been dieselised; the allocation of Pacifics at Camden and Crewe was run down and the displaced engines began to appear on unusual workings. There were even random arrivals at Manchester Victoria on up Glasgow trains until it was realised that the Preston-Bolton-Manchester route was not authorised for these engines! By 1960 'Duchesses' were still hauling the 'Royal Scot' daily and the 'Mid-day Scot' quite frequently, but they were also being demoted to working fitted and semi-fitted freight trains, while there was even a recorded case of a 'Princess' banking a freight train up Beattock. They had also put in appearances on the Euston-Wolverhampton trains, and were diagrammed to work the 09.35 from Wolverhampton regularly; this train had originally to be rerouted via Dudley Port until the Bescot route was cleared for Pacifics.

Early in 1961 Class 40 diesel power finally took over the 'Royal Scot', 'Mid-day Scot', 'Caledonian' and the West Coast Postal; in March the 'Princesses' were put into store at Carnforth, Kingmoor, Willesden and Rugby, as well as Crewe and Edge Hill. Most of them came out briefly in July for summer extra workings, but by September they were back in store; six were withdrawn in October/November. The remainder emerged again in January 1962 when the Class 40s encountered another bout of train heating boiler trouble, and some appeared on top class work. With the summer they hung on with duties progressively less demanding — parcels, fish and freight trains, leavened with the occasional express passenger job. They were seen on new routes, including Edinburgh-Dundee, and in September No 46200 worked an RCTS special to Llandudno. But it was the last fling. That month No 46209 was condemned, in October Nos 46201/3/8 followed suit, and Nos 46200/6 went in November, to render the class extinct.

Meanwhile the 'Duchesses' hung on; in March 1962 they lost the Birmingham-Glasgow jobs, but were usually available as stand-bys in case of diesel failure during the day; they were still fairly busy on the overnight sleeper trains. They began to appear in very unusual places on very mundane work — Marylebone, Callander, Windermere, Grangemouth, and between Edinburgh and Perth to instance a few — but clearly they were something of an embarrassment to the operators. In the autumn a number went into store and in December the first three were withdrawn — Nos 46227/31/2. As any major repairs became necessary — collision damage, frame fractures, or extensive firebox repairs — they were condemned. Many were in store for lengthy periods. In the summer of 1963 there was a minor swansong for them on Euston-North Wales trains, and late that year No 46239 was sent to Holyhead on loan. But withdrawals continued apace (13 in 1963); after three more went in February/March 1964, only 19 were left, half of which were in store.

Early in 1964 a proposition was examined to transfer the 11 engines in best condition to the Southern Region for working the Waterloo-Bournemouth expresses until electrification in 1967, but this fell through due to tight clearances and inadequate tender water capacity. Meanwhile, the 25kV electrification was bringing more difficulties for them at home; in March 1964 No 46254, working a fitted freight from Willesden, was failed at Nuneaton because there was no more coal at the front of the bunker, the coal pusher was *hors de combat* and the fireman was not allowed, for safety

reasons, to enter the bunker to pull coal forward! From 1 September they were prohibited from working under the wires south of Crewe station area (though there *were* subsequent cases of penetration all the way to Euston) for clearance reasons, and the cab sides of the remaining engines were adorned with the yellow diagonal stripe to indicate their banishment. But the yellow paint barely had time to dry before, with the end of the summer workings in September 1964, no fewer than 18 'Duchesses' were withdrawn. Only No 46256 *Sir William A. Stanier FRS* was kept for two weeks to work an RCTS special charter train on 26 September for which she had been specifically requested. She was condemned the following week, and Stanier's magnificent 'Duchesses' were no more. Or so we thought!

The 'Royal Scot' and 'Mid-day Scot'

Above left:
On a bright summer morning in 1951, No 46232 *Duchess of Montrose* runs off the troughs and approaches Bushey station with the down 'Royal Scot' loaded on 16 coaches. *Brian Morrison*

Left:
No 46221 *Queen Elizabeth* waits at Crewe to take over the down 'Mid-day Scot' on 4 August 1958. She will attach two through coaches from the Western Region. 'Princess' No 46210 is running tender-first to Crewe North shed after bringing in a train from the north. *Douglas Doherty*

Above:
The down 'Mid-day Scot' is on Dillicar troughs, with No 46249 *City of Sheffield* working hard to get the last bit of speed with which to rush the bank to Shap Summit. *Ian Allan Library*

Right:
At grips with the 1 in 75 of Shap, the down 'Royal Scot' is approaching Scout Green box in the care of No 46237 *City of Bristol*.
W. J. V. Anderson

Left:
Once over Shap Summit, it was coasting most of the way down to Carlisle. Here No 46224 *Princess Alexandra* **approaches Penrith with the down 'Royal Scot' in July 1951. The engine still has the tapered smokebox of her streamlined days. On the right, the single line of the CK&P comes down to the station.** *Derek Cross*

Below left:
Over the Border, Beattock bank was the next formidable obstacle. No 46245 has worked through from Crewe on the down 'Mid-day' and rushes through Beattock station while Class 5s wait their turn on freight. *W. J. V. Anderson*

Top right:
Greskine siding is empty as No 46231 *Duchess of Atholl* **thunders past with the 11-coach 'Royal Scot'.** *Eric Treacy/P. B. Whitehouse collection*

Right:
Waiting departure from Glasgow Central. The engine regulator checks that all is well with No 46221 *Queen Elizabeth* **working the up 'Royal Scot' and No 46220** *Coronation* **on the Glasgow-Birmingham.** *Douglas Doherty*

Below:
The long climb from Uddingston is over for No 46210 *Lady Patricia* **as she passes Beattock Summit box with the up 'Mid-day Scot'.** *Eric Treacy/ P. B. Whitehouse collection*

Above left:
No 46255 *City of Hereford* **puts up a magnificent display as she blasts up the 1 in 125 to Bessie Ghyll IB signals on the up 'Royal Scot'.** *W. J. V. Anderson*

Left:
Major effort; 11 months before withdrawal, No 46252 *City of Leicester* **cheerfully hauls at least 15 coaches round the Bessie Ghyll curves on the up 'Royal Scot' on 10 June 1962. Possibly due to diesel failure, the main train was combined with its Whit-Sunday relief train.** *J. S. Whiteley*

Below left:
Tebay on 3 August 1953; the up 'Mid-day Scot' coasts down from Shap Summit — 15 coaches behind No 46233 *Duchess of Sutherland* **— while a down express starts its unassisted climb. The Darlington line bears away to the right.** *A. G. Ellis*

Below:
The up 'Royal Scot' makes an unscheduled stop at Bletchley on 1 August 1954 for water, having been unable to get any on Castlethorpe troughs. *W. Philip Connolly*

The 'Caledonian'

Above left:
Coming up towards Scout Green box, 'City of Salford' is making all of 60mph on the 1 in 75. *W. J. V. Anderson*

Left:
Not much coal remains in the tender of No 46244 *King George VI* in charge of the up train as she approaches Bushey. *BRE LM Region*

Below:
Parting of the ways; the empty stock of the 'Caledonian' heads for Willesden, banked out of Euston by the train engine, appropriately No 46242 *City of Glasgow*, in September 1957. The engine will cross over to Camden shed for servicing. The train set appears to be a scratch one, as both the rear brake first and the kitchen car are ex-LMS vehicles.
P. Ransome-Wallis

The Birmingham-Glasgows

Left:
The down train is approaching Dillicar troughs and making speed behind de-streamlined No 46227 *Duchess of Devonshire* on 27 May 1952. *E. D. Bruton*

Below left:
What, one wonders, made the driver on No 46254 *City of Stoke-on-Trent* stop at Tebay for a banker on 25 September 1961? He is certainly not short of steam and the load of 14 coaches and a six-wheeled van is in no way exceptional. One of Tebay's parallel-boiler 2-6-4Ts gives a helping hand. Within a few months Class 40 diesels had taken over. *Derek Cross*

Top right:
No 46209 *Princess Beatrice* is at grips with Shap as she nears Scout Green box in the early 1950s. *Eric Treacy/ P. B. Whitehouse collection*

Right:
Made it! Shap Summit box looks down on *The Princess Royal* as she begins to accelerate her train off the 1 in 75 on 7 June 1952. *E. D. Bruton*

Below right:
On Sundays anything could happen. No 46253 *City of St Albans* has been diverted from Crewe through Manchester, and is here seen at Eccles. She is signalled for the line through Tyldesley to Springs Branch (now gone) where she will rejoin the West Coast main line. *J. R. Carter*

Above left:
No 46201 *Princess Elizabeth* blasts up Beattock bank and passes Harthope IB signal.
David Anderson

Above:
The up train approaches Thrimby Grange box in 1955 behind No 46206 *Princess Marie Louise*. *Eric Treacy/ P. B. Whitehouse collection*

Left:
After dragging 16 coaches and a van up to Shap Summit, No 46205 drifts down through the top cutting and past Milepost 37 towards Tebay. *Derek Cross*

The Sleepers

Left:
The driver of No 46210 *Lady Patricia* evidently thought it wise to take a banker to Beattock Summit rather than risk a lot of slipping on the morning dew.
Eric Treacy/P. B. Whitehouse collection

Above:
**Fifteen coaches are holding
No 46223 back as she fights
the 1 in 74 grade on about
50% cutoff approaching
Greskine box with banking
assistance.**
W. J. V. Anderson

Left:
**No 46256 *Sir William
A. Stanier FRS* passes
Greskine's down distant
signal in the early morning
with banking assistance in
the late 1950s. The
photographer was wont to
camp overnight at the
lineside to get pictures such
as this.** *W. J. V. Anderson*

The 'Merseyside' and others

Left:
**No 46208 *Princess Helena
Victoria* in full cry as she
comes out of Euston on to
Camden bank with the down
'Merseyside' in the early
1950s. This engine was
allocated to Edge Hill
continuously from
September 1951 until
withdrawal 11 years later.**
*Eric Treacy/P. B. Whitehouse
collection*

99

Left:
Sanders on and gently blowing off, No 46203 *Princess Margaret Rose* lifts a heavy Liverpool train up to the Regents Canal bridge at Camden. *Eric Treacy/ P. B. Whitehouse collection*

Below left:
Feeling replete after topping up her tender on Bushey troughs, de-streamlined No 46244 *King George VI* is making 60mph or more with the 15-coach 08.30 Euston-Liverpool on 28 April 1951. *E. D. Bruton*

Below:
Another classic Treacy picture; No 46211 *Queen Maud*, sanders on, fights her way up through the Lime Street rock cuttings with the up 'Merseyside Express'. *Eric Treacy/P. B. Whitehouse collection*

Right:
Round the curve from Edge Hill and past the shed coaling and ash plants, the original 'Princess' No 46200 accelerates an up express in the early 1950s. *Eric Treacy/ P. B. Whitehouse collection*

Below right:
No 46207 *Princess Arthur of Connaught* emerges smokily from Kilsby Tunnel on an up Liverpool train on 7 April 1953. *J. F. Henton*

Left:
It's almost all downhill now into Euston for No 46204 on the up 'Merseyside' as she passes Northchurch box on 16 August 1952.
E. D. Bruton

Below left:
Journey's end, and the 'Merseyside' rests in Platform 1 at Euston, its passengers gone. No 46208 will assist the stock up Camden bank before going on to the shed to be disposed.
Bill Stubbs collection

Running-in Turn

Above right:
Pristine after General Repair, No 46254 *City of Stoke-on-Trent* heads a three-coach Salop local out of Crewe. *Eric Treacy/ P. B. Whitehouse collection*

Right:
The return working of this running-in turn was a Plymouth-Manchester express from Shrewsbury. Here No 46250 makes the difficult start over the sharply-curved junction. Such starts were not made easier by the Western Region's continuing use of 25in vacuum for braking, making it necessary to 'pull the strings' to allow a 21in vacuum LM Region engine to release the brakes.
G. Wheeler

Driver's eye view

Above:
No 46257 working a Sunday Glasgow-Euston train diverted via Manchester comes up to a red aspect at Ordsall Lane. The tubular shaft to the reversing screw mounted underneath the platform is prominent in the foreground. *J. R. Carter*

Above right:
Fireman's view as No 46238 edges under the coaling plant at Crewe North.
J. R. Carter

Smoke Deflection

The smoke deflectors on the 'Duchesses' prevented formation of a vacuum along the smokebox sides which would suck smoke and steam down into the driver's line of vision. They did not prevent a small area of vacuum in front of the chimney, caused by the bluff smokebox front, into which smoke was drawn forward. This did not happen on the de-streamlined engines with sloping smokebox top.

Above right:
No 46227, working lightly at speed at Dillicar, shows the classic smoke pattern.
BR LM Region

Right:
No 46246 on the light eight-coach 'Royal Scot' on a still frosty morning in 1959 on which the steam hung almost motionless at ground level, nevertheless gives the enginemen a clear view.
W. J. V. Anderson

Water Troubles

Below:
The fireman on No 46247 *City of Liverpool* fails to get the scoop up quite in time on a down express on Newbold troughs north of Rugby.
W. J. V. Anderson

Left:
If you're going to make a splash, you might as well do it spectacularly! *The Princess Royal* **excels herself on Dillicar troughs with the up 'Mid-day Scot'.**
Eric Treacy/P. B. Whitehouse collection

The admiration of small boys

Centre left:
One serious number-taker with notebook; the others just savour the moment at Euston. *David Anderson*

Bottom left:
Only one lad is present to watch the departure of 'Coronation' from Edinburgh Princes Street on a morning local to Glasgow in August 1955.
David Anderson

Double-Headed

Top right:
Presumably 'Patriot' No 45542 is working home unbalanced as assistant to No 46248, on a Euston-Carlisle train arriving at its destination in August 1950. But what has happened to the headlamp over the left-hand buffer? *Derek Cross*

Centre right:
The night sleepers were always very heavy, and this one via the G&SW line is no exception, running to 16 coaches of which six are ex-LMS 12-wheelers weighing over 40 tons each. No wonder that No 46220 *Coronation* **takes Class 5MT No 44899 as assistant in April 1951, here seen at Polquhap Summit.**
Derek Cross

Carlisle

Right:
Carlisle No 3 box, behind the train, controlled the now-vanished junction to the Waverley line in the foreground. No 46255 passes on the 10.00 from Euston to Perth in July 1963.
P. J. Robinson

Above:
The 'Royal Scot' departs for Euston behind No 46236 *City of Bradford* as an early light-weight DMU arrives from the coast line.
Eric Treacy/P. B. Whitehouse collection

On Shed

Above left:
Camden; No 46211 *Queen Maud* has come in off the 'Merseyside', turned, and now awaits her turn under the coaling plant, where there appears to be some congestion. *Ian Allan Library*

Left:
No 46229 sits amongst the latter-day dirt and squalor of the ashpits at Edge Hill.
J. R. Carter

Left:
Crewe North, and *Duchess of Montrose* turns to find a vacant stall in the newer roundhouse section.
J. R. Carter

Below left:
Final preparations at Camden for a 'Duchess' before working a royal train. Mick Sparks, the chief locomotive inspector for the LM Region, is on the right; he will probably be on the engine to oversee the running. *Ian Allan Library*

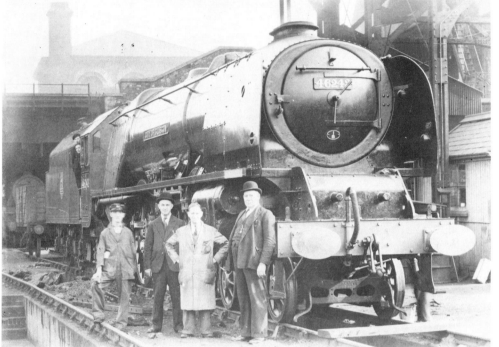

Climbing to Shap

Below:
Only four months before the withdrawal holocaust of September 1964, a well-turned out *City of Nottingham* takes water from Dillicar troughs while working as SLS special train. *W. J. V. Anderson*

Above left:
The diminutive Scout Green box rattles as the 10.40 Euston-Carlisle passes in charge of No 46228 *Duchess of Rutland*. At 28 May 1952, when this picture was taken, the tall LNWR up home signal with co-acting arms still survived. *E. D. Bruton*

Left:
The curves at Bessie Ghyll are the setting for a relief in front of the up 'Royal Scot' on Whit-Saturday 1963. With the six-coach load No 46233 *Duchess of Sutherland* is sustaining about 60mph up the 1 in 125 *P. J. Robinson*

Below:
The gradient eases slightly to 1 in 142 as No 46237 passes the limeworks at Harrison's Sidings.
Eric Treacy/P. B. Whitehouse collection

Above:
Approaching Shap station, No 46210 is talking loudly in the Glasgow-Birmingham train as she passes under the A6 road bridge.
W. J. V. Anderson

Left:
Her climbing over, No 46253 *City of St Albans* prepares to coast as she leaves Shap Summit behind and enters the rock cutting beyond.
Ian Allan Library

In Foreign Parts

Left:
Birmingham Snow Hill plays host to No 46237 *City of Bristol* on the 14.35 Wolverhampton-Paddington train in April 1955. This was during the period of her loan to Old Oak Common shed for dynamometer car trials on the Plymouth route.
B. Sackville

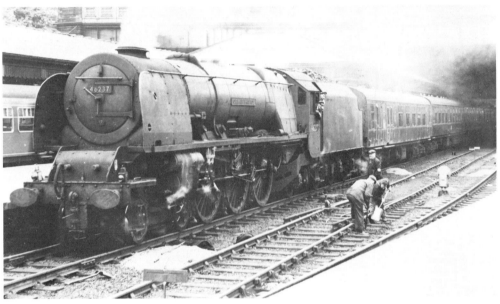

Top left:
In pouring rain, and assisted by No 5019 *Treago Castle* from Newton Abbot over the South Devon banks, No 46237 is forced to make an out-of-course stop at Totnes on 17 May 1955 (due to cattle on the line) during a dynamometer car test on the down 'Cornish Riviera'. *C. H. S. Owen*

Above left:
On the last run of the test series, on 20 May 1955, *City of Bristol* pulls out of Newton Abbot with the up 'Riviera'. *C. H. S. Owen*

Left:
In their latter days 'Duchesses' appeared from time to time at Edinburgh Waverley, usually on Perth workings. No 46237 awaits departure from platform 15 on such a train. *W. S. Sellar*

Below:
Intruder on the GN main line. No 46245 *City of London* heads a Home Counties Railway Society special from King's Cross to Doncaster Works, seen leaving Hadley Wood North Tunnel. *Brian Stephenson*

Miscellaneous Duties

Above:
No 46201 *Princess Elizabeth*, passing Grayrigg on a down express, shows the white feather.
Eric Treacy/P. B. Whitehouse collection

Left:
The day Euston-Perth train pulls away from Gleneagles in the early evening behind No 46257 *City of Salford*.
W. J. V. Anderson

Below left:
Quite common job for a Kingmoor Pacific latterly, No 46200 passes Friarton (Perth) with the 14.15 Aberdeen-Birmingham fish train. *W. J. V. Anderson*

Top:
**Smoked Haddock! No 46201
is working hard on the same
fish train on the climb from
Hilton Junction to
Gleneagles.**
W. J. V. Anderson

Above:
**No 46212 *Duchess of Kent*
detaches two special cattle
vans and a horsebox from
her down train at Carstairs.**
Photomatic

Left:
In their last years the 'Duchesses' were regular visitors to the North Wales coast line. Here No 46231 restarts the 09.20 Crewe-Holyhead train from Bangor on 7 April 1961. *R. E. James-Robertson*

Below left:
Confrontation at Chester! No 46238 and *Powderham Castle* stand chimney-to-chimney, for reasons not apparent. *J. R. Carter*

Final Duties

Below:
Even in the 1950s 'Duchesses' *did* sometimes get to work more humble duties; No 46225 is in charge of a down 'horse and carriage' passing Euxton Junction in June 1954. *Photomatic*

Above right:
The wires are up (but not yet energised) north of Crewe as *The Princess Royal* brings the 10.15 Glasgow-Euston past Hartford on 24 June 1961. *J. S. Whiteley*

Right:
The 17.30 stopping train from Glasgow to Carlisle (though with express headlamps) was a regular Pacific job in their last years. Here No 46222 *Queen Mary* storms out of St Enoch on 9 August 1961. The first four coaches are non-gangwayed stock.
Derek Cross

Below:
No 46223 is being used for a Glasgow-Ayr race special as she draws over the Ayr River bridge into the station on 15 July 1963. *Derek Cross*

Above right:
Class 40s have now displaced 'Duchesses' from the principal passenger trains — except in winter when the heating boilers fail! No 46229 *Duchess of Hamilton* is reduced to hauling a down parcels train on 26 July 1963 and having to wait for the road at Penrith while No D215 sweeps through on a Liverpool-Glasgow express. *Derek Cross*

Right:
This is ridiculous! No 46222 has charge of a two-coach Carlisle-Glasgow parcels train coasting down past Garrochburn box into Kilmarnock on 6 August 1963. *Derek Cross*

Below:
A joint RCTS/SLS Rail Tour on 27 September 1963 brought No 46238 *City of Carlisle* to the Settle & Carlisle line. She is seen passing Dent with the down train. Arten Gill viaduct is visible in the background. *G. W. Morrison*

Left:
No 46257 is getting away past Etterby Junction with the 18.00 Carlisle-Perth parcels in May 1964.
P. J. Robinson

Centre left:
The 16.00 Carlisle-Mitre Bridge milk train — which unusually ran with Class 1 headlamps — is work for No 46228 *Duchess of Rutland* in June 1964. A filthy Crewe North engine, she is making a determined effort to recover a 40-minute late start.
P. J. Robinson

Bottom left:
Irish meat in containers through Holyhead is the load behind No 46228, seen standing at Chester.
J. R. Carter

Right:
No 46248 *City of Leeds* makes loud music as she drags a fitted freight train up past Southwaite on 14 August 1964. The end came for this engine just three weeks later.
P. H. Wells

Below:
Much farther south, the wires are in place as No 46240 *City of Coventry* works a down fitted freight passing Ashton (between Hanslope and Roade) on 19 August 1964. She lasted a further three weeks before withdrawal. *K. C. H. Fairey*

Left:
Looking smart a fortnight before withdrawal, and with the overhead electrification gantries in position and her yellow stripe on the cabside, No 46239 *City of Chester* pulls out of Bletchley on 21 August 1964 with a Windermere-Euston express. *P. Hocquard*

Last Rites

Left:
Troon Harbour saw the destruction of a number of 'Duchesses', including No 46255, here being pushed (minus nameplates) past sister engine No 46238 into the breaker's yard on 2 December 1964. *J. L. Stevenson*

Below:
An unkempt Caprotti Class 5MT No 73143 drags No 46226 to the breaker's yard at Troon on 27 January 1965. She had been withdrawn 4½ months earlier. *Derek Cross*

9
Maintenance and Availability

Apart from random running repairs, depots carried out two groups of standard examinations (laid down in a booklet[122] universally known as 'MP11') between an engine's visits to main works. The first was based on days/weeks in traffic, and comprised:

'X' day and 'Boiler Full' exam	Every 6-8 days,
Washout and 'X' day exam	Every 12-16 days,

and multiples of these intervals at 3-5 weeks, 7-9 weeks and 9-15 weeks. The 'X' day examination schedule for Pacifics listed about a dozen items to be examined/tested to prevent random failures in traffic. The remaining time-based examinations were mainly concerned with boilers and steam fittings.

It was always LMS and LM Region policy that boilers should be washed out cold, the view being that proper examination of firebox water spaces, etc, was impossible under hot and steamy conditions. Cooling down and raising steam again had to be done fairly slowly to keep thermal stresses to a minimum. Boilers were cooled down by controlled cold water flushing at an increasing rate, a Pacific taking 6hr. After the actual washing-out process, using water jets and rodding, and the boilersmith's internal examination, the boiler was refilled with cold water and steam raised by natural draught (portable air or steam jets up the chimney were frowned on — unless there was a desperate shortage of engines, of course!), the process taking up to 8hr. If 'paper' availability was not to suffer, it was desirable to bring an engine for washout into the shed in the afternoon or evening — thus getting credit for utilisation that day — cool down overnight, wash out next morning, and start raising steam as early as possible during the afternoon; provided that steam was available (and so the engine theoretically available for work) by 22.00, the engine was 'available' on paper that day.

The second group of examinations was based on mileage run, and these were predominantly concerned with components subject to mechanical wear. They were done at multiples of 5-6,000 miles; almost all items were examined in position up to and including the 15-18,000-mile examination, without dismantling, the principal exception being the inside big ends. These were stripped down at 10-12,000 miles, mainly to check for cracking or lifting of the whitemetal linings. Piston rings were changed at 20-24,000 miles on Pacifics (one of only three classes so dealt with), since wear was then making it unlikely that they would run to the major mileage examination at 30-36,000 miles (the No 6 examination). At this, cylinders were opened up, all rings

renewed, and various other items dealt with (mechanical lubricators, anti-vacuum valves, axlebox flexible oil pipes, intermediate drawgear, etc) to fit the engine to run the same distance again without trouble.

This latter examination involved much stripping and renewal work, and often material had to be sent to works for attention beyond the scope of shed equipment, eg coupling rods for joint pin renewals, or piston valves with damaged heads. Traditionally the examination was always done at the concentration depot of the district to which the engine was allocated, but this could result in delays in the transport of material and spares. A postwar drive to increase availability led the Motive Power Department to carry out all valve and piston examinations for the English-based Pacifics at Crewe North shed, where components could be quickly taken into the works. A special squad of fitters performed this work to a very high standard, taking about five days unless there were supply problems.

As the mileage built up towards that for the second valve and piston examination, engines were carefully examined to ensure that the work would not be wasted by the need for shopping shortly afterwards; tyre wear and incipient boiler repairs were potential causes here. So the Mechanical Foreman needed to be a man of judgment, not to say some guile, in presenting his first Shopping Proposal (submitted after eight months from classified repair for the Pacifics). The aim was that the Shopping Bureau would give the benefit of any doubt and accept an engine for shops at that stage rather than get, perhaps, another 10,000 miles from it but need a valve and piston examination to achieve it before shopping at a second Proposal. If his report failed to ring true for any reason, or if there were specific defects at an unusually low mileage which needed looking into, he would have the Shopping Bureau Inspector — in the 1950s the respected but unloved Tommy Simnett, 'Tommy Two-thou' behind his back — to look the engine over, and there was no pulling the wool over *his* eyes! In practice, about half of all shoppings of 'Duchesses' for General or Intermediate Repairs occurred when a valve and piston examination was due.

Works Overhauls

All works repairs on Pacifics were done at Crewe, though there were isolated visits to St Rollox for casual repairs, and one 'Princess', No 46203, was given an Intermediate Repair at Derby in 1952 for special reasons.

(a) 'Princesses'

The works overhaul record of the 'Princesses', was, like the policeman's lot, not a happy one, for they spent more time in, and awaiting, works than any other comparable class.

The first two engines, after the additional shopping caused by boiler changes to provide high superheat, settled down to exchange their boilers at General Repairs from among the three (Nos 6048-50) which were suitable for their frames; the normal period between changes was 2-2½ years. An average of a little over four boiler changes a year was thus needed, but as with all new locomotive batches, there was bunching of repairs in the first few years, and 1937 saw nine boiler changes; this caused some extended times in works waiting for repaired boilers. When that peak had passed, boiler changes remained on a more even keel. The average mileage between General Repairs did not vary greatly over the years, though it reached its lowest figure in the immediate postwar period; the figures were:

1936-9	170,441
1940-5	160,900
1946-50	139,132
1951-9	174,702

Correspondingly there was an average of about 1.7 Service (or in BR parlance, Intermediate) Repairs per General Repair, though in the early postwar period, notwithstanding the low mileage between Generals, the number of Intermediates crept up to just over 2.1 per General Repair.

But the overall shopping history of the 'Princesses' can only be described as bad. Over and above the classified repairs referred to above, there were innumerable special shoppings for specific defects (excluding a disturbing sprinkling of rectification work immediately after classified repairs for defective work), which depots were not equipped to handle. Up to 1945 such 'Other' (in BR language, 'Casual') repairs had averaged 2.2 between Generals, but in 1946-50 this figure climbed to 3.9. Indeed, some engines spent a great deal of time in the works; an extreme example is shown below, though it is not now possible to identify the cause of each 'Other' repair. Typical causes were loose cylinders, fractured exhaust channels or leaking channel joints, damage arising from hot inside big ends, superheater header fractures, firebox expansion diaphragm defects, collision damage, and a variety of less common defects.

Engine No 6204 (Crewe North and Edge Hill)			
Repair	*Date stopped*	*Date to traffic*	*Weekdays out of traffic*
Heavy Service	2.9.47	15.10.47	38
Rectification	18.10.47	17.11.47	26
Light Other	20.11.47	11.12.47	19
Light Other	9.3.48	21.4.48	37
Not Classed	3.5.48	20.5.48	16
Light Intermediate	30.12.48	10.3.49	61
Not Classed	24.3.49	4.4.49	10
Light Casual	14.5.49	2.6.49	18
Light Casual	27.6.49	28.9.49	81
Light Casual	22.10.49	9.11.49	16
Heavy Intermediate	15.4.50	13.9.50	129

Despite the rising mileage between General Repairs the number of repairs of all kinds between Generals came down from 6 to 5. Not earth-shaking, but worthwhile. Similarly the percentage of weekdays spent under and awaiting works repair fell to about 17%. However, the number of Casual Repairs did not abate.

Summing up, the 'Princesses' always had a number of weak spots which made them 'tender' in service and were beyond the scope of LM Region depots to deal with. Once in the works, they fitted uneasily into Crewe's progressive belt system in the erecting shop, where pressure for repair berths in some cases encouraged the adoption of palliative short cuts which were less satisfactory than a fundamental repair. There are distinct signs in the shopping records that some of these repetitive casual repairs led to an increasing sense of desperation and an eventual classified repair which might have been better agreed at an earlier stage.

(b) 'Duchesses'
The shopping record of the 'Duchesses' was very much better. The average mileage between General Repairs was consistently higher:

1940-5	190,897
1946-50	205,255
1951-9	192,539

There was an average of 1.5 Service/Intermediate Repairs per General Repair, though in the case of the last five engines, fitted with manganese steel axlebox liners the average mileage between General Repairs was rather higher, at 224,309, while the number of Intermediate Repairs was reduced to 1.2, representing a substantial increase in mileage between classified repairs.

The position in respect of unclassified Casual Repairs, however, was far from satisfactory, though hardly in the 'Princess' category. Leaving aside those few visits concerned with special painting for naming ceremonies and similar events, they averaged 1.7 per General Repair, while in the case of the manganese linered engines this rose to 2.4 and on Nos 46256/7 was still higher at 2.7. It was disturbing that something like 15% of these Casual Repairs arose almost immediately after a classified repair; even though they were not recorded as rectifications of unsatisfactory repair work, there must have been a strong element of unsatisfactory work involved. A particularly bad example concerned No 46255, an Upperby engine, after her first General Repair:

Repair	*Date stopped*	*Date to traffic*	*Days out of traffic*
Heavy General	2/ 6/50	11/ 8/50	60
Not classed	23/ 8/50	30/ 8/50	6
Light Casual	3/10/50	4/11/50	28
Light Casual	26/ 2/51	6/ 4/51	33
Heavy Casual	13/ 4/51	12/ 5/51	25
Light Intermediate	25/10/51	27/11/51	28

But the position was somewhat patchy; by contrast, No 46238 only received four Casual Repairs during the whole of her 25-year life. The last two Pacifics signally failed to live up to their designers' hopes. Each had no less than *seven* Casual Repairs before the *first* General, and while No 46256 then settled down well, No 46257 continued her rake's progress, largely due to problems with the firebox rear bearer bracket loosening on the frames, and excelled herself with a chain of five Casual Repairs after her final General Repair in March 1959.

Availability

The Motive Power Department, with the CM&EE, naturally aimed to have locomotives available for traffic for as much of their time as possible. Taken over the fleet as a whole, the target availability was 85%. That did *not* mean in practice that all engines should be available 85% of the time, nor that 85% of engines should be available *all* the time; rather, that 85% of engines should be available for work for as long as possible (and not less than 2hr) each day. In fact the average hours off the shed for the fleet was over 12, and only a small minority, either before or after washout or repair, scraped in on the 2hr basis. In reality, 85% was extremely difficult to reach, and in the postwar years it needed favourable circumstances for a District (no statistics were produced for individual depots) to better 82-83%.

Now having a sizeable allocation of large passenger engines was *not* a formula for high availability, if only because of the frequency of 'X' examinations. Also, making their mileage faster than run-of-the-mill engines, they were stopped more frequently (and often longer) for mileage-based examinations; there was inherently more work to do with three or four cylinders.

Statistics are still in existence of availability for most locomotive classes for the 1950-7 period, as part of the Individual Costing of repairs, which was restarted after lapsing during the war. The table below shows details for the Pacifics, the 'Duchesses' being sub-divided into 'standard' engines (ie Nos 46220-52) and the two groups constituting the 'Roller Bearing Experiment', namely Nos 46253-55 and 46256/7:

| | Average weekdays/annum | | Availability (including available but not required) % | Miles per weekday available† |
	Under & awaiting Classified Repair in works	Under Repair and Examination at sheds		
'Princess'	64.0	58.6	60.4	292
'Duchess':				
Standard LM Reg	38.5	54.9	69.9	331
Standard Sc Reg	42.1	56.0	68.3	263
Nos 46253-5	41.6	61.9	67.1	325
Nos 46256/7	55.7	61.2	62.3	363
All 38 engines	40.5	56.0	68.9	316

† No allowance made for Sundays worked.

It will be seen that while the time spent at sheds under repair and examination was fairly uniform at around 55-58 weekdays per annum, the latter 'Duchesses' were marginally worse, probably due to their running greater mileages between works repairs and thus incurring more examinations at sheds. The 'Princesses' are seen to have spent much more time in works than the 'Duchesses', confirming what has been said earlier; the 'Duchesses' spent about 40 days per annum undergoing classified repairs in works, apart from Nos 46256/7, for which the figure was 40% higher. Accordingly, the availability of these two engines, at 62%, was hardly better than that of the 'Princesses' and compared badly with the 68-70% of their sisters. Since their annual mileage was little different the average miles run per *available* weekday, at 363, was better than the LM Region average of 336. The very poor utilisation on the Scottish Region, at 263 miles per available weekday, stands out.

Maintenance and Availability

Left:
Early in her career, No 6200 sits in the Crewe erecting shop undergoing a casual repair involving boiler work.
Photomatic

123

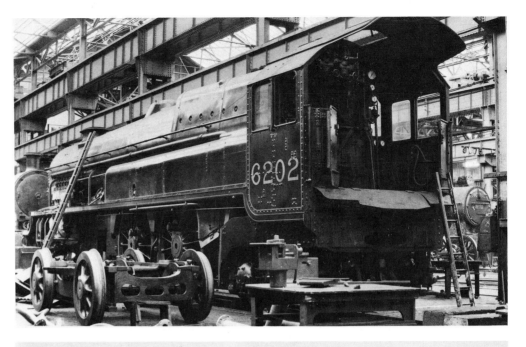

Right:
During one of her two returns to Crewe Works in 1935 for turbine or gear train repairs, No 6202 has the leading coupled wheels and gearcase removed.
Photomatic

Below right:
Waiting works. No 6200 sits on Crewe North shed with motion stripped down, waiting to be called in. In the background is the old suspension bridge (Midge Bridge) linking the old works with Crewe station; it was dismantled in 1939.
Real Photos (W9271)

Below:
The odd lady out, No 46205 sits outside Crewe North shed with inside piston valves removed on 18 May 1958. Whatever the attention needed — probably broken valve heads — it was done at the depot without the engine being shopped. *G. Wheeler*

10

Super-'Duchesses'

Almost from the moment in 1937 when the first 'Duchess' appeared, it was acknowledged within the CME Department that it was not the final solution. Neither the light 'Coronation Scot', taking 6½hr between Euston and Glasgow, nor the heavyweight possibilities of a 7hr journey time opened up by the *Duchess of Abercorn* tests in 1939 represented the maximum that could be done within the British loading gauge and weight limitations. There was a certain amount of commercial and operating pressure for higher speeds and heavier loads; the West Coast inability to match the LNER's 6hr timing to Edinburgh with a similar time to Glasgow (eight miles further) probably rankled at a time when air competition was showing signs of becoming a force to be reckoned with. It may well be that Stanier put what he could offer in the shop window to stimulate ideas. The outcome was that some scheming of more powerful express locomotives took place before World War 2 put an end to such exercises.

The assumed guidelines were the working of a 500-ton train between Euston and Glasgow in 6hr — double the load taken by *Princess Elizabeth* in 1936. To do this needed greater boiler power rather than greater tractive effort, and this could not be achieved without mechanical stoking. At the same time the influence of Andre Chapelon's work on refinement of the steam circuit and steam distribution was being felt in LMS drawing offices. A common feature throughout the design studies was the retention of six coupled wheels, which in view of the susceptibility to slipping (Chapter 8) was a dubious premise. There was an assumption that the Civil Engineer could be persuaded to accept a coupled axleload of 24 tons, perhaps by some further reduction in reciprocating balance.

There had been some early design work relating loosely to this theme, which had not borne fruit. Prompted by experimental work done by the Baltimore & Ohio RR in the USA, some scheming had been done on a watertube firebox for the 'Princess' boiler, and some drawings have survived at the NRM York. This work was stopped because of emerging problems with weight, and the difficulty of keeping 45sq ft of grate with the necessary size of the bottom tube headers. Water treatment, too, might have brought problems. In 1938, therefore, development work started on the idea of a conventionally-boilered super-'Duchess'.

It is an occupational hazard of locomotive engineers that they produce pet schemes for new machines, based on their own feelings and without guidance from above. LMS offices were no exception in this respect, and one or two of these have survived the holocaust to gain a spurious authenticity. For instance, an outline scheme exists for a four-cylinder compound 'Duchess', using the boiler little altered (except for the tube layout) but with a major redesign of the front end of the frames to carry inside low-pressure cylinders of no less than 25in diameter. This proposal carried no endorsement from Stanier; E. S. Cox in a letter to the author[123] described it as 'the merest fiction' and continued:

'Stanier may have seen it . . . but his whole consistent locomotive policy was non-compound. He would never have entertained such a design because . . . of doubts on its mechanical integrity'.

What *was* seriously looked at was a revamp of the 'Duchess' to give higher efficiency, and this got to the stage of proposing two such engines for the 1940 Building Programme. (The war led to their cancellation.) The boiler was to be redesigned for 300lb/sq in pressure, and the whole steam circuit was to be reworked on Chapelon principles from the regulator to the Kylchap double blastpipe, with particular reference to the valve ports and passages. It would have been unlikely to have had poppet valves.

The other serious scheme was designed to provide at one fell swoop 40% more power at 60mph than the 'Duchess', and dates from 1938 (Fig 36). To provide this power a bigger firebox with 70sq ft of grate was needed; to get adequate free gas area in proportion to this grate it was necessary to increase the boiler barrel diameter at the firebox end to 6ft 10½in. Such a boiler could only have been carried within the loading gauge by abandoning the Belpaire firebox and by reducing the coupled wheels to 6ft 6in diameter. The combustion chamber in the firebox was omitted in favour of a simple sloping throatplate, increasing the distance between tubeplates to 20ft 6in. The 48 superheater flues were enlarged to 5½in diameter; with 132 tubes 2½in diameter. This provided an enormous 9.58sq ft of free gas area (39% more than the 'Duchess') of which the superheater contributed 5.87sq ft or 61.3% — more than the *whole* area of a 'Princess'! Pressure was to be 300lb/sq in. It had the makings of a magnificent boiler, and probably would have been able to provide 55,000lb/hr of steam at high temperature. To use this steam, piston valve cylinders based on the 'Duchess' layout were shown; the diameter was increased to 17½in, but to avoid a very excessive tractive effort the valves would have had restricted maximum cutoff. The enormous firebox demanded a four-wheeled truck to carry its weight, making the engine a 4-6-4. The outline of this proposal carried the endorsement of Stanier's signature. There was a variant of this scheme, which had no official standing. It was much inferior in the boiler proportions, giving a free gas area of 8.24sq ft, representing only 11.75% of grate area.

These projects were stopped at the outbreak of war, but were by no means forgotten; indeed they were tinkered with during odd slack periods of design activity. Mention has been made in Chapter 7 of E. S. Cox's 1942 report on 'Postwar Developments' and its proposals for new 4-6-4 and 4-8-4 designs. The first was essentially the 1938 scheme. The coupled wheelbase was tightened up by 6in; while not shown, it could be expected that bar frames and roller bearings would have been used. The boiler was the same except that the firebox had reverted to Belpaire form; it was accommodated by pitching the boiler at 9ft 3½in above rail (the 'Duchess' was 2in higher) but the clearance for the trailing coupled wheel flanges must have been extremely tight. The tender was now shown to hold 12 tons of coal and 5,000gal of water, which with the higher superheat and thus lower specific water consumption should have given more margin to get through the 'desert' from Mossband to Pettinain troughs. The 4-8-4 mixed traffic engine (Fig 40) used the same boiler and tender, with 'Duchess'-size cylinders and 5ft 6in diameter coupled wheels. Bar frames were specifically shown, but no attempt was made to outline a satisfactory ashpan over and through the trailing truck; the front slope might have posed problems.

Splendid as the 4-6-4 concept was, its employment in the fell country would have been constrained by adhesion, and therefore the scheme for a 4-6-2+2-6-4 Garratt for passenger work north of Preston, advanced by the author in a previous book,[124] might well have been the better overall solution.

Below:
The 20.50 Perth-Euston catches the low evening sun shortly after passing Hilton Junction box, with No 46241 *City of Edinburgh* in charge. *W. J. V. Anderson*

11
Mishaps and Accidents

The fact that 51 locomotives should be involved in some 16 major accidents in no way reflects on the engines themselves; the services they worked were perhaps more vulnerable. But the Scottish section of the West Coast main line, and the 'Royal Scot' train, got more than their fair share of trouble.

Seven collisions overtook the Pacifics; in one of them a signalman's error was the direct cause. This was at Winsford on 17 April 1948, when the 17.40 Glasgow-Euston express was stopped by the pulling of the alarm chain between Winsford Junction and Station boxes and stood for 17min; the signalman in the Station box assumed it had passed unnoticed, cleared his block instrument and accepted the 18.25 Glasgow-Euston Postal hauled by No 46251, which hit the stationary train at no less than 45mph.

The other six collisions occurred after drivers had passed signals at danger, often in broad daylight. At Ecclefechan on 21 July 1941, No 6231 on the 13.00 Glasgow-Euston hit a freight train setting back into the up refuge siding; driver and fireman died. The position of the controls suggested that the driver had missed the distant signal and realised his mistake as he saw the home signal. At Hartford, on 6 October 1944, No 6230, working the 21.25 Euston-Glasgow, ran into a freight train at about 50mph, though the resulting damage was not extensive. On 18 May 1947 No 6235 on the up 'Royal Scot' hit a light engine at Lambrigg Crossing returning to Oxenholme after banking a train up Grayrigg. At Etterby Junction (north of Carlisle) on 16 August 1952 a 'Duchess' travelling tender-first light to Kingmoor shed struck the 23.40 Newcastle-Stranraer passenger train which was stopped at the home signal. Only seven weeks later came the holocaust at Harrow and Wealdstone, where on 8 October 1952 the 20.15 Perth-Euston, hauled by No 46242, overran the distant signal at caution and outer and inner home signals at danger and hit the 07.31 Tring-Euston commuter train standing in the up fast line platform, at speed. The driver and fireman were killed. Hardly had the noise of the impact died down when the 08.00 Euston-Liverpool, pulled by the rebuilt No 46202 and piloted by a 'Jubilee' (the driver of which died), ran into the piled-up wreckage at about 55mph. A total of 122 people lost their lives; it can be but small comfort that the resultant outcry stimulated the rapid development and adoption of the BR Automatic Warning System which has given a great boost to safety. Lastly, on 13 January 1960 No 46231 (an unlucky engine, for this was her third serious accident) collided in Carlisle station with the rear of the standing 11.00 Birmingham-Glasgow express and suffered extensive front end damage.

There were seven derailments of Pacific-hauled passenger trains, four of which were attributed to defective track. At Mossband on 15 May 1944, No 6225 on the 20.40 Euston-Glasgow and travelling at about 55mph, was derailed on poorly-founded track; a torn-up rail demolished Mossband signalbox. Three people died. On 21 July 1947 the 08.30 Euston-Liverpool, with No 6244, was totally derailed at Polesworth at 65-70mph. The engine had been recently shopped and was not responsible. (The author experienced some wild riding on rebuilt 'Royal Scots' on this stretch of track that year.) Fortunately, no one was killed. At Douglas Park (south of Uddingston) on 26 May 1949 No 46230 working the 22.10 Glasgow-Euston fell victim to a signalman's misdemeanour; the distant signal was clear, but the home signal had been put back and the loop facing points moved, and the train could not be stopped within the sighting distance. Again at Polesworth, on 19 November 1951, No 46252 on the 22.30 Glasgow-Euston was diverted through the fast-to-slow crossover at 55mph, the driver having missed the distant signal. On 8 August 1953 at Abington, No 46231 was in charge of the down 'Royal Scot' when the track buckled under the train due to high temperature, derailing the last seven coaches.

Two further derailments were of particular reference to the locomotives. On 21 September 1951 the leading bogie wheels of 'Princess' No 46207, working the 08.20 Liverpool-Euston, became derailed south of Weedon station. The engine continued thus for ¾-mile on straight flat-bottomed track through Stowe Hill Tunnel, but then came on to bullhead track, destroyed the rail fastenings and derailed almost the whole train, the engine finishing on its side in a field. A few days before the accident, because the left leading bogie wheel flange was wearing sharp, the two bogie axles and axleboxes had been changed over at Edge Hill shed. Unfortunately, some appalling fitting work was done; measurements of the fit of the boxes in the horns in their new positions, taken after the bogie was recovered to Crewe Works, showed:

L Ldg	R Ldg	L Trlg	R Trlg
.013in	.017in	.071in	.105in
interference	interference	clearance	clearance

effectively jamming the leading boxes in the horns. One marvels that it was possible to get them entered in the horngaps, let alone get the hornstay up afterwards. The bogie axle weights appeared reasonable. Even so, it was arguable whether the full facts were established; since the Stanier bogie frame itself carried no weight (this was transmitted from the side bolsters on to the bogie centre casting, from where the springs transferred it through the equalising beams direct to the axlebox tops) it was virtually free to rock independently of the axleboxes — and often did without affecting axle weights. So while no blame was directed at the track at the point of derailment, it seems likely that it made at least some contribution.

Another derailment, however, in Watford Tunnel on 3 February 1954, could be laid at the door of a whole host of engines, not just No 46250 whose train came to grief. A broken rail (the final break may well have occurred under the train, the up 'Royal Scot') derailed the rear bogie of the eighth coach at 65mph. The alarm chain was pulled, but with no noticeable effect as the train continued 1½ miles to Watford Junction; at the north end of the station the ninth and tenth vehicles also derailed at the fast-to-slow crossovers. The investigation brought to light a long and widespread history of rail corrosion and deteriorated fastenings, almost confined to the right-hand rail; the culprit was the discharge from the locomotives' continuous blowdown valve, which over many years had been led through the tender tank and deposited 2gal/min of boiler water on to the track just inside the RH rail. The discharge was promptly diverted into the ashpan on all engines.

The 'Duchesses' suffered two serious collapses of the inner firebox crown. On 10 September 1940, at short notice a passed fireman and passed cleaner from Polmadie were instructed to work the 'Royal Scot' from Glasgow with No 6224, the regular crew having been delayed by enemy action. The engine was ready prepared, but the inexperienced passed cleaner was clearly no match for a 'Duchess'; after stopping for a 'blow-up' at Carluke they restarted with water still low, and the sharp reversal of gradient at Craigenhill uncovered the firebox crown. The melting of the fusible plugs went unnoticed, and near Cleghorn the firebox collapsed. The young passed cleaner unfortunately paid with his life for his inexperience.

On 7 March 1948 No 6224 again suffered a firebox crown collapse, just 13 miles away at Lamington on the 21.25 Glasgow-Euston. The driver died and the fireman was severely injured. But this was no case of inexperience. On the previous day a driver at Polmadie had reported a serious discrepancy between the two water gauges, but the fitter who examined them failed to find the fault and the LH gauge was shut off. But those gauges were sorely wrong. An incorrect link between top and bottom shutoff cocks on the LH gauge meant that the two cocks were not in phase, while on the RH side one of the cock levers was wrongly fitted on the square end of the cock, so that when the bottom cock was open, the top one was shut. At the Carstairs stop, the fireman went to the shed to get a fitter to examine the engine for an audible steam blow in either the firebox or smokebox. The foreman and two fitters examined the engine and could hear the blow, but found nothing to account for it; yet at this stage at least one fusible plug had melted. The train went on, the crew satisfied that the water level was satisfactory, with disastrous results on the falling gradient to Lamington. The Polmadie fitter was blamed, and steps were taken to ensure that such a gauge defect could not recur.

Finally, three known incidents of inability to close the regulator. The first was at Watford Junction on 8 April 1939, with No 6234 on the 12.05 Euston-Crewe.[125] The train stopped short of the platform, but the wheels began to slip and continued at high speed for 5min with the train at a stand, wearing deeply into the rail heads. The slipping continued until one valve spindle broke. Six months later, on 31 October, the down 'Irish Mail' was involved in a similar incident at Headstone Lane, with No 6228. The driver came to a stand at a permanent way slack after failing to close the regulator. As was reported at the time:[126]

> '. . . for nearly 10min the engine pounded away
> with the wheels revolving . . . and the blast
> roaring up the chimney with brakes hard on. In
> the blackout . . . it was a sight worth seeing . . .'.

One would have thought that the combination of a full brake application and winding the reverser into mid-gear (equivalent to a cutoff of about 7%) would have been sufficient to stop the slip and thus, with no steam passing, enable the regulator to be shut. The modification of the main regulator valve stopped this sort of nonsense *unless there were serious water carryover*. Derek Cross recounted[127] such an incident in 1961 with a crew unfamiliar with their engine, No 46222. Trying to start the overnight sleeper train from Kilmarnock:

> '. . . the boiler was full and water surged through
> the valves, making it impossible to close the
> regulator . . . the engine slipped uncontrollably
> for some 15min without moving a foot. The noise
> was heard all over the town and it was a miracle
> that the engine stayed on the track . . . the rails
> were burned through to the web'.

Undoubtedly a 'Duchess' was a man's engine, and not for the boys!

Below:
The massive damage sustained by No 46242 *City of Glasgow* in the Harrow collision in October 1952 is evident in this picture taken at Harrow before the engine was dismantled for conveyance to the works at Crewe. The great structural strength of the boiler allowed it to survive almost undamaged, though the smokebox was mangled out of recognition. The front of the RH frame has been burned off, the entire inside cylinder flange has gone, and the outside cylinder has been sheared off through the barrel; the valve chest has completely gone.
Crown Copyright, National Railway

Bottom:
By contrast No 46202 looks superficially in much better shape. She is here seen in the works yard at Crewe, having been moved there on her own wheels.
Bill Stubbs collection

Appendices

1 Life of 'Princess' 4-6-2s

Number	Name	To traffic	Withdrawn	Mileage
6200	*The Princess Royal*	7/1933	11/1962	1,568,808
6201	*Princess Elizabeth*	11/1933	10/1962	1,526,807
6202*	—	6/1935	—	458,772
46202†	*Princess Anne*	8/1952	5/1954	11,443
6203	*Princess Margaret Rose*	7/1935	10/1962	1,494,484
6204	*Princess Louise*	7/1935	10/1961	1,373,945
6205	*Princess Victoria*	7/1935	11/1961	1,446,588
6206	*Princess Marie Louise*	8/1935	11/1962	1,552,133
6207	*Princess Arthur of Connaught*	8/1935	11/1961	1,502,705
6208	*Princess Helena Victoria*	8/1935	10/1962	1,449,634
6209	*Princess Beatrice*	8/1935	9/1962	1,578,045
6210	*Lady Patricia*	9/1935	10/1961	1,515,294
6211	*Queen Maud*	9/1935	10/1961	1,537,215
6212	*Duchess of Kent*	10/1935	10/1961	1,486,229

* Turbomotive; last in service 5/1950
† Rebuild of Turbomotive, non-standard with other engines

2 Life of 'Duchess' 4-6-2s

Number	Name	To traffic	S or NS	Double chimney	De-stream-lined	Withdrawn	Mileage
6220*	*Coronation**	6/1937	S	12/1944	9/1946	4/1963	1,321,682
6221	*Queen Elizabeth*	6/1937	S	11/1940	5/1946	5/1963	1,308,644
6222	*Queen Mary*	6/1937	S	8/1943	5/1946	10/1963	1,420,944
6223	*Princess Alice*	7/1937	S	11/1941	8/1946	10/1963	1,433,672
6224	*Princess Alexandra*	7/1937	S	5/1940	5/1946	10/1963	1,430,317
6225	*Duchess of Gloucester*	5/1938	S	6/1943	2/1947	9/1964	1,742,624
6226	*Duchess of Norfolk*	5/1938	S	7/1942	6/1947	9/1964	1,456,947
6227	*Duchess of Devonshire*	6/1938	S	12/1940	2/1947	12/1962	1,412,644
6228	*Duchess of Rutland*	6/1938	S	9/1940	7/1947	9/1964	1,394,049
6229*	*Duchess of Hamilton**	9/1938	S	4/1943	11/1947	2/1964	1,533,846†
6230	*Duchess of Buccleugh*	6/1938	NS	10/1940	—	11/1963	1,464,238
6231	*Duchess of Atholl*	6/1938	NS	6/1940	—	12/1962	1,472,439
6232	*Duchess of Montrose*	7/1938	NS	1/1943	—	12/1962	1,420,948
6233	*Duchess of Sutherland*	7/1938	NS	3/1941	—	2/1964	1,644,271
6234	*Duchess of Abercorn*	8/1938	NS	2/1939	—	1/1963	1,494,604
6235	*City of Birmingham*	7/1939	S	New	4/1946	9/1964	1,566,677
6236	*City of Bradford*	7/1939	S	New	12/1947	3/1964	1,629,412
6237	*City of Bristol*	8/1939	S	New	1/1947	9/1964	1,477,715
6238	*City of Carlisle*	9/1939	S	New	11/1946	9/1964	1,602,628
6239	*City of Chester*	9/1939	S	New	6/1947	9/1964	1,544,194
6240	*City of Coventry*	2/1940	S	New	6/1947	9/1964	1,685,042
6241	*City of Edinburgh*	4/1940	S	New	1/1947	9/1964	1,425,987
6242	*City of Glasgow*	5/1940	S	New	3/1947	10/1963	1,555,280
6243	*City of Lancaster*	6/1940	S	New	5/1949	9/1964	1,526,292
6244	*King George VI‡*	7/1940	S	New	8/1947	9/1964	1,395,153
6245	*City of London*	6/1943	S	New	8/1947	9/1964	1,408,315
6246	*City of Manchester*	8/1943	S	New	9/1946	1/1963	1,168,596
6247	*City of Liverpool*	9/1943	S	New	5/1947	5/1963	1,388,187
6248	*City of Leeds*	10/1943	S	New	12/1946	9/1964	1,136,599
6249	*City of Sheffield*	4/1944	NS	New	—	11/1963	1,098,157
6250	*City of Lichfield*	5/1944	NS	New	—	9/1964	1,353,526
6251	*City of Nottingham*	6/1944	NS	New	—	9/1964	1,236,546
6252	*City of Leicester*	6/1944	NS	New	—	5/1963	1,231,032
6253	*City of St Albans*	9/1946	NS	New	—	1/1963	932,417
6254	*City of Stoke-on-Trent*	9/1946	NS	New	—	9/1964	1,103,041
6255	*City of Hereford*	10/1946	NS	New	—	9/1964	836,858
6256	*Sir William A. Stanier FRS*	12/1947	NS	New	—	10/1964	1,016,060
46257	*City of Salford*	5/1948	NS	New	—	9/1964	806,758

* Nos 6220 and 6229 exchanged identities from January 1939 to February 1942
† Excluding mileage run in USA
‡ Carried name *City of Leeds* until April 1941

Left:
No 6200, undergoes clearance tests at Willesden Junction in the slow line platforms, 1933. The engine carries the early LMS enamel shed plate (1) for Camden.
Real Photos (10858)

Below:
Gleaming in the station lights, Upperby 'Duchess' No 46238 waits for her train in her home city. *R. Wright*

3 Valve Events

'Princess' 4-6-2s, Nos 6203-12
Walschaerts Valve Gear, inside admission 8in dia piston valves.

Steam Lap:	1¾in
Lead:	¼in
Exhaust Clearance:	Nil
Maximum Travel:	Outside, 7.25in Inside, 7.28in

Nominal cutoff %	Valve travel in	Lead in F	B	Port opening in F	B	Cutoff % F	B	Release % F	B	Compression % F	B
Outside:											
40	4.81	.26	.24	.57	.68	40	42½	79	77	77	79
25	4.32	.26	.24	.39	.43	25	28½	71	70	70	71
20	4.19	.26	.24	.34	.34	20	22½	67	67	67	67
15	4.10	.26	.24	.29	.29	15	16½	62	62	62	62
Inside:											
40	4.81	.26	.24	.62	.69	40	43½	79½	76½	76½	79½
25	4.37	.26	.24	.41	.44	25	28½	71½	70½	70½	71½
20	4.25	.25	.25	.35	.35	20	21½	67	66½	66½	67
15	4.12	.25	.25	.31	.31	15	15½	62	62	62	62

'Duchess' 4-6-2s, Nos 6220-6257
Walschaerts Valve Gear, inside admission 9in dia piston valves.

Steam Lap;	1¾in
Lead:	¼in
Exhaust Clearance:	¹/₁₆in
Maximum Travel:	7.03in

Nominal cutoff %	Valve travel in	Lead in F	B	Port opening in F	B	Cutoff % F	B	Release % F	B	Compression % F	B
40	4.75	.25	.25	.62	.62	44	38½	80	76	76	80
25	4.34	.25	.25	.42	.42	29	24½	72½	68	68	72½
20	4.19	.25	.25	.34	.34	22½	18½	67½	63½	63½	67½
15	4.06	.25	.25	.28	.28	17	13½	62½	58½	58½	62½

4 Boiler Proportions and Ratios

Class	Max Barrel Dia	Length between tubeplates	Superheater Flues No	OD and gauge	Elements	Small Tubes No	OD (11swg unless stated)	A/S Ratio	Free Gas Areas Flues	Tubes	Total	FGA of s'heater as % of total	Grate Area sq ft	Total FGA as % of Grate Area	Remarks	Dynamometer Car Testing
GWR Great Bear	6ft 0in	22ft 7in	21	4¾in 7swg	1⅜in	141	2½in	1/482	1.35	3.96	5.31	25.4	41.8	12.7		
GNR 'A1'	6ft 5in	19ft 0in	32	5¼in 5/32in	1½in	168	2¼in‡	1/462	2.68	3.64	6.32	42.4	41.2	15.3		
NER 'A2'	6ft 0in	21ft 0in	24	5¼in 5/32in	1½in	119	2¼in‡	1/510	2.01	2.58	4.59	43.8	41.0	11.2		
LNER 'A3'	6ft 5in	18ft 11¾in	43	5¼in 5/32	1½in	121	2¼in‡	1/462	3.61	2.62	6.23	57.9	41.2	15.1		
CR diagram 1913	5ft 8in	22ft 0in											37.0		McIntosh proposal	
LMS diagram 1924		19ft 0in	32	5⅛in 7swg	1½in	168	2¼in	1/456	2.62	3.73	6.35	41.3	42.0	15.1	Hughes proposal	
LMS diagram 1926	5ft 9⅞in	17ft 0in	32	5⅛in 7swg	1½in	172	2⅛in	1/436	2.68	3.36	6.04	44.4	43.5	13.9	Fowler proposal	
'Princess':																
6200/1 as built		20ft 9in	16		1⅜in	170	2¼in	1/498	1.33	3.78	5.11	26.0		11.4	Blrs 6048/9	6200/1, 1933
		20ft 9in	16		1⅜in	168	2¼in	1/498	1.33	3.73	5.06	26.3		11.2	Blr 6049 with improved washout provision	
6203 as built		19ft 3in	24		1⅛in	141	2¼in	1/463	2.32	3.13	5.45	42.6		12.1	Blr 9101	6203, Nov-Dec 1935
6204-6 as built		19ft 3in	24		1¼in	141	2¼in	1/463	2.16	3.13	5.29	40.8		11.8	Blrs 9102-4	
6207-12 as built		19ft 3in	32		1¼in	112	2¼in	1/463	2.89	2.49	5.38	53.7	45.0	12.0	Blrs 9105-9, 9235	6209, Nov-Dec 1935 6212, April-May 1936 6210, Oct 1936
Principal variations:	6ft 3in			5⅛in 7swg												
		20ft 9in	32		1¼in	112	2¼in	1/469	2.89	2.49	5.38	53.7		12.0	Blrs	6200, May-June 1935
		20ft 9in	32		1⅛in	119	2⅜in	1/469	3.09	2.98	6.07	50.9		13.5	Blrs 6048/9	6201, Nov 1936
		19ft 3in	32		1¼in	119	2⅜in	1/435	2.89	2.98	5.87	49.2		13.0		
		19ft 3in	32		1½in	119	2⅜in	1/435	2.41	2.98	5.39	44.7		12.0		
		19ft 3in	32		1¼in	123	2⅜in	1/435	2.89	3.08	5.97	48.4		13.3		
		19ft 3in	32		1½in	123	2⅜in	1/435	2.41	3.08	5.49	43.9		12.2		
'Turbomotive':																
6202 as built		19ft 3in	32		1¼in	112	2¼in	1/463	2.89	2.49	5.38	53.7		12.0	Blr 9100	
	6ft 3in	19ft 3in	40	5⅛in 7swg	1in trifurc	81	2¼in	1/463	3.66	1.80	5.46	67.1	45.0	12.1	Blr 9236	6202, Oct 1936
		19ft 3in	40		1in trifurc	101	2⅜in	1/453	3.66	2.53	6.19	59.1		13.8	Blr 9236	6202, June 1937
'Duchess':																
Standard		19ft 3in	40		1in trifurc	129	2⅜in	1/435	3.66	3.23	6.89	53.1		13.8		
6256/7 as built	6ft 5½in	19ft 3in	40	5⅛in 7swg	1in/1½in	129	2⅜in	1/435		3.23			50.00		5P4 elements	46256, March 1948
Proposed Developments:																
'Duchess' 1938	6ft 5½in		40†			129†							50.0		300lb/sq in boiler	
4-6-4 1938/42	6ft 10⅜in	20ft 6in	48	5½ 7swg	1in trifurc†	158	2½in	1/438	5.37	4.43	9.80	54.8	70.0	14.0	300lb/sq in boiler	

* 10swg   † Assumed, not specific   ‡ Boiler used on No 46212, 1954-58 and 46208, 1960-62

5 'Turbomotive': Crewe Works Repair History

Serial No	Date on works	Miles since new	Reason for shopping	Modifications made	Weekdays out of traffic
1	Aug 1935	6,100	Oil leak from turbine bearings. Water in roller bearing axleboxes	Axlebox oil seals	26
2	24 Sept 1935	9,164	Failure at Liverpool — damage due to reverse turbine dog clutch not engaging	See text	77
3	15 Jan 1936	12,644	Failure at Euston — reverse turbine dog clutch not engaging	See text	18
4	15 May 1936	40,653	Failure of reverse turbine bearings	Bearings and lube oil supply	35
5	14 July 1936	45,688	Oil leak from turbine bearings	New 40-element boiler (9236) fitted	16
6	28 Jan 1937	78,812	Failure at Willesden — forward turbine rotor jammed	Stator diaphragm locking arrangement. Sludge removal cover fitted to oil tank	64
7	Oct 1937	122,127	Routine repairs	Control gear and control box in cab. Vent. louvres added to turbine casing	22
8	29 Nov 1937	125,791	Failure of reverse turbine bearings	Bearings and lube oil system	16
9	2 June 1938	158,502	Light Service Repair	Forward turbine thrust bearing drain pipes, distant reading indicator fitted to main oil tank	123
10	8 Feb 1939	177,413	Failure at Leighton Buzzard — forward turbine spindle fractured	See text. New control box. Smoke deflectors	148
—	Sept 1939-July 1941		Withdrawn and stored due to war		
11	Sept 1941	195,370	Failure of reverse turbine	Additional Worthington oil pump for reverse turbine	257
12	1 Aug 1942	—	Light Casual Rep	—	7
13	21 Nov 1942	219,243	Oil leakage from both turbines	—	42
14	11 June 1943	249,261	Failure at Camden — failure of flexible drive at driving axle. Heavy General Repair	See text — final drive gearwheel springs	378
15	18 Dec 1944	252,473	Failure of reverse turbine bearing — oil passage obstructed at General Repair	—	27
16	12 April 1945	270,233	Oil leakage from turbine bearings	—	43
17	12 July 1945	—	Light Casual Rep	—	12
18	9 March 1946	306,683	Heavy General Rep	—	337
19	16 Aug 1947	333,984	Not classed	—	21
20	23 Sept 1947	334,444	Not classed	—	20
21	5 Dec 1947	345,913	Light Casual Rep	Additional oil tank	25
22	16 April 1948	369,014	Light Casual Rep	—	280
23	13 June 1949	382,286	Light Casual Rep	—	9
24	27 Sept 1949	402,988	Not classed	—	16
25	27 Dec 1949	414,577	Not classed	—	22
26	18 Feb 1950	412,626	Not classed	—	4
27	17 March 1950	426,902	Not classed	—	22
28	May 1950	431,720	Heavy General Rep	Rebuilt as reciprocating engine	708

6 Depot Allocations

	'Princesses'	'Duchesses'
July 1939		
Camden	6200/3-5/7-12	6220-8/30-4/6
Crewe North	—	6229/35
Longsight	6201/6	—
July 1944		
Camden	—	6225-9/37-41/3-8
Crewe North	6206-12	6233-6/52
Edge Hill	6200/1/3-5	—
Polmadie	—	6220-4/30-2/42/9-51

July 1952

Camden	—	6225/9/36/7/9-42/4/5/7/9/ 6250/2/6/7
Crewe North	6205/6/9-12	6233-5/43/6/8
Edge Hill	6201/4/7/8	—
Upperby	—	6226/8/38/51/3-5
Polmadie	6200/3	6220-4/7/30-2

July 1958

Camden	—	6229/36/9-42/5/7/54/6/7
Crewe North	6203/5/6/9/11/2	6220/1/5/8/34/5/46/8/9/ 51-3
Edge Hill	6200/4/7/8	—
Upperby	—	6226/33/7/8/43/4/50/5
Polmadie	6201/10	6222-4/7/30-2

Right:
No 6201 on the ashpit at Crewe North in 1937/8.
Real Photos (9342)

7 Mileage run: 'Princess' 4-6-2s

Year	Average	Annual mileage Maximum	Minimum
1936	88,799	108,360	67,464
1937	73,326	85,168	61,712
1938	76,926	89,055	67,657
1939	65,122	84,162	50,076
1940	62,991	73,027	44,395
1941	60,897	75,867	40,375
1942	56,119	72,920	42,229
1943	52,262	65,184	30,340
1944	53,536	72,767	35,058
1945	50,853	60,244	37,509
1946	55,726	72,008	40,846
1947	44,026	52,846	36,395
1948	49,567	60,934	35,007
1949	47,293	62,096	30,548
1950	49,081	62,328	24,746
1951	49,510	75,729	26,618
1952	55,027	69,582	44,562
1953	58,379	66,601	47,364
1954	56,337	63,041	45,868
1955	56,814	74,485	42,257
1956	56,644	67,373	44,968
1957	56,518	76,408	47,713
1958	53,166	59,988	41,979
1959	45,157	65,888	38,644
1960	45,548	67,327	27,108

8 Mileage run: 'Duchess' 4-6-2s

Year	Average	Annual mileage Maximum	Minimum
1938	66,787	69,163	63,289
1939	76,968	95,917	60,093
1940	72,941	92,696	53,082
1941	71,024	91,696	50,329
1942	67,656	77,937	45,369
1943	71,082	89,591	56,720
1944	68,083	82,091	40,435
1945	67,836	90,429	49,247
1946	73,598	93,228	48,435
1947	55,270	75,613	36,378
1948	65,278	82,821	46,006
1949	64,049	88,441	36,865
1950	67,229	88,950	47,131
1951	67,633	88,245	53,521
1952	67,387	89,601	40,424
1953	66,258	90,220	13,953†
1954	69,440	91,734	48,475
1955	65,535	92,974	40,828
1956	69,640	94,114	39,970
1957	66,070	86,531	33,707
1958	69,001	86,120	42,654
1959	65,671	95,633	41,310
1960*	65,145	84,439	46,098

* Based on only 24 engines; mileage no longer recorded for remaining 14 engines.
† Engine No 46242 after Harrow accident, 8 October 1952.

9 Average Annual Mileage at Principal Depots

(Complete calendar years only)

Depot	Class	1936-9	1940-5	1946-50	1951-9
Camden	'Princess'	77,383	67,632	—	—
	'Duchess'	77,937	73,699	69,815	75,935
Crewe North	'Princess'	—	50,547	48,985	57,042
	'Duchess'	—	63,521	62,213	70,839
Edge Hill	'Princess'	—	57,195	50,525	52,379
(Liverpool)	'Duchess'	—	—	—	—
Upperby	'Princess'	—	—	—	—
(Carlisle)	'Duchess'	—	—	56,295	63,473
Polmadie	'Princess'	—	—	—	53,029
(Glasgow)	'Duchess'	—	64,565	57,973	54,572

10 Preserved Locomotives

'Princess' 4-6-2s:

| 6201 | *Princess Elizabeth* | Princess Elizabeth Locomotive Society, Hereford |
| 46203 | *Princess Margaret Rose* | Midland Railway Trust, Butterley |

'Duchess' 4-6-2s:

46229	*Duchess of Hamilton*	National Railway Museum, York (on loan from Butlins Ltd)
6233	*Duchess of Sutherland*	Bressingham Hall, Diss
46235	*City of Birmingham*	Birmingham Museum of Science & Industry

An interesting survey of the work of the preserved No 46229 *Duchess of Hamilton*, mainly on the Settle and Carlisle line, is contained in the November 1983 issue of *Railway World*. The engine was taken out of service late in 1985 for general repair.

Above:
On 31 October 1982, No 46229 was working a 'Welsh Marches Pullman' from Hereford to Newport and back to Shrewsbury. Here she pulls away from Newport on the Usk river bridge. *David Eatwell*

11 Gradient Profiles

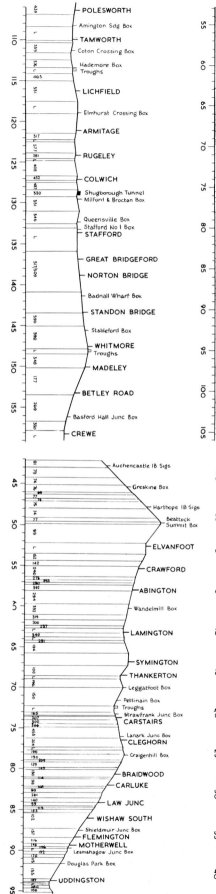

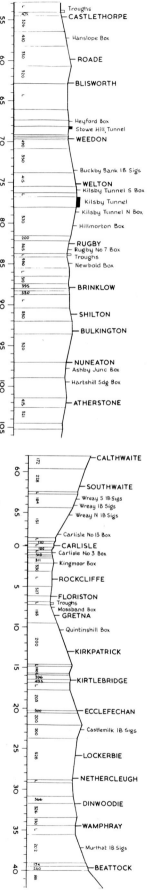

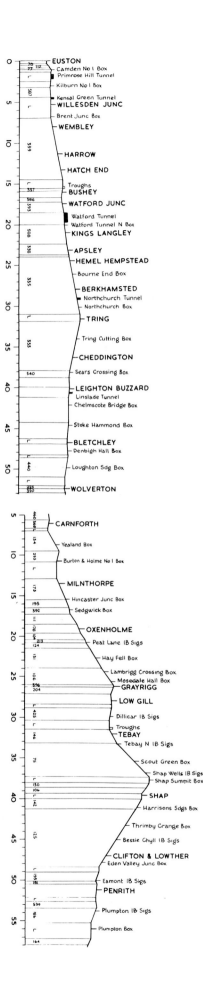

Above left:
On her way to Carlisle for an Open Day, No 6201 *Princess Elizabeth* passes Dent with a single brake third in tow on 4 July 1980.
J. H. Cooper-Smith

Above:
No 6201, now based at Hereford, is south of Dorrington and climbing hard to Church Stretton on 14 February 1981 with a 'Welsh Marches Express'.
P. Claxton

Left:
***Princess Elizabeth* bursts out of Dinmore Tunnel with a north-bound 'Welsh Marches Pullman' on 20 March 1982.**
J. H. Cooper-Smith

137

Left:
Given a cosmetic overhaul at Crewe after withdrawal and sold to Butlins for static exhibition at Minehead, No 6229 *Duchess of Hamilton* is being hauled through Mangotsfield on 18 April 1964 by No 6825 *Llanfair Grange*.

Following retrieval from Minehead in 1975 and another cosmetic overhaul at Swindon, *Duchess of Hamilton* was exhibited at the National Railway Museum, York. Three years later she was removed for restoration to full working order'[128] and in 1980 returned to main line service.

Left:
On her first full-scale outing after repair, No 46229 takes the first of two 'Limited Edition' 12-coach trains out of York on 10 May 1980 on a circular route via Leeds and Harrogate.
J. H. Cooper-Smith

Below:
A northbound 'Cumbrian Mountain Express' pauses at Dent on 10 August 1982.
J. H. Cooper-Smith

Above left:
The down 'Cumbrian Mountain Pullman' emerges from Blea Moor Tunnel on 12 March 1983.
J. H. Cooper-Smith

Above:
Passing Blea Moor box and under the shadow of Ingleborough on 26 March 1983, No 46229 (carrying a 'Thames-Clyde Express' headboard) has a 13-coach 'Thames-Eden Pullman'.
J. H. Cooper-Smith

Left:
Four weeks later, *Duchess of Hamilton* is working another 'Thames-Eden Pullman' approaching Birkett Tunnel.
Dr L. A. Nixon

Above left:
No 46229 stands in Platform 9 at York, under the magnificent curved roof, waiting to depart for Scarborough on 21 August 1983. *J. H. Cooper-Smith*

Above:
Duchess of Sutherland was also preserved by Butlins after cosmetic overhaul, this time at Heads of Ayr. Here she rests on Ayr shed on 2 October 1964 before making the short journey to Heads of Ayr camp along with 'Terrier' tank No 32662. *Derek Cross*

Centre left:
Six and a half years later she was brought out and taken to Bressingham, even incurring legal action on the way. Here she is all ready to leave Ayr shed on her journey south. *Derek Cross*

Left:
Restored to working order at Bressingham and magnificently finished, No 6233 now potters back and forth along a few hundred yards of track giving footplate rides.
J. H. Cooper-Smith

Left:
**On 8 November 1980
No 46229 hauled a '150th
Anniversary of Mail by Rail'
special to York, here seen
climbing away from Leeds.**
J. H. Cooper-Smith

References

Chapter 1
1. Stock as at 31 December 1931.
2. 'A Modern Locomotive History. 10 Years Development on the LMS, 1923-32', E. S. Cox. Proc Inst Loco E, Vol 190, 1946.
3. *Railway Magazine*, August 1932.
4. *Railway Magazine*, October 1932.
5. *West Coast 4-6-0s at Work*, C. P. Atkins. Ian Allan, 1981, Chapter 10.
6. E. S. Cox, op cit (2), Fig 9.

Chapter 2
7. *SLS Journal*, January 1979, supplemented by comments from K. R. M. Cameron.
8. 'The Metallurgy of a High-Speed Locomotive', *Railway Gazette*, 25 February 1938.
9. See *Stanier 4-6-0s at Work*, A. J. Powell. Ian Allan, 1983, p64/5.
10. *Loco Profile No 37*, 'LMS Pacifics', J. W. P. Rowledge. Profile Publications, 1974.
11. *The LMS 'Duchesses'*, ed Douglas Doherty, MAP, 1973.
12. *Railway Gazette*, 15 September 1933.
13. *Through the Links at Crewe*, P. G. Johnson. Bradford Barton.
14. *SLS Journal*, January 1979.
15. *British Locomotives from the Footplate*, O. S. Nock. Ian Allan, 1950, Chapter 6.

Chapter 3
16. Weight taken from dynamometer car report. Contemporary accounts give the load as 14 coaches, 500 tons tare.
17. *Railway Magazine*, October 1933.
18. *Railway Magazine*, November 1933.
19. *Railway Magazine*, June 1934.
20. Note deleted.
21. Discussion on paper by R. C. Bond, Proc Inst Loco E, Vol 191, 1946.
22. *Railway Magazine*, December 1936.
23. *Railway Magazine*, March 1937.
24. *Railway Magazine*, July 1938.
25. Note deleted.
26. *Railway Gazette*, 13 April 1934.
27. *Railway Magazine*, September 1935.
28. *William Stanier*, O. S. Nock. Ian Allan.
29. *Railway Magazine*, April 1939.
30. 'Performance and Efficiency Tests of LM Region "Duchess" class 4-cyl 4-6-2 Express Locomotive No 46225', Report No R13, Rugby Testing Station, July 1938. Resistance figures given in 'Developments in Locomotive Testing', S. O. Ell, Proc Inst Loco E, Vol 235, 1953, Fig 19.

31. *Railway Magazine*, July 1936.
32. *Railway Magazine*, July 1936.
33. *Railway Magazine*, September 1936.
34. *Railway Magazine*, July 1936.
35. *Railway Magazine*, September 1936.
36. *Railway Magazine*, September 1936.
37. P. G. Johnson, op cit (14).
38. O. S. Nock, op cit (16).
39. *Railway Magazine*, September 1936.
40. *Railway Magazine*, July 1938.
41. *Railway Magazine*, July 1938.
42. *Railway Magazine*, March 1936.
43. *Railway Magazine*, March 1936.

Chapter 4
44. CME Derby report dated 31 July 1935, not issued in numbered series.
45. Dynamometer Car Report No 64.
46. Dynamometer Car Report No 71.
47. *Railway Magazine*, December 1935.
48. *Railway Magazine*, September 1935.
49. *Railway Magazine*, April 1939.
50. *Railway Magazine*, January/February 1946.
51. *Railway Magazine*, December 1936.
52. 'Ten Years Experience with the LMS 4-6-2 Non-Condensing Turbine Locomotive No 6202', R. C. Bond. Proc Inst Loco E, Vol 191, 1946.

Chapter 5
53. *SLS Journal*, June 1936.
54. *SLS Journal*, October 1979.
55. *Railway Magazine*, January 1937.
56. O. S. Nock, op cit (28).
57. CME Derby report dated November 1936, not issued in numbered series.
58. *SLS Journal*, September 1974.
59. *SLS Journal*, March/April 1947.
60. O. S. Nock, op cit (28).
61. Note deleted.
62. P. G. Johnson, op cit (14).
63. *Railway Magazine*, August 1937.
64. Note deleted.
65. H. A. V. Bulleid, letter to the author.
66. *British Pacific Locomotives*, C. J. Allen. Ian Allan.
67. *Railway Magazine*, July 1938.
68. *Railway Magazine*, January 1941.
69. *Railway Magazine*, January 1941.
70. *SLS Journal*, February 1939.

Chapter 6
71. *SLS Journal*, November 1938.

72. *Railway Magazine*, December 1936.
73. CME Derby report dated February 1939, not issued in numbered series.
73a. This double blastpipe had two plain 5¼in dia caps in lieu of a single, 5¹¹/₁₆in dia cap. They were much too large — even the twin 'Duchess' caps were only 4⁷/₁₆in dia — and steaming would have been very adversely affected.
74. *Stanier 4-6-0s at Work*, A. J. Powell. Ian Allan, 1983.
75. *Railway Magazine*, May 1939.
76. A. J. Powell, op cit (74).

Chapter 7
77. *Railway Magazine*, January/February 1943.
78. *Railway Magazine*, February 1959.
79. 'Report on Postwar Investigation', E. S. Cox. CME Dept report dated 17 June 1944.
80. *Living with London Midland Locomotives*, A. J. Powell. Ian Allan, 1977, Fig 2. A. J. Powell, op cit (74), Fig 10.
81. 'Report of the Locomotive Testing Committee on the Locomotive Interchange Trials, 1948'. The Railway Executive.
82. *The Locomotive Exchanges*, C. J. Allen. Ian Allan, 1949.

Chapter 8
83. *Railway Magazine*, July 1955.
84. *Trains Illustrated*, February 1956.
85. *Railway Magazine*, March 1954.
86. *Trains Illustrated*, September 1954.
87. *Trains Illustrated*, October 1959.
88. *Trains Illustrated*, November 1960.
89. *Trains Illustrated*, February 1955.
90. *Trains Illustrated*, January 1959.
91. *Railway Magazine*, July 1955.
92. *Railway Magazine*, September 1958.
93. *Railway Magazine*, March 1954.
94. *Railway Magazine*, June 1954.
95. *Railway Magazine*, January 1961.
96. *Trains Illustrated*, November 1959.
97. *Railway Magazine*, September 1960.
98. *Main Lines Across the Border*, O. S. Nock and Eric Treacy. Nelson, 1960.
99. *Railway Magazine*, November 1957.
100. *Railway Magazine*, September 1960.

101. *Railway Magazine*, December 1955.
102. *Railway Magazine*, December 1954.
103. Note deleted.
104. *Railway Magazine*, November 1957.
105. See C. J. Allen *Railway Magazine*, April 1954.
106. *Railway Magazine*, March 1960.
107. 'Exploring Adhesion with British Rail's Tribometer Train', D. J. Watkins. *Railway Engineering Journal*, July 1975. I Mech E.
108. *Railway Magazine*, March 1960.
109. *Trains Illustrated*, February 1954.
110. *Railway Magazine*, November 1957.
111. *Railway Magazine*, March 1958.
112. A. J. Powell, op cit (12).
113. *Railway Magazine*, March 1956.
114. *Railway Magazine*, September 1960.
115. *Railway Magazine*, January 1958.
116. *Trains Illustrated*, March 1954.
117. *Railway Magazine*, January 1952.
118. *Railway Magazine*, February 1955.
119. *Railway Magazine*, January 1958.
120. *Trains Illustrated*, July 1955. *Railway Magazine*, September 1956. *Railway Magazine*, July 1960.
121. *Trains Illustrated*, March and April 1956.

Chapter 9
122. Standard Examination Schedule, MP 11, issued by the Superintendent of Motive Power, Euston.

Chapter 10
123. E. S. Cox, letter to the author dated 12 September 1984.
124. A. J. Powell, op cit (80), Chapter 14.

Chapter 11
125. *SLS Journal*, June 1939.
126. *SLS Journal*, December 1939.
127. *Locomotives Illustrated*, No 16, 'Stanier Pacifics', Derek Cross.

Appendix 10
128. For further details see *46229 Duchess of Hamilton*, M. Blakemore and M. Rutherford, Friends of the National Railway Museum, 1984.

Index